— Stories from God's Word Series —

Bible Treasures

I SAMUEL to MALACHI

Edited by Amber Bennett

CHRISTIAN LIBERTY PRESS • ARLINGTON HEIGHTS, ILLINOIS

Stories in this Bible storybook are adapted from *The Child's Story Bible*
Volumes 1 & 2, 1935; Volume 3, 1936. By Catherine Frances Vos (Smith).
Originally published by Wm. B. Eerdmans Pub. Co. Public Domain.

A publication of
Christian Liberty Press
502 West Euclid Avenue
Arlington Heights, Illinois 60004
www.christianlibertypress.com
www.shopchristianliberty.com

Compiled and edited by Amber Bennett
Copyediting by Diane C. Olson
Layout by Bob Fine and Edward J. Shewan
Cover design by Bob Fine
Cover illustration by David Bergquist
Text illustrations by Keith R. Neely
Activity illustrations by David Bergquist and Drew Roland

Scripture taken from the New King James Version®. Copyright © 1982 by Thomas Nelson, Inc.
Used by permission. All rights reserved.

Catechism questions and answers are from *First Catechism* (copyright © 2003, Great Commission Publications, Inc.). Used by permission.
First Catechism, from which questions and answers appear in this curriculum, is available in booklet form from Christian Liberty Press.

ISBN 978-1-932971-92-7 (print)
ISBN 978-1-932971-93-4 (eBook PDF)

Printed in the United States of America

Contents

Introduction

Bible Treasures: 1 Samuel to Malachi is a children's Bible storybook written specifically for first graders, though children of many ages will enjoy the familiar stories and accompanying pictures. As the title implies, this book focuses on stories found within the books of 1 Samuel through Malachi. Characters such as Job, Samuel, David, Solomon, Elijah, Elisha, Jonah, Isaiah, Jeremiah, Daniel, Esther, Ezra, Nehemiah, and others are brought to life within these pages.

Bible Treasures is based on a thirty-six week school year. Each week consists of four Bible lessons and one review lesson. While this may seem like a lot of stories for young children, this format is intended to provide the children with a comprehensive, chronological overview of the Bible books of 1 Samuel through the major prophets and Jonah. The stories naturally follow one another and are short enough that they can easily be reread as often as your student desires and your time allows.

Each weekly lesson also includes questions about the Bible story, one thought question, a weekly Bible memory verse, and a question from *First Catechism* (copyright © 2003, Great Commission Publications). The story questions are easily answered in a few words. The thought questions are meant to promote thought and discussion between you and your student and may be done orally. The memory verses and catechism questions are meant to be memorized by your student in order to help hide God's Word and truth in his or her heart. Teachers and parents are encouraged to review the weekly Bible verse and appropriate catechism question each day to help their students memorize them more quickly.

A review lesson is provided at the end of each week. This lesson reviews the weekly Bible verse and catechism questions from the week. This review will also, as the weeks pass by, begin including catechism questions from previous lessons and from *Bible Treasures: Genesis through Ruth*. A fun activity, meant to help students review some of the week's Bible lessons, is also provided in the review lesson at the end of each week.

An answer key is provided at the end of this book. The answers correspond to the questions listed at the end of each Bible story, the weekly review questions, and activity questions, if applicable. No answers are provided for the thought questions, as they are meant merely to help guide discussion.

Amber Bennett

Unit 1   Job Is Tested

LESSON 1

Job's Wealth

Job 1:1–12

Before we learn about the kings of Israel, we need to look at an important man from the Old Testament. His name was Job, and he lived in a country called Uz.

Though we do not know very much about where or when Job lived, the Bible does tell us that Job was a righteous man. The word *righteous* means "acting in a right way and dealing fairly with others"; a righteous man loves God and seeks to obey all He commands. Job was a righteous man because he loved God very much and lived to serve Him. Job hated evil, and the Lord blessed him with great wealth and happiness.

God gave Job ten children, seven sons and three daughters. Job also had 7,000 sheep, 3,000 camels, 500 yoke of oxen, 500 female donkeys, and a great house full of people. Job was the richest man alive in his country.

Job's sons regularly met together in each other's houses to eat and drink. They invited their sisters to come to the feasts, as well. Then Job would bless his children and, in case one of them had sinned before God, offer sacrifices for each one of them. Thus, Job was rich and happy in the life he lived before God.

Job's righteousness did not go unnoticed. God saw His faithful servant and was pleased with the way he lived. One day, "the sons of God came to present themselves before the Lord" (Job 1:6). This meant that God's angels came into His presence. Satan, the wicked angel who had fallen into sin, also came.

God asked Satan where he had come from. Satan answered that he had been coming and going across the face of the earth. Then the Lord asked Satan if he had noticed His servant Job. He told Satan that there was no one like Job, for he was blameless in all his doings. The word *blameless* means "no fault can be found"; this means that no one could find fault with anything Job said or did.

Satan had noticed Job. He thought Job only worshiped God because God protected him from evil and blessed him in everything he did. He told God, "But now, stretch out Your hand and touch all that he has, and he will surely curse You to Your face!" (Job 1:11).

Then the Lord gave Satan permission to do whatever he wanted to Job, just as long as he did not hurt Job himself. So Satan went out from before the Lord.

Questions

1. How many children did Job have? _____

2. Who appeared before the Lord with the other angels? _____

3. God gave Satan _____ to do whatever he wanted to Job.

Thought Question

Why do you think God might have given permission for Satan to hurt Job?

Catechism

Question 58: What must you do to be saved?
Answer 58: I must repent of my sin and believe in Christ as my Savior.

Memory Verse

2 Timothy 3:16
All Scripture is given by inspiration of God, and is profitable for doctrine, for reproof, for correction, for instruction in righteousness.

To the Teacher : Take time to go over the meanings of the following italicized words from the verse: *inspiration* means "God breathed"—that is, God influenced the authors of Scripture as they wrote; *profitable* means "helpful, beneficial, useful"—that is, God's Word is very helpful. The next four words describe how God's Word is profitable: *doctrine* means "teaching, rules to be followed"; *reproof* means "judging, rebuking"; *correction* means "making or setting right"; *instruction* means "teaching what should be obeyed."

LESSON 2

The Destruction of Job's Wealth

Job 1:13–22

One day, Job's sons and daughters had come together as they often did. They were eating and drinking in the house of their oldest brother.

That same day, a messenger came to Job and told him that the oxen had been out plowing. The donkeys were out with the oxen. Suddenly, a band of raiding warriors called Sabeans had come up. The Sabeans had taken all the oxen and all the donkeys. With swords, they had also killed all the servants who were there. The servant who came to tell Job what had happened was the only servant who survived.

While this first servant was still talking, a second servant ran up. He told Job that the fire of God had come down from heaven and burned up all Job's sheep along with all the servants who were watching them. This servant was the only one who escaped, and he had immediately come to tell Job what had happened.

Before the second servant was done talking, a third servant ran up to talk to Job. This one told Job that a band of Chaldeans had come and raided the camels and killed the servants. The camels were all gone, and the servants were dead.

Once again, only the servant who came to tell Job what had happened survived the attack.

This was all terrible; but while the third servant was speaking, a fourth came running to Job. He had the worst news of all, for all of Job's children were dead. A great wind had come up from the wilderness and struck the house where Job's children were eating and drinking. The house collapsed, and everyone inside died except for one servant who immediately came to tell Job the bad news.

Job stood up and tore his clothes. He shaved his head in a sign of mourning. Then he bowed down and worshiped God. He said, "Naked I came from my mother's womb, and naked shall I return there. The LORD gave, and the LORD has taken away; blessed be the name of the LORD" (Job 1:21).

Although Job was very sad, he did not blame the Lord for anything that had happened. He knew the Lord had given him everything he had, and he knew the Lord had the ability to take everything away. In all of this, Job did not sin against the Lord.

Questions

1. Job's sheep died when a great _____ from heaven burned them up.

2. Job's children died when a great _____ collapsed their house and killed them.

3. Job was very sad when he lost everything, but he _____ the Lord anyway.

Thought Questions

Everything we have was given to us by God. Does it make sense to say that we rely on God for our very lives? Do you know that God can take away anything He has given us at a moment's notice?

Catechism

Question 58: What must you do to be saved?
Answer 58: I must repent of my sin and believe in Christ as my Savior.

Memory Verse

2 Timothy 3:16
All Scripture is given by inspiration of God, and is profitable for doctrine, for reproof, for correction, for instruction in righteousness.

LESSON 3

Job's Illness

Job 2:1–13

Another day came when the sons of God presented themselves before the Lord of heaven and earth. Once again, Satan was among them. He came before the Lord just as before.

Again, God asked Satan where he had been. And again, Satan answered that he had been coming and going on the earth. This time, God asked Satan, "Have you considered My servant Job, that there is none like him on the earth, a blameless and upright man, one who fears God and shuns evil? And still he holds fast to his integrity, although you incited Me against him, to destroy him without cause" (Job 2:3). This verse says that Job held fast to his *integrity*, which means that he faithfully held fast to what he knew was right and did not change.

Satan, however, was unimpressed with Job's faithfulness to God. He told God that Job was content to worship God as long as he himself was healthy. Satan said that if God would hurt Job himself, then the man would curse God to His face.

So God allowed Satan to continue to test Job. This time, Satan was allowed to do whatever he wanted to Job's physical body as long as he did not kill him.

Then Satan left God's presence. With very little left to take from Job, Satan struck the man with painful boils, which are sores that swell and become infected. From the top of his head to the bottoms of his feet, Job was covered with these boils. He was so miserable that he sat in the middle of a pile of ashes and scraped at his skin with a broken piece of pottery.

When Job's wife saw all the terrible things that had happened to her husband, she became very angry. She told Job, "Do you still hold fast to your integrity? Curse God and die!" (Job 2:9).

Job, however, would not curse God. He warned his wife that speaking such things against God was foolish. He added, "Shall we indeed accept good from God, and shall we not accept adversity?" (Job 2:10).

Once again , even though Job was in a great deal of pain, he was righteous and blameless in his words and actions. Job did not sin against God.

After this, three of Job's friends heard what had happened to Job. So they traveled to see him. Eliphaz the Temanite, Bildad the Shuhite, and Zophar the Naamathite came to mourn with Job and to comfort him.

When they came close to their friend, they did not even recognize him. Then they tore their clothes and sprinkled dust on their heads in mourning with their friend. Finally, they sat down with Job for seven days and nights. During those seven days and nights, Job's friends did not speak a single word to him, for they saw that his grief was very great.

Questions

1. Satan was allowed to make Job _____ this time.

2. Job's wife told Job he should _____ God and die.

3. Three _____ came to visit Job.

Thought Question

What does it mean to "hold fast to your integrity"?

Catechism

Question 58: What must you do to be saved?
Answer 58: I must repent of my sin and believe in Christ as my Savior.

Memory Verse

2 Timothy 3:16
All Scripture is given by inspiration of God, and is profitable for doctrine, for reproof, for correction, for instruction in righteousness.

LESSON 4

Job's Three Friends

Job 3:1–10:22

After the seven days and nights were over, Job began to speak. He cursed the day he was born, saying it would have been better if he had never been born at all. He wished he had died at birth instead of living a life so full of grief and pain. Job was so miserable that he wished he was dead.

Then Job's friend Eliphaz began to talk to Job. He thought that Job must have sinned to bring such terrible tragedies upon himself. He claimed that no one who was upright, or good, would be cut off and destroyed the way Job had been. He thought that only those who were wicked would be touched by trouble.

Eliphaz talked for a long time, warning Job of what happens to men who ignore God's judgment on sin. He told Job that if he would just find out what sin had caused his troubles and repent before God of that sin, then God would lift him up and deliver him from trouble.

Although much of what Eliphaz said sounded good and was even true, he did not understand God's workings as well as he thought he did. He also did not understand Job's true situation.

Job answered Eliphaz but continued to say that he was right.

He had not sinned. Instead, God was working in his life for other reasons. He said, "Oh … that it would please God to crush me, that He would loose His hand and cut me off!" (Job 6:9). He also told Eliphaz to stop accusing him of sin. He wished for the kindness of friends instead of accusations.

Job made sure to tell his friends that he was innocent of sin. Then he began to cry out to God, asking what he had done.

After this, Job's second friend, Bildad, began to speak. He told Job that there must be sin in his life and that he must repent. He thought that if Job were truly righteous, then God would already have blessed him once again.

Once again, Job answered his friend. He knew that the Lord was mighty in all things and would punish the wicked. God's ways are not man's ways. He knew his troubles were coming from God, but he did not know why.

Mostly, Job did not understand why God, who had created him, would want to destroy him. He did not understand how his suffering could glorify God. He knew his troubles were not punishment for sin, but he did not understand why he was being troubled.

Questions

1. Job's friends thought his unconfessed _____ caused all his troubles.

2. Job disagreed with his friends because he said that he had not _____.

3. Job did not understand how his suffering could _____ God.

Thought Question

How might Job's suffering have brought glory to God?

Catechism

Question 58: What must you do to be saved?
Answer 58: I must repent of my sin and believe in Christ as my Savior.

Memory Verse

2 Timothy 3:16
All Scripture is given by inspiration of God, and is profitable for doctrine, for reproof, for correction, for instruction in righteousness.

LESSON 5

Week 1 Review

2 Timothy 3:16

Catechism

Question 1: Who made you?

Question 2: What else did God make?

Question 3: Why did God make you and all things?

Question 58: What must you do to be saved?

To the Teacher : The answers to catechism questions 1–3 are found on page 265.

Activity

Number the Order of Events

Number the parts of Job's story in order from one to four.

_____ Job's three friends come to visit.

_____ Job gets boils.

_____ Satan first appears before God.

_____ Job's children are killed.

Unit 2   *Job Is Restored*

LESSON 6

The Advice of Job's Friends

Job 11:1–31:40

This time, Zophar answered Job. He accused Job of mockery and empty words. He told Job that the trouble he was enduring was less than what his sin deserved. Zophar also told Job to repent from whatever sin was in his life.

Again, Job answered his friends. He told them that he was not arguing about whether or not the Lord had done these things to him. He simply disagreed with his friends on why God had done these things. Job only wanted to "speak to the Almighty, and … desire to reason with God" (Job 13:3).

Job told his friends they were not helping at all. In fact, they were making things worse. Then he prayed to God, begging Him to show him if there was sin in his life that needed to be forgiven. Once again, he asked God to let him die.

Then Eliphaz spoke again and accused Job of being foolish. He claimed that Job did not know anything that he and the other two friends also knew.

So Job answered again and called his friends miserable comforters. He wanted true comfort and not the false comfort of friends who accused him of sin. Then Job prayed to God once again, asking for relief from all of his troubles, including the trouble of his so-called friends.

Instead of listening to Job, Bildad answered again and reminded Job that God punishes the wicked for their sin. Those who do not repent of their sin will die in wickedness and be forgotten.

So Job told his friends that if he had sinned, then it was his own sin. Yet he warned his friends that they were sinning against him. He reminded his friends of the terrible things that were happening and how he was despised by everyone. Finally, he said, "Have pity on me, O you my friends…. Why do you persecute me as God does?" (Job 19:21–22). Yet while he claimed that God was persecuting him, he also reminded his friends that he trusted God, his Redeemer. Job knew that his Redeemer was alive. He wanted one day to see God with his own eyes.

Job's friends refused to listen. They continued to tell Job that he was wicked and needed to repent. They warned him again and again about what happens to wicked people. They even bluntly accused Job of wickedness.

Job also continued to defend himself and his righteousness. He spoke of God's wisdom and his friends' foolishness. He reminded his friends of what he had been and what he was now. He ended by asking once again why God was working against him. He thought that because he had lived a righteous life, he should not have to suffer.

Questions

1. Were Job's friends helpful? _____

2. Job knew that his Redeemer was _____ and wanted to see _____ with his own eyes.

3. Job's friends accused him of _____.

Thought Question

How could Job claim that God was persecuting him and yet still trust God?

Catechism

Question 59: How do you repent of your sin?
Answer 59: I must be sorry for my sin, and hate and forsake it.
(The word *forsake* means "to turn away from completely"; we must completely turn away from our sin.)

Memory Verse

2 Timothy 3:17
That the man of God may be complete, thoroughly equipped for every good work.

LESSON 7

Elihu's Wisdom

Job 32:1–37:24

After many long arguments, Job's friends finally stopped answering Job. They realized he would not change his position.

Then another man began to speak. His name was Elihu. He had been with Job and his friends for a while and had heard much of what was said. Yet he had been quiet because he was younger than all the other men and thought it would be best for the older, wiser men to speak.

Yet after he heard all their arguing, Elihu became angry. He was angry at Job because Job was justifying himself as righteous instead of justifying God for being righteous.

First, Elihu reprimanded Job's three friends for being unable to answer their friend with true wisdom. Then Elihu spoke directly to Job. His answer to all of Job's complaints about why God was working against him was this: "God is greater than man" (Job 33:12).

Although he was young, Elihu had been given God's understanding. He knew that God does all things well in His own time. God does not have to give an account of His actions to men. He can do whatever He wants, for whatever reason He wants, whenever He wants.

Elihu proclaimed God's justice in all things before Job and his friends. He begged Job to listen and understand that God is far above man in all of His works.

Elihu explained how God sets up and destroys the ways of all men. He knew that God controls every single thing that happens on this earth for His own glory, and not for the glory of any man, even a righteous one.

That was why Elihu was displeased with Job, for Job was acting self-righteous; that is, he thought his own words and deeds were right and that his friends' were wrong. He knew he was not being punished for sin and thought he did not deserve the suffering he had endured. However, Elihu reminded Job that only God is truly righteous and that only God can do what is right and just.

Finally, Elihu proclaimed God's goodness and majesty to Job and his friends. He explained that, while God was working in the lives of all men, He was doing so with justice and goodness. With *justice*, God judges in a fair and right way; with *goodness*, God acts in an honorable and kind way. Although it might be hard to see at times, God is working for the good of His people and the destruction of the wicked. God does only what is good. Thus, Elihu reminded Job to praise God for His majesty and all His good, marvelous works.

Questions

1. Elihu did not speak earlier because he was _____.

2. In response to Job's complaints against God, Elihu said that God is _____ than man.

3. Who alone is truly righteous? _____

Thought Question

Why is it important to remember that, while God works for the good of His people, He is ultimately working for His own glory?

Catechism

Question 59: How do you repent of your sin?
Answer 59: I must be sorry for my sin, and hate and forsake it.

Memory Verse

2 Timothy 3:17
That the man of God may be complete, thoroughly equipped for every good work.

LESSON 8

God Answers Job

Job 38:1–40:5

When Elihu was done speaking, God Himself spoke to Job out of a whirlwind. God told Job, "Now prepare yourself like a man; I will question you, and you shall answer Me. Where were you when I laid the foundations of the earth? Tell Me, if you have understanding. Who determined its measurements? ... Or who laid its cornerstone, when the morning stars sang together, and all the sons of God shouted for joy?" (Job 38:3–7).

God continued to ask Job questions, and Job could not answer any of them. They were all questions that God alone could answer, for God alone is the all-powerful Creator of heaven and earth. He alone created mankind.

God reminded Job that even though he had lived many years on the earth, he was still ignorant of the ways of God. The wisdom of man was foolishness in the eyes of God. He asked Job, "Who has put wisdom in the mind? Or who has given understanding to the heart?" (Job 38:36). Any wisdom that man may have has been given by God.

God spoke to Job for quite a while. He went through much of creation, reminding Job that He alone is God. He alone created nature, and He alone upholds nature still.

It was God, not Job or any other man, who gave boundaries to the sea and told the waves where to stop. God alone controls the clouds, the wind, the rain, the hail, the thunder, the lightning, and the snow. God placed the stars in the sky and controls all things over the earth.

God asked if Job could provide meat for the wild lions. He asked if Job knew when the wild mountain goats gave birth or if he had given the horse its strength. He asked if the hawk flew by Job's wisdom, or if the eagle mounted at Job's command to make its nest up high.

Through all of this, Job was silent. He knew that God did not actually expect answers, for he could give none. God alone is all powerful and can accomplish all the workings of the earth.

Finally, God asked, "Shall the one who contends with the Almighty correct Him? He who rebukes God, let him answer it" (Job 40:2).

This time, Job did answer. He told God, "Behold, I am vile; what shall I answer You? I lay my hand over my mouth. Once I have spoken, but I will not answer; yes, twice, but I will proceed no further" (Job 40:4–5).

Questions

1. God spoke to Job from a _____.

2. Job could not answer any of God's questions because only God knew the _____.

3. Who, alone, is all-powerful? _____

Thought Question:

How can people get wisdom?

Catechism

Question 60: Why must you hate and forsake your sin?
Answer 60: Because sin displeases God

Memory Verse:

2 Timothy 3:17
That the man of God may be complete, thoroughly equipped for every good work.

LESSON 9

Job Is Restored

Job 40:6–42:17

After Job acknowledged that he could not answer God, God spoke to him once more from the whirlwind.

Once again, God told Job to prepare himself. This time, God directly addressed Job's complaints. He said, "Would you indeed annul My judgment? Would you condemn Me that you may be justified? Have you an arm like God? Or can you thunder with a voice like His?" (Job 40:8–9).

God told Job that, if he was like God, then he should be able to clothe himself in majesty and make the proud humble. He should be able to put the wicked in their place and save himself with his own hand.

God also mentions two animals that are no longer living. Although we do not know exactly what they were like, we do know they were very large animals. God tells Job to look at the behemoth who "moves his tail like a cedar.... His bones are like beams of bronze, his ribs like bars of iron" (Job 40:17–18).

Then God speaks of Leviathan and asked, "Shall one not be overwhelmed at the sight of him [the Leviathan]? No one is so fierce that he would dare stir him up" (Job 41:9–10).

God was pointing out the behemoth and Leviathan as examples of His own strength. He had created these huge, fierce animals. If no one wanted to stir up a behemoth or Leviathan, God asked, "Who then is able to stand against Me?" (Job 41:10). God is far more powerful than any of the mightiest creatures on earth.

When God was done speaking, Job answered Him and said, "I know that You can do everything, and that no purpose of Yours can be withheld from You.... Therefore I have uttered what I did not understand, things too wonderful for me, which I did not know.... Therefore I abhor myself, and repent in dust and ashes" (Job 42:2–6).

After Job repented, God spoke to Job's three friends. He told them to go and sacrifice for their sins, for they had not spoken rightly of God as Job had. So Eliphaz, Bildad, and Zophar offered sacrifices to God, and Job prayed for them.

Then the Lord restored to Job twice as much as he had before. His friends and family returned to him and comforted him. He was given 14,000 sheep, 6,000 camels, 1,000 yoke of oxen, and 1,000 female donkeys. He also had seven more sons and three more daughters.

Thus the Lord blessed the end of Job's life more than the beginning. Job lived 140 more years and saw his children and grandchildren for four generations.

Questions

1. God asked Job about the Leviathan and the _____,
   _____.

2. _____ made these animals, yet He is more powerful than they were.

3. God blessed Job at the end of his life by giving him _____ as much as he had before.

Thought Question

What does Job mean when he tells God, "No purpose of Yours can be withheld from You?"

Catechism

Question 60: Why must you hate and forsake your sin?
Answer 60: Because sin displeases God

Memory Verse

2 Timothy 3:17
That the man of God may be complete, thoroughly equipped for every good work.

LESSON 10

Week 2 Review

Memory Verse

2 Timothy 3:16–17

Catechism

Question 4: How can you glorify God?

Question 5: Why are you to glorify God?

Question 6: Is there more than one true God?

Question 59: How do you repent of your sin?

Question 60: Why must you hate and forsake your sin?

To the Teacher :   The answers to catechism questions 4–6 are found on page 265.

Activity

True or False

1. Job was a very rich man who lived in Uz. **True/False**

2. God allowed Satan to kill Job. **True/False**

3. Job cursed God because his wife told him to. **True/False**

4. Job's three friends wanted Job to confess his sin. **True/False**

5. Elihu waited to speak because he was older than the others. **True/False**

6. Elihu told Job that God always does what is just and right. **True/False**

7. God is the only one who is truly righteous. **True/False**

8. God restored to Job twice as much as he had before. **True/False**

Unit 3   *God Speaks to Samuel*

LESSON 11

Hannah's Prayer

1 Samuel 1:1–20

Now we shall return to the land of Israel as the people began to search for a king.

At the end of the time when judges ruled Israel, a man named Elkanah lived in Israel. He had two wives. Elkanah loved his wife Hannah very much, even though Hannah had no children. Elkanah's other wife, Peninnah, had many children. This made Hannah very sad, for in those days every wife wanted to have many children. Hannah felt disgraced that she had no children while Peninnah had a wonderful family. Hannah became very unhappy. She wanted the Lord to give her children.

Now Elkanah was a godly man who taught his family to fear God. Every year, he brought the family to Shiloh so they could worship God in the tabernacle. Even at the tabernacle, Hannah was not happy. Peninnah was jealous that Elkanah loved Hannah the most, so she bragged about all of her children to Hannah. Hannah would cry and not eat.

One year, Elkanah tried to comfort Hannah. He said, "Why do you weep? Why do you not eat? And why is your heart grieved? Am I not better to you than ten sons?" (1 Samuel 1:8). Hannah listened to her husband, but she still wanted a child.

After the family finished eating and drinking, Hannah went alone to the tabernacle. She began to pray to God, asking Him to give her a son. She promised that if God would give her a son, then she would give the boy back to the Lord. Hannah's son would serve God his whole life. As a sign of that promise, the boy's hair would never be cut.

Hannah prayed very earnestly to God from her heart. Her lips were moving, but no words were coming out.

The priest of the tabernacle at this time was named Eli. He saw Hannah praying, but saw that only her lips were moving. He did not understand that Hannah was praying deeply from her heart. He asked her, "How long will you be drunk?" (1 Samuel 1:14).

Hannah answered, "I have drunk neither wine nor intoxicating drink, but have poured out my soul before the LORD" (1 Samuel 1:15).

So Eli said, "Go in peace, and the God of Israel grant your petition which you have asked of Him" (1 Samuel 1:17).

Hannah went home with Elkanah and the rest of the family. Very soon, God answered her prayer. Hannah had a baby boy. She named him *Samuel*, which means "Asked of God."

Questions

1. Who prayed earnestly to God for a son? _____

2. Who was the priest at the tabernacle? _____

3. What did Hannah name her son? _____

Thought Question:

Why was it important for Hannah to go directly to God with her request for a son?

Catechism

Question 61: What does it mean to believe in Christ?

Answer 61: To trust in Christ alone for my salvation

Memory Verse

Psalm 23:1

The LORD is my shepherd; I shall not want.

LESSON 12

Samuel

1 Samuel 1:21–2:36

The year after Samuel was born, Hannah did not go with Elkanah to Shiloh. Samuel was too young to go, so she stayed with him. She told Elkanah that she would go when Samuel was older, "then I will take him, that he may appear before the LORD and remain there forever" (1 Samuel 1:22).

When Samuel was four or five years old, Hannah took him and went with the rest of the family to Shiloh. She and Elkanah took Samuel to Eli, the priest. Hannah told Eli, "As your soul lives, my lord, I am the woman who stood by you here, praying to the LORD. For this child I prayed, and the LORD has granted me my petition … as long as he lives he shall be lent to the LORD" (1 Samuel 1:26–28). Then she prayed to God, blessing and thanking Him.

Hannah left Samuel with Eli so that he could grow up in the tabernacle. From that day on, Samuel lived with Eli and helped in the tabernacle.

Every year after that, when Elkanah and his family came to Shiloh, Hannah would come to worship God and to visit her son. Each year she brought Samuel a little robe she had made.

Eli blessed Elkanah and Hannah saying, "The LORD give you descendants from this woman for the loan that was given to the LORD" (1 Samuel 2:20). And God did bless them. Hannah had three more boys after Samuel, as well as two girls.

Now Eli was a godly man who worshiped God, but he had two wicked sons named Hophni and Phinehas. When they were younger, they had done wicked things, and Eli had been too gentle with them. Now they were grown men, and they were still doing wicked things. Eli spoke with his sons about their wickedness, but they would not listen to their father.

Then God told Samuel to tell Eli some bad news. Because Eli had allowed his sons to become so wicked, God would no longer let Eli's family be the priests of God. There would never again be old men in Eli's family, for his two sons would die on the same day, and all of Eli's descendants would die young. God would appoint another priest who would be a righteous man.

Too late, Eli learned that God always holds parents responsible for how they bring up their children. When your father and mother correct you, remember that they are doing what God has commanded them to do.

Questions

1. Samuel did most of his growing up in the _____.

2. Eli's sons were very _____.

Thought Question

Why should God hold parents responsible for training their children and teaching them about God?

Catechism

Question 61: What does it mean to believe in Christ?
Answer 61: To trust in Christ alone for my salvation

Memory Verse

Psalm 23:1
The LORD is my shepherd; I shall not want.

LESSON 13

The Voice of God

1 Samuel 3:1–21

One evening, Samuel went to bed as he usually did. In the night, he woke up and heard someone call for him. He thought Eli needed him, so he ran to the room where Eli slept. He told Eli, "Here I am, for you called me" (1 Samuel 3:5). Eli had not called, however. He sent Samuel back to his room to lie down.

Soon, Samuel heard his name being called again. He jumped and ran to Eli. Yet once again, Eli had not called for Samuel. The third time this happened, Eli realized that it was the Lord who was calling to Samuel. He sent the boy back to bed and told him that if the Lord called again, he should answer.

So Samuel went back to bed. Once more, the Lord called, "Samuel! Samuel!"

This time, Samuel stayed in his room and answered, "Speak, for Your servant hears" (1 Samuel 3:10).

The Lord told Samuel that He would indeed do everything He had promised to do to Eli. God would send a punishment on Eli because Eli had not punished his sons and did not tell them to turn them away from their wickedness.

Samuel lay still the rest of the night. In the morning, he opened the doors of the tabernacle as he usually did. He was afraid to tell Eli what the Lord had told him.

Eli, however, wanted to know what the Lord had said. He called Samuel to him and asked what God had told him. So Samuel told Eli everything that the Lord had said during the night.

When Eli heard everything, he said, "It is the Lord. Let Him do what seems good to Him" (verse 18).

After that, Samuel stayed with Eli. As Samuel grew older, it became clear to everyone in all of Israel that God was with Samuel, for God often spoke to Samuel after that night.

Questions

1. Whom did Samuel think was calling him? _____

2. Eli told Samuel that _____ was calling him.

3. God told Samuel He would send a _____ on Eli because he did not punish his sons.

Thought Question

When Eli heard what God had told Samuel, why did he answer, "It is the Lord. Let Him do what seems good to Him"?

Catechism

Question 62: Can you repent and believe in Christ by your own power?
Answer 62: No. I cannot repent and believe unless the Holy Spirit changes my heart.

Memory Verse

Psalm 23:1
The Lord is my shepherd; I shall not want.

LESSON 14

Bad News

1 Samuel 4:1–18

Samson, one of Israel's judges, had destroyed many wicked Philistines when he was alive. Yet Samson had been dead for a long time, and the Philistines had become strong once again.

The Israelites fought against the Philistines and were badly beaten. About 4,000 Israelite soldiers were killed. The elders of Israel came together to discuss how they could beat the Philistines. They said, "Let us bring the ark of the covenant of the LORD from Shiloh to us, that when it comes among us it may save us from the hand of our enemies" (1 Samuel 4:3).

Do you remember that the ark of the covenant was very sacred? The word *sacred* means "set apart for service and worship" of God. Therefore, the ark was kept in the holy of holies, where no one was allowed to go except the high priest once a year. Even when Israel traveled, they covered the ark so that no one could see it. The people, however, thought the ark could save them, so they wanted to take the ark into battle with them. Yet the people could only be saved by obeying God and repenting of their sins.

Eli's wicked sons agreed to bring the ark into battle. When they brought the ark into the Israelite camp, the people shouted so loudly that the Philistines heard and wondered what the noise was. Someone told the Philistines that the ark of God had been brought into the Israelite camp.

The Philistines were terrified. They remembered the stories of the God of Israel and how He had destroyed many nations for His people. The Philistines thought they might lose the battle, but they did not want to lose to Israel, so they fought very hard.

Israel lost the battle, and 30,000 Israelites were killed. Eli's sons, Hophni and Phinehas, were both killed. The worst thing was that the Philistines captured the ark of the covenant.

A man of Israel ran all the way back to Shiloh to tell Israel what had happened. When he told the people what had happened, the whole city cried out in grief.

Blind old Eli was sitting on a seat by the side of the road. He was afraid for the ark of the covenant, so he sat and waited for news. When he heard the cry of the city, he wanted to know what had happened.

The messenger came to Eli and told him that he had fled from the battle. Then he told him that Israel had lost and that many men were dead, including Hophni and Phinehas. Finally he said, "the ark of God has been captured" (1 Samuel 4:17).

Eli listened to the news with fear. God had fulfilled His promise and punished Eli's sons for their wickedness. Then Eli heard about the ark. This news was too much for him. Eli fell backwards off his chair, broke his neck, and died.

Questions

1. The elders of Israel wanted to bring the _____ of the _____ into battle.

2. During the battle, the Philistines killed 30,000 Israelites and _____ the ark.

Thought Question

Why would Eli be more afraid for the ark of the covenant than for his sons?

Catechism

Question 62: Can you repent and believe in Christ by your own power?
Answer 62: No. I cannot repent and believe unless the Holy Spirit changes my heart.

Memory Verse

Psalm 23:1
The LORD is my shepherd; I shall not want.

LESSON 15

Week 3 Review

Memory Verse:

Psalm 23:1

Catechism

Question 7: In how many Persons does this one God exist?

Question 8: Name these three Persons.

Question 9: What is God?

Question 61: What does it mean to believe in Christ?

Question 62: Can you repent and believe in Christ by your own power?

To the Teacher :   The answers to catechism questions 7–9 are found on page 265.

Activity
Matching

Draw lines to match the descriptions to the people who match them.

1. Prayed for a son   Hannah

2. Killed Eli's sons   Samuel

3. Was called by God when he was a boy   Eli

4. Died when he heard that the ark was taken   Philistines

Unit 4 — Saul Anointed King

LESSON 16

The Ark of God

1 Samuel 5:1–7:2

The Philistines took the ark to their city of Ashdod. A temple of the fish-god Dagon was in Ashdod. The Philistines brought the ark into the temple and set it next to their idol.

In the morning, the Philistines found that their god Dagon had fallen down on his face in front of the ark of God. They picked up their idol and set it where it belonged. But the next morning, Dagon had fallen on his face again. This time, his hands and his head had broken off.

The people of Ashdod became ill, and many died. Finally, the people said, "The ark of the God of Israel must not remain with us, for His hand is harsh toward us and Dagon our god" (1 Samuel 5:7). So the men of Ashdod called a meeting of all the lords of the Philistines to see what to do with the ark.

The lords decided to send the ark to Gath, another Philistine city. God sent a nasty disease to the people of Gath, and many of them died, as well. The ark stayed with the Philistines for seven months. The entire time it was there, God sent plagues and sickness to the Philistines.

Eventually, the Philistines decided they were too afraid to keep the ark in their country. They called their magicians and priests together to decide what to do with the ark. The magicians said that the ark should be sent back to Israel along with some presents to glorify the God of Israel.

So the Philistines made a new cart and hitched up two cows whose young calves had just been taken from them. They put the ark and the presents on the cart and sent the cart down the road to Beth Shemesh, which was in Israel. They said that if the cows took the cart straight to Israel, then they would know the sickness was from God. However, if the cows turned around and came back to their calves, then the sickness was not from God.

The cows never looked back. They walked straight to Beth Shemesh. The lords of the Philistines followed the cart until it reached Beth Shemesh. At this time, the wheat was being harvested in Israel. All the people of the town were out in the fields gathering wheat. They saw the ark of their God coming down the road with the Philistine lords following behind.

Some Levites, who were the only ones allowed to touch the ark, took the ark and the presents and set them on a stone. Then they offered burnt offerings and sacrifices to the Lord.

Yet the Israelites of Beth Shemesh did a very wrong thing too. Some of the Israelites came to the ark, opened the lid, and looked inside. This was wrong because no one was allowed to touch the ark except for the Levites. God punished them immediately by killing more than 50,000 men.

Thus, the Israelites were afraid to keep the ark in Beth Shemesh. They sent word to another city in Israel called Kirjath Jearim. They asked the men in that city to take the ark. So the men of Kirjath Jearim came and carried the ark to their city. The ark stayed in Kirjath Jearim for twenty years.

Questions

1. What was the Philistines' idol called? _____

2. What kind of animal pulled the ark to Israel? _____

3. The men of Beth Shemesh were _____ to keep the ark.

Thought Question

Why did the idol Dagon fall over when the ark was placed beside it?

Catechism

Question 63: How can you get the help of the Holy Spirit?
Answer 63: God has told us to pray for the Holy Spirit's help.

Memory Verse

Psalm 23:2
He makes me to lie down in green pastures; He leads me beside the still waters.

LESSON 17

Samuel as Judge

1 Samuel 7:3–15

Samuel was now a man. He had been a good boy who listened to the Lord, and he grew into a good man who loved the Lord. God loved Samuel, too.

Eli had judged Israel for forty years. After he died, Samuel became judge. God spoke to Samuel as He had talked to Moses and Aaron. Israel was greatly comforted that God was again speaking to His people through a prophet. Many Israelites had begun to worship idols, but now they remembered that they were God's people. They longed to return to the Lord and worship only Him.

Samuel told them that if they put away their idols and worshiped only God, then God would take them back and deliver them from the Philistines. The Israelites listened to Samuel.

Then Samuel called a gathering of all the people at Mizpah. They were to confess their sins there and ask God to forgive them. For a whole day, the people fasted and confessed their sins. Samuel prayed for them all day long.

When the Philistines heard of this great meeting, they thought it would be a good chance for them to make war. So they marched an army towards Mizpah. When the Israelites found out what the Philistines were doing, they were very afraid. They asked Samuel not to stop praying for them. So Samuel prayed and offered up a lamb as a burnt offering. As Samuel offered the lamb, God began to help Israel.

The heavens grew black, wind blew, and rain came pouring out of the sky. Huge thunder claps sounded from heaven, and lightning flashed across the sky. The Philistines became so confused in the storm that they turned and ran away while the Israelites chased them and won the victory.

After the battle, Samuel took a great stone and set it up where the battle had been. He called the stone *Ebenezer*, which means "Thus far the Lord has helped us." The Philistines had been so badly beaten that they did not bother Israel as long as Samuel was alive.

Every year after that, Samuel visited different cities in Israel before returning to his home in Ramah. He judged Israel everywhere he went. The people no longer served idols but God. They were peaceful and happy with Samuel as their judge.

Questions

1. Who became judge when Eli died? _____

2. Who fought the Philistines for Israel? _____

Thought Question

Why does God defend His people when they obey Him and worship Him?

Catechism

Question 63: How can you get the help of the Holy Spirit?

Answer 63: God has told us to pray for the Holy Spirit's help.

Memory Verse

Psalm 23:2
He makes me to lie down in green pastures; He leads me beside the still waters.

LESSON 18

A King for Israel

1 Samuel 8:1–9:21

Samuel continued to judge Israel as he grew old. He had a family too. When his sons grew up, Samuel made them judges over Israel; but Samuel's sons were not good judges the way that Samuel was.

Israel's elders came to Samuel and asked him to give them a king to rule over them, just like the other nations. Samuel was not happy, but he was not sure what to tell the people. So he did what all good men should do when they are in trouble—he prayed to the Lord.

God told Samuel to listen to the people, "for they have not rejected you, but they have rejected Me" (1 Samuel 8:7). God was Israel's King. The people did not need an earthly king, and they should not have asked for one. They thought they wanted to be like the nations around them, but they would soon be sorry that they had asked for a king other than God.

Samuel warned the people that their king would take their sons and daughters to serve him. He would take away their fields to give to people he would choose. The people would have to pay heavy taxes. Even when Samuel warned them that they would be sorry, the people wanted their own way. So a king was found.

In the tribe of Benjamin, there was a rich man named Kish who had a son named Saul. In all of Israel there was not a finer, more handsome man than Saul. He was a whole head taller than all the other men in Israel.

Now Kish had many donkeys. One day, some of his donkeys wandered away and were lost. Kish told his son, "go and look for the donkeys" (1 Samuel 9:3). Saul and a servant went out to look for the donkeys. They hunted for a long time, but they could not find the donkeys. Finally, Saul told the servant that they should go home before his father began worrying about them.

The servant told Saul that before they left they should go up to the city because he knew that Samuel lived there. So the two men went up to the city. On the way, they met some young girls who were going out to draw water. The men asked if the prophet of God lived nearby. The girls answered that Samuel was close and that he was sacrificing to God that day.

Saul and his servant hurried into the city. Soon they met Samuel himself, who was going up to sacrifice.

Samuel knew that Saul was coming, for God had told him the day before. God had told Samuel that when Saul arrived, Samuel should anoint him as king over Israel. As Saul walked up, God told Samuel, "This one shall reign over My people" (1 Samuel 9:17). At the same moment, Saul walked up to Samuel and asked where the prophet of God lived.

Samuel answered that he was the prophet of God. Then Samuel invited Saul to spend the day with him. Then, even though Saul had not asked about the donkeys, Samuel said, "But as for your donkeys that were lost three days ago, do not be anxious about them, for they have been found" (1 Samuel 9:20). Then he surprised Saul even more by telling him he was the man all Israel was looking for.

Saul did not understand what Samuel meant. He was confused, and Samuel did not yet tell him that God had chosen him as the first king of Israel.

Questions

1. What did Israel want Samuel to choose for them? _____

2. Samuel was _____ when he heard what the people wanted.

3. Who came to Samuel looking for lost donkeys? _____

Thought Question

Why is it important to ask the Lord before making big decisions, as Samuel did before choosing a king?

Catechism

Question 64: How long ago did Christ die?

Answer 64: About two thousand years ago

Memory Verse

Psalm 23:2
He makes me to lie down in green pastures; He leads me beside the still waters.

LESSON 19

Saul

1 Samuel 9:22–10:27

Saul spent the day with Samuel. The next morning, Saul and his servant wanted to go home. Samuel went with them to the edge of the city. Then he told Saul, "Tell the servant to go on ahead of us. But you stand here awhile, that I may announce to you the word of God" (1 Samuel 9:27).

Saul's servant left, but Saul stayed with Samuel. Then Samuel took a bottle of oil and emptied it over Saul's head. He kissed Saul and told him that the Lord had anointed him king over His people Israel.

Then Samuel told Saul that three things would happen to him on his way home. First, two men would tell him that his father was worrying about him. Next, he would meet three men who would give him bread. Finally, Saul would join a company of prophets.

All of these signs came true as Saul returned home. He prophesied with the company of prophets when the Spirit of God came upon him. Then Saul went home and told his family that he had spoken with Samuel; but he did not tell them that Samuel had said he would be king.

A week later, Samuel sent word to the tribes of Israel to come together. He wanted to announce the new king publicly.

When all the people arrived, Samuel chose out the tribe of Benjamin so that all the people knew from which tribe their king was chosen. Then Samuel called out one family. The men of that family came forward, and Saul's name was called, but Saul could not be found.

Saul knew that he would be chosen as king, but he was afraid. He did not want to face all the people of Israel, so he hid. The people asked the Lord what they should do, and the Lord told them that Saul was hiding among the bags and equipment they had brought.

So the people found Saul and brought him out before all of Israel. Then Samuel told the people, "Do you see him whom the LORD has chosen, that there is no one like him among all the people?" (1 Samuel 10:24).

So all the people shouted, "Long live the king!" (1 Samuel 10:24). The people of Israel were very happy to have a king and to be like other nations.

Questions

1. Who anointed Saul? _____

2. What was Saul doing when his name was called? _____

3. Who was the first human king of Israel? _____

Thought Question

Why might the people have been so happy to have Saul as king?

Catechism

Question 64: How long ago did Christ die?

Answer 64: About two thousand years ago

Memory Verse

Psalm 23:2

He makes me to lie down in green pastures; He leads me beside the still waters.

LESSON 20

Week 4 Review

Memory Verse

Psalm 23:1–2

Catechism

Question 10: Where is God?

Question 11: Can you see God?

Question 12: Does God know all things?

Question 63: How can you get the help of the Holy Spirit?

Question 64: How long ago did Christ die?

To the Teacher : The answers to catechism questions 10–12 are found on page 265.

Activity

Fill in the Blank

Word Bank: Benjamin   face   God   hid   judge   king   Philistines   Saul

1. The _____ took the ark of the covenant to their own heathen temple.

2. The Philistines' idol fell on its _____ before the ark of the covenant.

3. Samuel grew up to be a _____ of Israel.

4. The Israelites claimed that they wanted a _____ to be like the nations.

5. _____ was the true King of Israel.

6. Samuel anointed _____ as the first human king of Israel.

7. Saul was from the tribe of _____ .

8. Saul _____ with the bags and equipment because he was afraid.

Unit 5 — *Fighting Israel's Enemies*

LESSON 21

Saul Saves the Eyes of His People

1 Samuel 11:1–15

Remember that the tribes of Reuben, Gad, and half of Manasseh had settled on the eastern side of the Jordan River. A people called the Ammonites had lived near there when Israel first entered the land. Israel did not fight with Ammon because the Ammonites were the children of Lot, Abraham's nephew.

So the Ammonites still lived near Israel. Their king was named Nahash, and he was a cruel and wicked man. He gathered an army and marched against Jabesh Gilead, one of Israel's cities on the east bank of the Jordan This was very wrong of Nahash, for Israel had not tried to fight against Ammon.

The people of Jabesh Gilead were afraid when they saw Nahash's army. They went out to the army and tried to make peace with Nahash. They promised that if Nahash would not kill them, then they would be his servants. Nahash, however, was not satisfied with their offer. Instead, he said, "On this condition I will make a covenant with you, that I may put out all your right eyes, and bring reproach on all Israel" (1 Samuel 11:2).

The men of Jabesh Gilead were even more afraid. They asked Nahash for seven days to send for help. Messengers ran to a city where Saul lived. All the people began to weep when they heard what had happened. As they cried out, Saul came to them and asked why everyone was so upset. When he heard the story, he became very angry.

Then the Spirit of the Lord came upon Saul and made him brave and strong. Saul took a yoke of oxen, cut them in pieces, and sent them to all the tribes of Israel along with a message: "Whoever does not go out with Saul and Samuel to battle, so it shall be done to his oxen" (1 Samuel 11:7).

All the men of Israel came quickly to Saul until he had an army of 330,000 men. Now that they had a leader, they were happy to go and fight.

After dividing his men into three companies, Saul hurried across the Jordan River. The Israelites met the Ammonites early in the morning. Nahash's army was beaten so badly that no two of his soldiers were left together.

This great victory made Saul the hero of Israel. The people were willing to do anything for this strong, handsome soldier who had led them so well. Not everyone in Israel was happy at first with Saul as their king. After this victory, however, the Israelites were willing to kill anyone who had not wanted Saul to be king. Yet Saul answered, "Not a man shall be put to death this day, for today the LORD has accomplished salvation in Israel" (1 Samuel 11:13).

Then the Israelites went to Gilgal where they sacrificed to God who had given them the victory. After that, they publicly made Saul their king.

Questions

1. Nahash wanted to put out the right _____ of the Israelites.

2. _____ led the people into battle.

3. Was anyone unhappy to call Saul king after the battle? _____

Thought Question

Why was it important that the Spirit of the Lord came upon Saul so that he could lead?

Catechism

Question 65: How were sinners saved before Christ came?
Answer 65: By believing in the promised Messiah

Memory Verse

Psalm 23:3
He restores my soul; He leads me in the paths of righteousness for His name's sake.

LESSON 22

Saul's Unlawful Sacrifice

1 Samuel 13:1–23

Saul reigned as king for several years. He chose 3,000 men to be warriors with him. He led 2,000 men, and his oldest son, Jonathan, led the other thousand.

Jonathan and his men attacked a small group of Philistines, but soon all the Philistines had heard about it. They were angry with Israel and brought together a huge army to fight.

So Saul called all of Israel to come to him. The Israelites were terrified, but they followed. Now Saul was set for battle against the Philistines, but he was to wait for Samuel to come and sacrifice to God first. Saul waited for seven days, and still Samuel did not come.

Then Saul became impatient and offered a burnt offering himself. As soon as he was done, Samuel arrived and asked, "What have you done?" (1 Samuel 13:11). Saul tried to excuse himself by saying that he needed the people to be brave and that Samuel had been late.

Samuel did not accept any excuses. Saul was not a priest and was not supposed to sacrifice to God. Samuel told Saul that the Lord would have made Saul's family kings in Israel forever. Now that Saul had acted foolishly, though, God would choose another king. God would find a man after His own heart.

Then Samuel rose and went away while Saul prepared for battle. Israel did not have very many men compared to the Philistines. This was not their worst problem, however.

The Israelites also had no swords, spears, or other weapons. The Philistines had made sure that no one in Israel was able to make swords and spears. They did not want the Israelites to have weapons to fight them. So instead, the Israelites would have to fight with axes and farm tools. Only Saul and Jonathan had swords.

Questions

1. Who was Saul's son? _____

2. Instead of waiting for Samuel, Saul offered a burnt _____ himself, which was against God's Law.

Thought Question

Why was it important for Saul to wait for Samuel, even though he was afraid and impatient?

Catechism

Question 65: How were sinners saved before Christ came?
Answer 65: By believing in the promised Messiah

Memory Verse

Psalm 23:3
He restores my soul; He leads me in the paths of righteousness for His name's sake.

LESSON 23

Jonathan

1 Samuel 14:1–48

Jonathan, Saul's son, was a brave warrior who trusted in God. He took his armorbearer and went up to the Philistine camp. He did not tell his father what he was doing, so no one knew that Jonathan and his armorbearer were gone.

When they were close to the Philistine camp, Jonathan told his armorbearer, "It may be that the LORD will work for us. For nothing restrains the LORD from saving by many or by few" (1 Samuel 14:6). The man who carried Jonathan's armor said that he would follow Jonathan.

So Jonathan went out and showed himself to the Philistines. He told his armorbearer that if the Philistines told them to wait where they stood, then they would wait. However, if the Philistines called for them to come up to the camp, then they would go up, and this would be the sign that the Lord had given the Philistines into their hands.

When the Philistines saw Jonathan and his armorbearer, they called for the men to come up to the camp. So Jonathan and his armorbearer went into the Philistine camp. That day, the Philistines fell before Jonathan so that he and his armorbearer killed twenty men. Then the earth began to shake, and the Philistines were so confused that they began to fight each other.

Saul and his men heard a great uproar in the Philistine camp. They wondered what was happening. They called together all the men and discovered that Jonathan and his armorbearer were not with them. Then Saul took the whole army and went to the Philistine camp. There, he found the Philistines fighting each other. So the Lord saved Israel from the Philistines that day.

Saul had a problem, however. Earlier in the day, he had made an oath that anyone who ate any food before the Philistines were completely defeated would be punished. Jonathan had not heard his father's oath because he was not in the camp. After the first fight against the Philistines, the Israelites came across some honey in the forest. Jonathan ate some honey, and the army was afraid for him because of his father's oath.

Later, Saul inquired of the Lord, asking if he should go down to finish fighting the Philistines. When God did not answer, Saul knew that someone had eaten food. He was so angry that he promised to kill the man who had eaten food. Then he discovered that Jonathan was the man who had eaten food.

Jonathan was upset with his father. He knew that the men would have fought better and truly defeated the Philistines if they had been able to eat before the battle. But he said, "I only tasted a little honey…. So now I must die!" (1 Samuel 14:43). And Saul agreed. He was willing to kill his own son.

The Israelite army, however, was not willing to let Jonathan die. They rescued Jonathan from Saul that day saying, "Shall Jonathan die, who has accomplished this great deliverance in Israel? Certainly not! As the LORD lives, not one hair of his head shall fall to the ground, for he has worked with God this day" (1 Samuel 14:45).

Then Saul no longer pursued the Philistines, and the Philistines went to their own homes. So Saul continued to rule Israel and fight against all of Israel's enemies.

Questions

1. Jonathan and his _____ left camp to fight the Philistines.

2. Who fought with Jonathan and his armorbearer? _____

3. Saul had told the people they could not _____ before the battle.

Thought Question

"Nothing restrains the LORD from saving by many or by few" (1 Samuel 14:6). What does this quote mean?

Catechism

Question 66: Before Christ came, how did believers show their faith?
Answer 66: By offering the sacrifices God required

Memory Verse

Psalm 23:3
He restores my soul; He leads me in the paths of righteousness for His name's sake.

LESSON 24

Cumulative Review 1

Job, Samuel, and Saul

1. What did Hannah name her son? _____

2. Israel wanted Samuel to choose a _____ for them.

3. Who was the first human king of Israel? _____

4. Who was Saul's son? _____

Oral Questions

1. What did God give Satan permission to do to Job?

2. What did Job's friends think was causing Job's troubles?

3. What was Elihu's answer to Job's complaints against God?

4. List at least three things that God controls.

Catechism

Question 66: Before Christ came, how did believers show their faith?
Answer 66: By offering the sacrifices God required

Memory Verse

Psalm 23:3
He restores my soul; He leads me in the paths of righteousness for His name's sake.

LESSON 25

Week 5 Review

Memory Verse

Psalm 23:1–3

Catechism

Question 13: Can God do all things?

Question 14: Where do you learn how to love and obey God?

Question 15: Who wrote the Bible?

Question 65: How were sinners saved before Christ came?

Question 66: Before Christ came, how did believers show their faith?

To the Teacher : The answers to catechism questions 13–15 are found on page 265.

Activity

Maze: Help Jonathan and his armorbearer reach the Philistine camp.

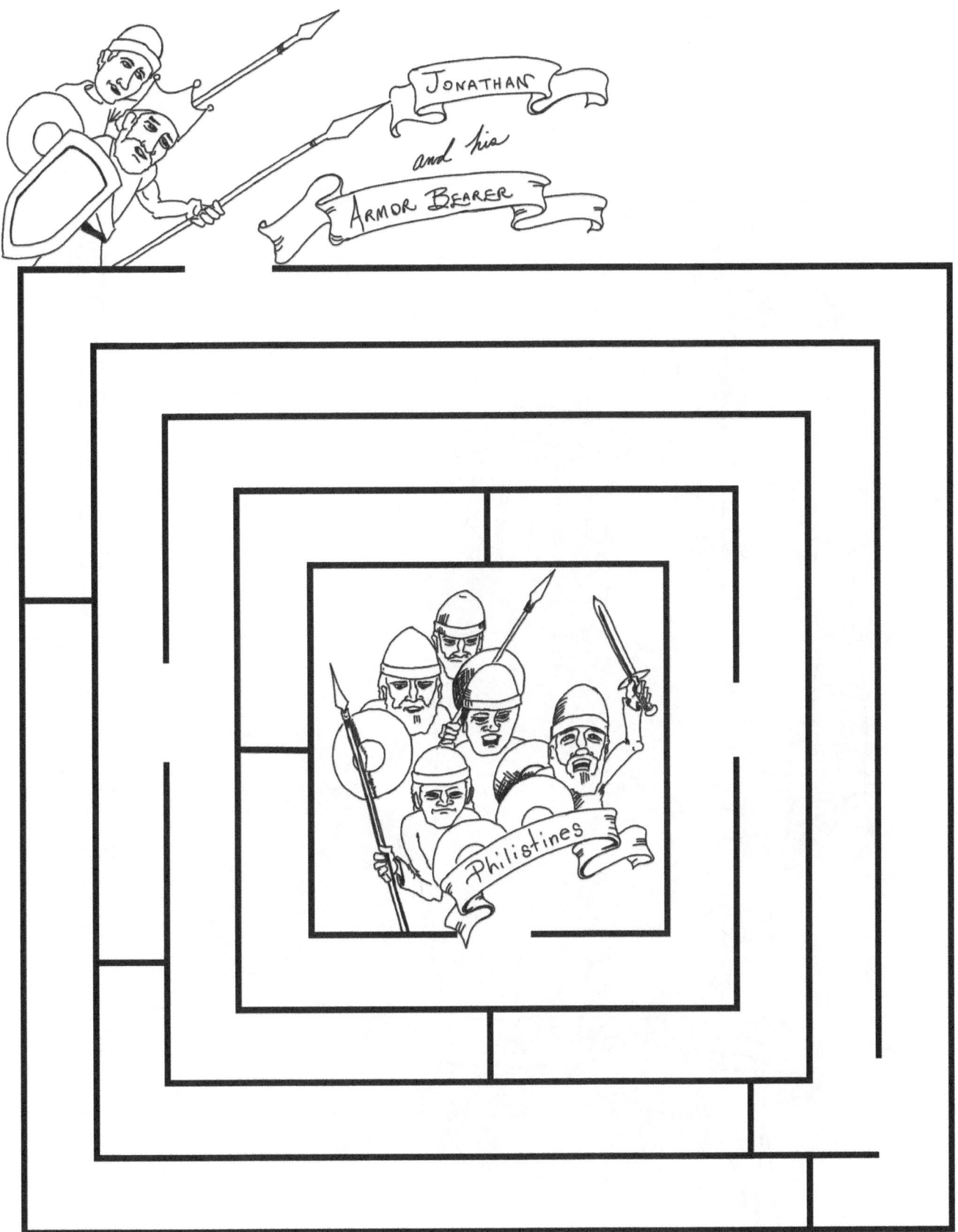

Unit 6   David Anointed King

Saul Loses the Kingdom

1 Samuel 15:1–35

Back when Israel was leaving Egypt, a group of people called the Amalekites had given them a lot of trouble. Joshua had fought the Amalekites while Moses prayed, but the Amalekites had been so wicked that God had promised to have war with them forever.

After Saul had been king of Israel for several years, Samuel came to him with a message from God: "Now go and attack Amalek, and utterly destroy all that they have, and do not spare them" (1 Samuel 15:3).

Saul collected his soldiers and counted them—210,000 soldiers were ready for war. With this army, Saul marched south to the desert where the Amalekites lived.

The Israelites won a great battle against Amalek. Saul killed all the people, as God had commanded. However, he and his soldiers did not kill all the animals as God had told them to do. In addition, Saul captured Agag, the king of Amalek, and kept him alive.

That night, God told Samuel, "I greatly regret that I have set up Saul as king, for he has turned back from following Me, and has not performed My commandments" (1 Samuel 15:11).

Samuel was upset and cried out to the Lord all night long. In the morning, he went to find Saul. The king met him joyfully and expected Samuel to be pleased with him. However, Samuel just said, "What then is this bleating of the sheep in my ears, and the lowing of the oxen which I hear?" (1 Samuel 15:14).

Saul tried to excuse himself and say that the animals were kept as sacrifices for God, but Samuel told Saul to be quiet. Then he told Saul what God had said the night before. He reminded Saul that God had made him king and that he owed obedience to God. Samuel told Saul plainly that he had disobeyed God in not destroying everything that belonged to Amalek.

Saul tried again to say he had done the right thing, but Samuel told him that God was much more pleased with obedience than with sacrifices. Then Samuel said, "Because you have rejected the word of the LORD, He also has rejected you from being king" (1 Samuel 15:23).

Then Saul, who still did not understand, asked Samuel to come and worship with him. He seemed to think that God might forget to punish him or forget that he had sinned. Yet Samuel would not go with Saul. Instead, he told Saul one last time that God would not let Saul remain as king.

As Samuel turned to leave, Saul reached out and grabbed the edge of Samuel's robe. The robe tore in Saul's hands. Then Samuel said, "The LORD has torn the kingdom of Israel from you today, and has given it to a neighbor of yours, who is better than you" (1 Samuel 15:28).

Then Samuel ordered the people to bring Agag to him. Agag thought that if the Israelites were going to kill him, they would have done it already. He thought he was safe, but Samuel killed Agag before the Lord with his own hand.

Finally, Samuel returned to his house in Ramah. Even though he mourned for Saul, he never went to see that king of Israel again.

Questions

1. What group of people was Saul supposed to destroy? _____

2. God said, "I greatly _____ that I have set up Saul as king."

3. God took the _____ of Israel away from Saul.

Thought Question

Why does God want obedience instead of sacrifices?

Catechism

Question 67: What did these sacrifices represent?
Answer 67: Christ, the Lamb of God, who would come to die for sinners

Memory Verse

Psalm 23:4

Yea, though I walk through the valley of the shadow of death, I will fear no evil; for You are with me; Your rod and Your staff, they comfort me.

LESSON 27

How a Shepherd Was Anointed King

1 Samuel 16:1–23

After a time, God told Samuel to fill his horn with oil and to go down to see a man named Jesse who lived in Bethlehem. God had chosen one of Jesse's sons to be the new king of Israel.

Samuel was afraid to go down. He thought that Saul would kill him if he discovered that he was anointing a new king. So God told Samuel to bring a sacrifice to Bethlehem and invite Jesse to the sacrifice. Samuel obeyed God and did everything He said.

Now Jesse was the grandson of Ruth and Boaz. He had many fine, strong sons. They went to Samuel when he invited them.

When Samuel saw Jesse's oldest son, Eliab, he thought for sure that he would be God's chosen. Eliab was tall and strong. God said, "Do not look at his appearance or at his physical stature, because I have refused him. For the LORD does not see as man sees; for man looks at the outward appearance, but the LORD looks at the heart" (1 Samuel 16:7).

So Samuel looked at Jesse's second son, Abinadab. Again, God said no. Then the third son, Shammah, was rejected. One by one, seven of Jesse's sons were not chosen by God to be king.

Samuel looked around and found that there were no more sons. He asked Jesse if all of his sons were there. Jesse answered that his youngest son, David, was at home keeping the sheep. Then Samuel sent for David and would not sit down until the youngest boy came to see him.

David finally came in from the fields. He was a young man, and good-looking. He had a fresh, healthy color in his face from being outside day after day with the sheep.

When David arrived, God told Samuel, "Arise, anoint him; for this is the one!" (1 Samuel 16:12). Samuel went to David and anointed him with oil as his brothers stood by and watched. The Spirit of the Lord came upon David from that day onward.

Then Samuel returned to Ramah. David would not publicly be recognized as king for many years, for Saul was still king, even though the Spirit of God was no longer with him. His disobedience had shown that his heart was not good. When God's Spirit left Saul, an evil spirit came to trouble him.

Some of Saul's servants told the king to look for a man who was skilled in playing the harp. Then, whenever the king was troubled by the evil spirit, the harp's music would soothe him.

Saul agreed. One of his servants knew of a shepherd boy who played the harp very well. The boy was a son of Jesse named David. Then Saul commanded David to come live in the palace. Whenever the evil spirit came upon Saul, David played his harp for the king and the evil spirit would leave.

Questions

1. Whose house did Samuel visit in Bethlehem? _____

2. Which of Jesse's sons was anointed as king? _____ , his youngest son

3. What instrument did David play for Saul? _____

Thought Question

What does God mean when He says that man sees only the outward appearance of man, but that He looks at man's heart?

Catechism

Question 67: What did these sacrifices represent?
Answer 67: Christ, the Lamb of God, who would come to die for sinners

Memory Verse

Psalm 23:4
Yea, though I walk through the valley of the shadow of death, I will fear no evil; for You are with me; Your rod and Your staff, they comfort me.

LESSON 28

David and Goliath

1 Samuel 17:1–32

Saul had trouble with the Philistines the entire time he was king. Over and over again, the Philistines came to fight Israel. A short time after David was anointed, the Philistines gathered an army and came once again. Saul and his soldiers went out to meet them. The armies camped on separate mountains with a valley to separate them.

With the Philistine army was a man named Goliath of Gath. He was more than nine feet tall! Goliath was a giant. He dressed in metal from head to foot. He held an enormous spear that a normal man could not even pick up.

Every day, Goliath came out of the Philistine camp and shouted a challenge across to the other mountain where Israel was camped. He challenged, "Choose a man for yourselves, and let him come down to me. If he is able to fight with me and kill me, then we will be your servants. But if I prevail against him and kill him, then you shall be our servants and serve us…. I defy the armies of Israel this day" (1 Samuel 17:8–10).

The Israelites were terrified. Not one man from the army of Israel wanted to fight against the Philistines, not even King Saul.

Since Saul was away at war, David had gone home to his father to care for the sheep. Several of his older brothers had joined Saul's army. One day, Jesse told David to take some food to the Israelite camp for his brothers and to bring back word of how his brothers were doing.

David left his sheep with a keeper and left early for the battlefield. When he reached the army, the men were just getting ready to go out to battle. David ran to find his brothers. As he spoke with his brothers, Goliath came out of the Philistine camp and began to challenge Israel, just as he had for forty days. David heard everything Goliath said and saw the men of Israel's army run and hide.

Some soldiers near David told him about the giant. They also said that Saul had promised great riches to the man who killed Goliath. Saul had even promised to give that man his daughter in marriage. Still, not a man in the army wanted to fight Goliath. They were all convinced that they would lose.

David answered, "For who is this uncircumcised Philistine, that he should defy the armies of the living God?" (1 Samuel 17:26). David believed that God was more powerful than any giant and would help His people.

Some of the men told Saul what David had said, so Saul called David to him. Then David told Saul, "Let no man's heart fail because of him [Goliath]; your servant will go and fight with this Philistine" (1 Samuel 17:32). When no man of the army would fight Goliath, David, a young shepherd boy, decided to fight for them.

Questions

1. What was the giant's name? _____

2. Who wanted to fight the giant? _____

Thought Question

Why was David so upset when he realized that no one from Israel would fight Goliath?

Catechism

Question 68: How many offices does Christ fulfill as the promised Messiah?
Answer 68: Christ fulfills three offices.

Memory Verse

Psalm 23:4
Yea, though I walk through the valley of the shadow of death, I will fear no evil; for You are with me; Your rod and Your staff, they comfort me.

LESSON 29

David Kills a Giant

1 Samuel 17:33–58

Saul was afraid for David at first. He tried to convince David that he was too young and small to fight Goliath. Yet David told Saul about being a shepherd in his father's fields and how he had killed a lion and a bear. David knew that the real reason he would beat Goliath was that God was with him. He told Saul, "The LORD, who delivered me from the paw of the lion and from the paw of the bear, He will deliver me from the hand of this Philistine" (1 Samuel 17:37). Saul agreed to let David fight Goliath.

However, Saul thought David would be safer if he wore some armor. So he gave David all his own armor to go into battle. David could not move in the armor, though, and he took it off. He preferred to battle with his own weapons—a sling, some stones, and the strength of the Lord.

So David went down to a stream that was in the valley between the two mountains where the armies were camping. From the streambed David took five smooth stones and placed them in his shepherd's bag. Carrying those, his staff, and his sling, David ran towards Goliath.

Goliath was insulted because David was only a boy, not a warrior. He said, "Am I a dog, that you come to me with sticks?" (1 Samuel 17:43). David kept walking forwards. He was not afraid of Goliath. He told Goliath that even though the giant had bigger weapons, David was fighting in the name of the Lord. He told Goliath that the Lord would let David kill him. David wanted all the people to know that God did not save with swords and spears. The Lord would defeat Goliath any way He chose.

When David said all of this, Goliath came forward to kill him. David ran towards the Philistine. He put his hand into his bag, brought out a stone, and placed it in his sling. He slung the stone right at the giant. The stone hit Goliath's forehead and sank in deep. Goliath fell face downward on the ground.

David ran up to the giant. He pulled Goliath's sword out of the sheath and cut off the giant's enormous head with it.

All of the Israelites and Philistines were watching the fight. When the Philistines saw that their champion was dead, they ran away as fast as they could. The men of Israel shouted out loud and chased the Philistines all the way back to the gates of the Philistine cities.

Many Philistines were killed that day. It was also on this day that Saul began to notice the young man, David, who had done such a brave deed.

Questions

1. Whom did David trust to win the battle? _____

2. How many stones did David pick up? _____

3. David cut off Goliath's head with the giant's _____.

Thought Question

Do you think it was a good thing or a bad thing that Saul began to notice how brave David was? Why?

Catechism

Question 68: How many offices does Christ fulfill as the promised Messiah?
Answer 68: Christ fulfills three offices.

Memory Verse

Psalm 23:4
Yea, though I walk through the valley of the shadow of death, I will fear no evil; for You are with me; Your rod and Your staff, they comfort me.

LESSON 30

Week 6 Review

Memory Verse

Psalm 23:1–4

Catechism

Question 16: Who were our first parents?

Question 17: How did God create man?

Question 18: Of what were our first parents made?

Question 67: What did these sacrifices represent?

Question 68: How many offices does Christ fulfill as the promised Messiah?

To the Teacher : The answers to catechism questions 16–18 are found on page 265.

Activity
Matching

Match the people on the right to their actions on the left.

A. Defeated a giant   _____ Saul

B. Anointed a new king   _____ God

C. Sacrificed without waiting for Samuel   _____ Samuel

D. Taunted God's people   _____ Goliath

E. Took Israel away from Saul   _____ David

Unit 7   Saul Seeks to Kill David

LESSON 31

David in Trouble

1 Samuel 18:1–19:19

Saul was so pleased with David's bravery in battle that he kept David with him at the palace. Saul's son Jonathan became very good friends with David. Jonathan loved David more than he loved himself, and David loved Jonathan, too. They were godly friends who made a covenant together. Then Jonathan gave David his own robe, armor, sword, bow, and belt. Because he was Saul's oldest son, Jonathan's possessions were very nice, but he gave them to David because he loved his friend.

So David continued living at the king's court. He went wherever Saul sent him and did what Saul told him. Wherever David went, the people loved and respected him. Soon Saul made David the captain of his army.

One day, as David was returning from a battle with the Philistines, the women of the cities they passed through came out to meet King Saul. They danced and played instruments and sang, "Saul has slain his thousands, and David his ten thousands" (1 Samuel 18:7).

When Saul heard what the women sang, he became angry and jealous of David. He began to worry that the people would begin to love David so much that they would want him as king instead of Saul.

The next day, the evil spirit came upon Saul. David played his harp for Saul as he had done before. This time, however, Saul was holding a spear in his hand. He began to hate David so much that he threw the spear at David, trying to kill him. David managed to escape, even when it happened a second time. After that, Saul did not want David in his house. He sent him into the army and made him captain of 1,000 men. By this time, David had grown to be a strong man, and the Lord was with him.

Saul began to be even more afraid of David because he was brave and wise. He knew the people loved David, though, so he could not have him killed. Instead, he decided to try to have David killed in battle.

Now Jonathan was not the only member of Saul's family who loved David. Saul's daughter Michal also loved David. David loved Michal, too. Saul told David that if he killed 100 Philistines, then he could marry Michal. David went out willingly with his 1,000 men.

Saul hoped David would be killed by the Philistines. Instead, David and his men killed 200 Philistines, and Saul kept his promise. David married Michal, and Saul continued to grow more and more afraid of David because everyone, even his own children, loved him.

Then Saul tried a different approach. He told Jonathan and his servants to kill David. Jonathan was greatly displeased. He found David and warned him. He told David to hide for a little while. David listened to his friend, and Jonathan went back to Saul and spoke well of David. He reminded Saul of all that David had done for him.

Saul was ashamed and promised not to kill David. So Jonathan brought David back to the king's court and presented him to Saul. David lived in the court until he went out to fight the Philistines. Again, he won a great victory.

Once again Saul became jealous of the young warrior. The evil spirit also bothered him, so David came to play his harp. Yet Saul tried to kill him with a spear again. David escaped, and the spear stuck in the wall.

This time, however, Saul was so angry that he sent men to David's house to kill him. Saul's daughter, Michal, defeated her father's plans. She let David out through a window. David ran away and stayed with Samuel for a while.

Questions

1. Who was David's best friend? _____

2. Whom did David marry? _____

3. Saul was _____ of David because the people liked him.

Thought Question

Why might Saul have been so terrified of David?

41

Catechism

Question 69: What are they?

Answer 69: The offices of a prophet, of a priest, and of a king

Memory Verse

Psalm 23:5

You prepare a table before me in the presence of my enemies; You anoint my head with oil; my cup runs over.

LESSON 32

David and Jonathan

1 Samuel 20:1–42

David knew he could not hide from Saul forever. He soon came back and secretly met with Jonathan. He asked what he had done to make Saul so angry. He knew Saul wanted to kill him.

Jonathan was very upset. He did not think Saul would kill David after he had promised he would not. He did not think Saul would plan something like that and not tell him. However, David reminded Jonathan that Saul knew they were friends and might not trust him because he had already saved David once.

Then David asked Jonathan to do something for him. The next three days were feast days. Jonathan and David were supposed to be there. David asked Jonathan to talk to Saul for him. When Saul asked why David was not there, Jonathan was supposed to tell him that David had gone home to sacrifice with his family. If Saul was fine with that answer, then David was safe. If Saul was angry, then David would have to run away.

Jonathan agreed. He promised to tell David what Saul said. Jonathan might have been king one day, following in his father's footsteps; but he understood that God wanted David to be the next king. He was not jealous of David. Instead, he made another covenant with David, asking for David's kindness not only to him, but also to all of his children. David promised to care for Jonathan's family.

Then Jonathan hid David in the fields. When he brought news of Saul's anger, he would bring his bow and a boy to find his arrows. If he told the boy to find his arrows on this side, then David would know he was safe. But if Jonathan told the boy that the arrows were beyond him, then David should run away.

So David hid for three days while Jonathan went to the feast of the New Moon. When Saul asked about David, Jonathan answered as David had instructed. Saul flew into a rage. In front of everyone at the table, he began to yell at Jonathan and say very harsh things to him.

Jonathan was angry, too. He asked his father, "Why should he be killed? What has he done?" (1 Samuel 20:32). Saul was so angry with Jonathan that he cast his spear at him, his own son, as he had done with David several times.

Jonathan became so angry that he got up and left the feast. He refused to eat anything, for he knew his father was treating David shamefully. The next morning, he brought a little boy down to where he knew David was hiding. When he fired his arrows, he called to the little boy, "Is not the arrow beyond you? Make haste, hurry, do not delay" (1 Samuel 20:37–38).

David knew that he must flee, or he would be killed. First, though, Jonathan sent the little boy away with his bow and arrows. He knew he would have to say good-bye to his best friend. David and Jonathan both wept as they said good-bye.

Jonathan said, "Go in peace, since we have both sworn in the name of the LORD, saying, 'May the LORD be between you and me, and between your descendants and my descendants, forever" (1 Samuel 20:42). Then the two friends went their ways, David into the desert and Jonathan back to the palace.

Questions

1. _____ sought out help from Jonathan.

2. Saul tried to _____ his own son, Jonathan.

Thought Question

Why would it be important for David and Jonathan to make a covenant to care for each others' families?

Catechism

Question 69: What are they?
Answer 69: The offices of a prophet, of a priest, and of a king

Memory Verse

Psalm 23:5
You prepare a table before me in the presence of my enemies; You anoint my head with oil; my cup runs over.

LESSON 33

David the Outlaw

1 Samuel 21:1–23:29

David began to run away from Saul. First, he went to visit a priest named Ahimelech. The priest gave David some bread and Goliath's sword, which had been stored there, as a weapon. Sadly, a wicked man named Doeg was also staying near the priest. He saw David there, and David knew that Doeg would tell Saul.

So David ran until he reached Gath, the Philistine city. Even there, some men went to the Philistine king about David and asked if he was the one all of Israel was praising. The king called David to him. To avoid being captured, David pretended to be crazy. He scratched at the doors and let spit run into his beard. The Philistine king said, "Have I need of madmen?" (1 Samuel 21:15).

David escaped that time, but knew he had to move on again. Praying to God to help him, he took refuge in a big cave called the cave of Adullam in the country of Judah. When David's brothers and father heard where David was hiding, his whole family went and joined him. In fact, many Israelites who did not like Saul joined David in the cave. Before long, David had 400 men that followed him.

Afraid that Saul would find them, David moved his men far away from Israel. They went to Moab, where David arranged a safe place for his mother and father to stay, for they were too old to continue following David. David's parents stayed there the whole time David ran from Saul. Soon God sent the prophet Gad to tell David to return to Judah. David and his 400 men obeyed.

Meanwhile, Saul was angry that he could not find David. The wicked man Doeg came and told Saul where he had seen David. When Saul found out that Ahimelech had helped David, he killed the priest and his family. One of Ahimelech's sons escaped and ran to find David. David was distressed when he heard what happened. He promised that Ahimelech's son would be safe with him.

Then the Philistines started causing trouble again. David asked God if he should go and fight them. David and his men, who numbered about 600 by then, obeyed God and fought the Philistines. They won, too, but Saul heard about the battle and brought an army down to capture David.

David hid in the wilderness, and Saul could not find him no matter how hard he hunted. Jonathan was there too, and he heard where David was hiding. He went down and encouraged his friend.

In this place, there was a city that was not friendly to David. They offered to help Saul catch his enemy. Saul was pleased, and he soon knew exactly where David was hiding. He took his army to find David.

Just in time, David heard of Saul's army coming. He and his men began to run away, but Saul's army was very close. There seemed to be no chance for David to escape. Suddenly, a messenger came to Saul and said, "Hurry and come, for the Philistines have invaded the land" (1 Samuel 23:27). Saul had to take his whole army and go fight the Philistines. David was safe for the moment.

Questions

1. David escaped from the Philistine king by pretending to be _____.

2. Saul _____ the priest who helped David.

3. Who went down to encourage David? _____

Thought Question

Why do you suppose Saul was unable to find David and capture or kill him?

Catechism

Question 70: How is Christ your prophet?
Answer 70: Christ teaches me the will of God.

Memory Verse

Psalm 23:5
You prepare a table before me in the presence of my enemies; You anoint my head with oil; my cup runs over.

LESSON 34

David Spares Saul

1 Samuel 24:1–22

David took his men and hid in the wilderness of En Gedi, which was near "the Rocks of the Wild Goats." The little army hid in a cave there.

Meanwhile, Saul fought the Philistines. When he had driven off his enemy, he took 3,000 of his best soldiers and went to the wilderness to hunt for David.

Saul even found the exact cave that David and his men were hiding in, but he did not know it. He went inside the cave but did not see David and his men. David was close enough to Saul that he was able to cut off a corner of Saul's robe. His men wanted him to kill Saul, but David would not. He said, "The Lord forbid that I should do this thing to my master, the Lord's anointed, to stretch out my hand against him, seeing he is the anointed of the Lord" (1 Samuel 24:6).

As Saul left the cave, David followed him and called out to him. Saul turned around and saw that the very man he was hunting was calling out to him.

David told Saul not to believe anyone who said David wanted to hurt the king. "Look," David said, "this day your eyes have seen that the Lord delivered you today into my hand in the cave, and someone urged me to kill you. But my eye spared you" (1 Samuel 24:10). David promised that he would not try to kill Saul. He also said that if Saul kept hunting him when he had done nothing wrong, then God would judge Saul.

Saul knew that everything David said was true. When he heard all the words David had to say and saw that David had spared his life, he felt very ashamed. He answered David, "You are more righteous than I; for you have rewarded me with good, whereas I have rewarded you with evil.... And now I know indeed that you shall surely be king, and that the kingdom of Israel shall be established in your hand" (1 Samuel 24:17, 20).

Then Saul asked David to promise him that he would not kill all of Saul's family and children when he became king. David promised, and then Saul went home. David and his men went up to the stronghold of En Gedi; however, Saul could not be trusted. At any moment, he might become angry again and decide to hunt David down and kill him.

Questions

1. David's men wanted him to kill _____ when he entered the cave.

2. David _____ Saul's life instead.

3. Saul knew that David would someday become _____ of Israel.

Thought Question

Why would Saul make David promise not to kill his family and children?

Catechism

Question 70: How is Christ your prophet?
Answer 70: Christ teaches me the will of God.

Memory Verse

Psalm 23:5
You prepare a table before me in the presence of my enemies; You anoint my head with oil; my cup runs over.

LESSON 35

Week 7 Review

Psalm 23:1–5

Catechism

Question 19: What else did God give Adam and Eve besides bodies?

Question 20: Do you have a soul as well as a body?

Question 21: How do you know your soul will last forever?

Question 68: How many offices does Christ fulfill as the promised Messiah?

Question 70: How is Christ your prophet?

To the Teacher :   The answers to catechism questions 19–21 are found on page 265.

Activity
Number the Order of Events

Number the parts of David's story from one to four.

_____ Saul throws a spear at David, trying to kill him.

_____ Saul kills the priests who helped David.

_____ Jonathan tells David to run away.

_____ David spares Saul's life in the cave.

Unit 8 — King Saul's Decline

LESSON 36

A Wise Wife and Foolish Husband

1 Samuel 25:1–42

At this time, the good old prophet Samuel died. All the people of Israel went to Ramah to mourn for him. David could not go, for Saul was still hunting for him.

Instead, David took his army south of the Dead Sea into the Wilderness of Paran, another rough country. On his way, he had to pass by a farm that belonged to a very rich man named Nabal. Nabal was cross and selfish, but he had a beautiful wife who was sensible and generous. Her name was Abigail.

It was the time of year when sheep were sheared. Nabal had many sheep, so he hired some men to come work for him. He prepared a great deal of food and held a feast for all his workers.

David often had a hard time finding enough food for all of his followers. When he heard that Nabal was having a feast, he sent ten young men to Nabal with a message: "Now I have heard that you have shearers. Your shepherds were with us, and we did not hurt them, nor was there anything missing from them all the while they were in Carmel…. Therefore let my young men find favor in your eyes, for we come on a feast day. Please give whatever comes to your hand to your servants and to your son David" (1 Samuel 25:7–8).

Nabal responded rudely to David's messengers and told them he would give David nothing. When David heard how rude Nabal had been, he became so angry that he told his men to get ready. They were going to punish Nabal.

In the meantime, one of Nabal's servants heard what David was planning and ran to Abigail. He told her how David had sent messengers, how Nabal had responded rudely, and how David was on his way to punish Nabal.

Wise Abigail acted quickly. She took 200 loaves of bread, two big, full wineskins, five cooked sheep, five measures of parched wheat, 100 clusters of raisins, and 200 cakes of figs. She loaded all the food onto donkeys and sent it all off with some servants to David. Then she rode another donkey behind the gift of food. She, however, did not tell Nabal what she was doing.

As soon as Abigail saw David, she got off her donkey and bowed to the ground before him. She apologized for how her husband had acted. Then she said, "For the LORD will certainly make for my lord [David] an enduring house, because my lord fights the battles of the LORD, and evil is not found in you throughout your days" (1 Samuel 25:28).

When David heard Abigail's apology, he was pleased. He told her she gave blessed advice and agreed not to punish Nabal. Then Abigail went home.

There, Nabal was having his great feast. He was very drunk, and Abigail did not tell him what she had done. In the morning, when Nabal was no longer drunk, Abigail did tell him what had happened and how much danger he had been in. When Nabal heard this, he was so frightened that his heart almost stopped beating. About ten days later, the Lord struck Nabal, and he died.

When David heard of Nabal's death, he sent some messengers to Abigail to ask her to come and be his wife. So Abigail mounted her donkey and went to live with David.

Questions

1. David wanted to punish Nabal because of his _____.

2. _____ was Nabal's wise wife.

3. Nabal's wife told him all that happened; ten days later, God struck him, and Nabal _____.

Thought Question

Why did God kill Nabal?

Catechism

Question 71: How is Christ your priest?
Answer 71: Christ died for my sins, and continues to pray for me.

Memory Verse

Psalm 23:6
Surely goodness and mercy shall follow me all the days of my life, and I will dwell in the house of the Lᴏʀᴅ forever.

LESSON 37

David Spares Saul Again

1 Samuel 26:1–27:12

Saul did not keep his promise of not hurting David. The people living near David were not friendly to the outlaw and told Saul where David was hiding. Saul and an army of 3,000 soldiers went to hunt for David in the wilderness. Soon David's spies were telling him that Saul was hunting them once more.

One night, David and his soldiers went to the place where Saul and his soldiers were camping. God sent a sound sleep on the Saul's soldiers. David and one of his companions, Abishai, walked quietly through the camp, and not one of Saul's men woke up. Saul was sleeping, and his general Abner was sleeping nearby.

Saul's spear was stuck in the ground at Saul's head, and a pitcher of water stood nearby. Abishai wanted to kill Saul, but David said, "Do not destroy him; for who can stretch out his hand against the LORD's anointed, and be guiltless?" (1 Samuel 26:9).

Instead, David took the spear and the pitcher of water and, with Abishai, went to the top of a hill some distance away. Then David called down to Saul's general Abner and asked why he had not properly guarded the king. He made sure Abner knew that he had taken the spear and the water.

Saul woke up and recognized David's voice. He called out to David, and David answered. He asked Saul to stop hunting him, for he had done nothing wrong.

Saul answered, "I have sinned. Return, my son David. For I will harm you no more, because my life was precious in your eyes this day" (1 Samuel 26:21). Then David returned Saul's spear and prayed that, as he had spared Saul's life, so the Lord might spare him from all tribulation.

Finally, Saul blessed David and went on his way. David still did not trust Saul, however, so he took his 600 men along with their families and crossed over into the Philistine lands.

The king of this land was friendly to David. When David asked him, the king gave him the town of Ziklag. Here, David was joined by even more Israelites. Many people wanted to follow David instead of Saul.

Sometimes, David and his army would go out and attack another Philistine town or city. They would destroy the city and everyone in it so that no one could bring word to the Philistine king of what was happening. Then he would tell the king that he had destroyed an Israelite town. The king believed him and thought David was a faithful servant who hated Israel.

Questions

1. David took a _____ and a _____ of water from Saul.

2. What town did the Philistines give David? _____

Thought Question

Why did David not trust Saul when he promised not to hunt David anymore?

Catechism

Question 71: How is Christ your priest?
Answer 71: Christ died for my sins, and continues to pray for me.

Memory Verse

Psalm 23:6
Surely goodness and mercy shall follow me all the days of my life, and I will dwell in the house of the LORD forever.

LESSON 38

Saul and the Witch

1 Samuel 28:3–25

A little while after David spared Saul's life for the second time, the Philistines got ready for another big battle against Israel.

King Saul gathered his army together and went out to meet the Philistines. When he saw how big the enemy army was, he became afraid. Before going into battle, he inquired of the Lord about what was going to happen, but the Lord did not answer him.

So Saul told his men to find him a witch, a woman who claimed to be able to talk to the spirits of dead people. These witches, or mediums (NKJV), were wicked people, and Saul had outlawed them from the land of Israel some time ago. Still, Saul's men found one witch who still lived in the nearby town of En Dor.

Then Saul disguised himself and went to En Dor to inquire of the witch. When he came to her, he asked her to call up a spirit for him. The witch answered that she could not, for King Saul had outlawed such practices. So the disguised Saul swore to the witch that she would not be put to death for calling up a spirit.

When the witch asked whose spirit she should call, the king answered, "Bring up Samuel" (1 Samuel 28:11).

Now Samuel had been dead for some time. Saul knew that Samuel had been able to talk to God, and he wanted Samuel to talk to God for him now, even though he was dead.

Suddenly, the witch actually saw Samuel. Immediately, she knew that the man who was standing in the room with her was the king. She was afraid, but Saul told her not to fear him. Instead, he asked about Samuel.

The witch told Saul that an old man wearing a robe had come up out of the earth. Saul bowed himself before Samuel, but Samuel asked, "Why have you disturbed me by bringing me up?" (1 Samuel 28:15).

Saul talked with Samuel and told him everything that was happening. The Philistines were attacking, God had left him, and Saul no longer knew what to do. He wanted Samuel to tell him what to do.

Samuel, however, was greatly displeased. He told Saul that the Lord was doing all He had promised. He was tearing the kingdom away from Saul. The Lord had become Saul's enemy. Then Samuel said that the very next day, Saul and his sons would die and the Philistines would defeat the Israelites.

When he heard these words, Saul was deeply distressed and shaken. He fell to the ground filled with fear. Then the witch and Saul's men convinced him to get up and eat something. So Saul ate and left the witch's home and returned to his camp.

Questions

1. Saul was _____ when he saw the enemy army.

2. Whom did the witch call up for Saul? _____

3. Samuel told Saul that he and his _____ would all die.

Thought Question

Why was it terribly wicked for Saul to go to a witch for help?

Catechism

Question 72: How is Christ your king?
Answer 72: Christ rules over me, the world, and Satan; and He defends me.

Memory Verse

Psalm 23:6
Surely goodness and mercy shall follow me all the days of my life, and I will dwell in the house of the LORD forever.

LESSON 39

David Defeats the Amalekites

1 Samuel 29:1–30:25

After some time, the Philistines got ready for another big battle against Israel. David and his men went up to the Philistine city Gath to go with them against Israel. The lords of the Philistines were afraid to take David into battle with them. They thought he would turn against them in the battle. They still remembered that people had sung about David killing tens of thousands of people.

So David and his men turned back to their town. When they got there, they found that the wandering tribes of the desert, the Amalekites, had burned Ziklag and escaped, taking all of the women and children from Ziklag with them.

When the men saw what had happened, they lifted up their voices and wept. Then David asked the Lord if he should pursue the Amalekites. God told him to go and promised he would recover everything that had been stolen. So David and 400 men went after the Amalekites, but they did not know which way the thieves had gone.

In a field, they found a sick man who had been left behind by his Amalekite master. He was almost dead of starvation, for he had had nothing to eat or drink in three days and nights. The Israelites gave him some food and water and then asked if he knew where the Amalekites were.

The man did know, and he agreed to take David's men there if they promised not to kill him or give him back to the Amalekites.

In their camp, the Amalekites were feasting and celebrating because they had taken so much treasure from the Philistines and from Judah. David attacked them at once. The armies fought all night and all the way until the next evening. All the Amalekites were killed except for 400 young men who escaped on camels.

David's men got back everything that had been stolen from them, including their wives and children. Besides that, they took everything that had belonged to the Amalekites who had been killed.

As David and his 400 men returned home, they met the other 200 of David's warriors. These men had been too tired to continue and fight the Amalekites. Some of David's warriors did not want to share the treasure from the fight with the 200 men who had not fought. David was displeased and told the men that all of the treasure would be shared equally among the men who had fought and the men who had not. No one would be left out.

After all these things, David and his men returned to Ziklag.

Questions

1. The _____ did not let David fight with them.

2. The Amalekites had burned _____ while David and his warriors were away.

Thought Question

Why would David find it important to make sure everyone got an equal share of the treasure taken from the Amalekites?

Catechism

Question 72: How is Christ your king?
Answer 72: Christ rules over me, the world, and Satan; and He defends me.

Memory Verse

Psalm 23:6
Surely goodness and mercy shall follow me all the days of my life, and I will dwell in the house of the LORD forever.

LESSON 40

Week 8 Review

Psalm 23:1–6

Catechism

Question 22: In what condition did God make Adam and Eve?

Question 23: What covenant did God make with Adam?

Question 24: What is a covenant?

Question 71: How is Christ your priest?

Question 72: How is Christ your king?

To the Teacher : The answers to catechism questions 22–24 are found on page 265.

Activity

True or False

1. Nabal was a wise man who wanted to help David. **True/False**

2. Nabal's wife was named Abigail. **True/False**

3. Abigail saved her husband by bringing David food and advice. **True/False**

4. God killed Nabal for his wickedness. **True/False**

5. David wanted to kill Saul when he found him asleep. **True/False**

6. David trusted Saul when Saul said he was sorry. **True/False**

7. Saul was wicked to ask a witch for advice. **True/False**

8. Samuel said that Saul and his sons would die the next day in battle. **True/False**

Unit 9   David Becomes King

LESSON 41

Saul's Death

1 Samuel 31:1– 2 Samuel 1:27; 1 Chronicles 10:1–7

The next day, there was a great battle on the mountain of Gilboa. The Philistines fought hard and gained the victory over the Israelites. Many Israelites were killed.

Even Jonathan and two of Saul's other sons were killed on Mount Gilboa, just as Samuel had said. Saul was followed by the Philistines' archers, and they hit him with arrows so that he was wounded. He was afraid that if the Philistines captured him they would torture him. So he asked his armorbearer to kill him. When his armorbearer refused to do such a terrible thing, Saul took his own sword and stuck it in the ground with the point up. Then he fell on his sword and killed himself. When the armorbearer saw what had happened, he fell on his own sword and died, as well.

As soon as the rest of the Israelites realized that Saul and his sons were dead, they turned and ran. After the battle, the Philistines came to the battlefield to strip the dead and take any treasures they could find. They were very excited when they found the bodies of Saul's sons. When they found Saul's body, they rejoiced. The Philistines cut off Saul's head and took his armor. They sent news of Saul's death to all their land. Then they put Saul's armor in one of their temples.

Most shocking, they took the bodies of Saul and his sons and hung them on the wall of one of their cities. They were trying to insult the people who had once claimed Saul as their king. That night, however, some brave Israelites from

Jabesh Gilead came and took the bodies down and buried them under a tree. All the Israelites mourned for seven days after Saul's death.

All this time, David had known nothing about Saul's death or Israel's defeat. Two days after he and his men returned from defeating the Amalekites, a young man came into their town. His clothes were torn and he had earth on his head, so David knew he brought news and asked where he had come from.

The man answered that he had come from Israel. David and his men listened eagerly as the man told of the battle. When they heard that Saul and his sons had been killed, they began to mourn.

Thinking he might gain a reward, the young man who brought the news told David how he knew Saul was dead. He claimed Saul had asked to be killed, so he had reached out his hand and killed him. He even brought Saul's crown and bracelet as proof. Instead of rewarding the man, David had the man executed for killing God's anointed king.

Then David and his men mourned for Saul and for Jonathan. David even wrote a song called "The Song of the Bow" to remember Saul and Jonathan. He and the rest of his men sang out, "How the mighty have fallen, and the weapons of war perished!" (2 Samuel 1:27).

Questions

_____

1. Saul was wounded, and his armorbearer refused to kill him, so he fell on his own _____ .

2. The men of Jabesh Gilead _____ the bodies of Saul and his sons.

3. David wrote "The _____ _____ _____ _____" to remember Saul and Jonathan.

Thought Question

Why would David mourn for Saul, who had tried so hard to kill him?

Catechism

Question 73: Why do you need Christ as your prophet?
Answer 73: Because I am ignorant by nature

Memory Verse

Galatians 5:22
But the fruit of the Spirit is love, joy, peace, longsuffering, kindness, goodness, faithfulness,

LESSON 42

David as King

2 Samuel 2:1–5:9

With Saul and his sons dead, Israel had no king. David was to be the next king, so he asked God where he should go. The Lord sent David to Hebron. The men of Judah were ready, and they made David king over them. Then David blessed the men of Jabesh Gilead for burying Saul and his sons.

However, not all of Israel wanted David as king. Saul's general, Abner, took Saul's youngest son, Ishbosheth, and made him king of the rest of Israel. For seven years, David ruled over Judah and lived in Hebron.

Abner came out to meet Joab, who led some of David's troops. They agreed to let some of the men compete before them, but all the men who fought died. So all the men began to fight, and a huge battle started. Abner's forces were defeated, and he began to run away.

Now Joab had two brothers. One was Abishai, who had gone with David into Saul's camp and taken his spear and water jug. The other was Asahel, who was very fast. Asahel chased Abner and caught up with him. Abner told him to go back, but Asahel would not, so Abner killed him. This made Joab and Abishai very angry. They followed Abner all the way back to his own land where more soldiers waited to protect him. Joab and Abishai returned home, but did not forget Abner.

War continued between Abner and David for a long time. David began to have sons. He also continued winning, and Saul's house grew weaker and weaker. Finally, Ishbosheth made Abner angry, and Abner decided to become David's ally against Saul's son. David agreed that Abner could be on his side if he brought Michal, Saul's daughter and David's first wife, to him. They had been separated the entire time Saul hunted David in the wilderness.

Abner sent Michal to David and began to tell all of Israel that they should anoint David as king. Soon he came to David, and David threw a feast for him.

Before long, Joab and the troops he led came in with much treasure. They had been out fighting for David, and they had won. When Joab heard that Abner had come, he went straight to David. He thought Abner had come to deceive David, but David would not listen.

So Joab went out and sent a message after Abner. He called Abner in from where he had been staying and went to speak to him. In private, Joab stabbed and killed Abner because he had killed his brother Asahel.

When David heard what had happened, he mourned for Abner so that all of Israel knew he had not wanted the man killed. He also cursed the house of Joab.

When Ishbosheth heard that Abner was dead, he lost his courage. Before long, the two captains of his own troops came and killed him. They took Ishbosheth's head and brought it to David, hoping he would be pleased. Again, David was not happy. He had these two captains killed, and he buried Ishbosheth properly.

Then all of Israel came to Hebron and anointed David as king. So David moved into Jerusalem, the stronghold of Zion, which would become the royal city and was often called "the City of David" (2 Samuel 5:7). He ruled Israel wisely because God was with him.

Questions

1. Who made Ishbosheth king? _____

2. Which tribe chose David as king? _____

3. _____ is called the "City of David."

Thought Question

Why was David angry with Joab for killing Abner?

Catechism

Question 73: Why do you need Christ as your prophet?
Answer 73: Because I am ignorant by nature

Memory Verse

Galatians 5:22
But the fruit of the Spirit is love, joy, peace, longsuffering, kindness, goodness, faithfulness,

LESSON 43

The Ark Comes to Jerusalem

2 Samuel 5:10–7:17

David was thirty when he became king, and he reigned over Israel for forty years. In Jerusalem, he built a large palace with fine cedar trees that were sent to him by Hiram king of Tyre. He also built other houses and was a prosperous king with many wives and sons. He continued fighting and beating the Philistines. Most importantly, David obeyed God, and God was with him.

After some time, David remembered that the ark of God was still in Kiriath Jearim. It had been there for twenty years, ever since the Philistines had captured and returned it.

So David rose up and went with his people to bring the ark into Jerusalem. The people put the ark on a new cart which was driven by two men. Everyone else walked beside the cart while David played his harp and praised God. Many people played different instruments. They were overjoyed to be bringing the ark home.

In one place along the road, the oxen pulling the cart stumbled because the path was rough. Uzzah, one of the men driving the cart, reached out a hand to steady the ark and keep it from falling. God became angry, for no one was to touch the ark. So God struck Uzzah, and the man died immediately.

When Uzzah died, David and the people became frightened. David cried out, "How can the ark of the LORD come to me?" (2 Samuel 6:9). Instead of bringing the ark straight to Jerusalem, David had the people bring the ark to a nearby house. The ark stayed there for three months, and God blessed the family that lived there.

Hearing that God was blessing the people who kept the ark, David gathered enough courage to bring the ark all the way to Jerusalem. This time, the Levites carried the ark as God

had commanded. Once more, David and the people danced and sang as they went along. With music, dancing, and rejoicing, the ark was brought into Jerusalem where a tent had been made ready to receive it.

The people offered sacrifices to God, and David appointed some of the Levites to take care of the ark. He also blessed all the people and gave them food.

When David went home, his wife Michal was waiting for him. She had seen David leaping and dancing among the people and did not like his behavior. She spoke harshly to David, but he answered that the Lord had made him king, "Therefore I will play music before the LORD" (2 Samuel 6:21). The Lord punished Michal for this by not allowing her to have any children.

Once again, the worship of God centered around the ark of God. Yet David realized there was a problem: he had a huge palace while the Lord's ark was set up in a tent. David wanted to build a splendid house for God.

God sent word to the prophet Nathan, who went and told David what God had said. God had been with Israel for a long time, from bringing them out of Egypt and through the wilderness; but He had never asked Israel to build a house for Him. God had taken David from the sheep fields and made him a king.

That night, God promised that He would not depart from David's children. However, God's holy temple could not be built by someone whose life had been filled with war. David's son would be king after him, and that son would build God's house. David was humble when he heard God's promise. He did everything he could to get things prepared for when his son would build God's house.

Questions

1. What did David bring to Jerusalem? _____ of _____

2. God killed Uzzah for _____ the Law; no one was to touch the ark.

3. Who would build God's house? _____ _____

Thought Question

Why did God kill Uzzah for touching the ark?

Catechism

Question 74: Why do you need Christ as your priest?
Answer 74: Because I am guilty of breaking God's law

Memory Verse

Galatians 5:22
But the fruit of the Spirit is love, joy, peace, longsuffering, kindness, goodness, faithfulness,

LESSON 44

David as Warrior and Friend

2 Samuel 8:1–10:19

David fought many wars. God gave him victories over his enemies, the Philistines. David beat them so badly that they fled from the battlefield. Then David gathered up their wicked idols and burned them.

The Israelites also made servants of the Moabites who lived on the east side of the Jordan. Then David marched north and defeated all the wicked people who lived there. Finally, David marched south and defeated the nations there. Long ago, God had promised to give Israel all of the land that David was conquering. Under David's rule, the people gained a lot of land and treasure. David brought much of the treasure back to Jerusalem and saved it to help build God's house.

When David had defeated many nations and knew that his kingdom was safe, he began to look for any of Saul's descendants who were still alive.

David sent for Ziba, an old servant of Saul's, and asked about Saul's family. Ziba told David about Mephibosheth, who was Jonathan's son. Mephibosheth was five when Saul and Jonathan were killed. When news of their deaths arrived, a nurse picked the boy up to run and hide him. In her haste, she dropped the boy, and he had been unable to walk ever since.

David called Mephibosheth to him. Mephibosheth came, but he was afraid David might want to kill him for being related to Saul. Instead, David said, "Do not fear, for I will surely show you kindness for Jonathan your father's sake" (2 Samuel 9:7). So King David returned all of Saul's lands to Mephibosheth. Ziba farmed the land for him, and Mephibosheth lived at the palace and ate at the king's table. Thus David remembered his covenant with Jonathan.

After that, David went back to war. Do you remember Nahash, the wicked king of Ammon who wanted to put out the eyes of the people of Jabesh Gilead? This king died, and his son, Hanun, began to rule.

David politely sent messengers to Hanun in order to comfort him at the death of his father, but Hanun's advisors told him that the messengers were probably spies. Hanun believed his advisors. He took David's messengers and shaved off half of their beards and cut off half of their clothes. This was a shameful thing to do in those days, and David's messengers were ashamed.

When David heard what had happened, he was angry. He told his messengers to stay in Jericho, which was empty, until their beards grew again. Then he sent his finest soldiers, led by his general, Joab, into Ammon to fight Hanun.

Hanun knew there was going to be a big battle. He sent word to other kings along the river and asked for help. Many kings answered, and Joab sent word asking David for help. With many more men, David went and joined Joab. Together, they fought against all the other nations. Because God was on their side, the Israelites won. The other nations became Israel's servants. David was now a very great king. All the other nations were afraid of him, for God was on his side.

Questions

1. Jonathan's son, Mephibosheth, was crippled when he was _____ years old.

2. David showed kindness to Mephibosheth for _____ sake.

Thought Question

Why were so many kings afraid of David?

Catechism

Question 74: Why do you need Christ as your priest?
Answer 74: Because I am guilty of breaking God's law

Memory Verse

Galatians 5:22
But the fruit of the Spirit is love, joy, peace, longsuffering, kindness, goodness, faithfulness,

LESSON 45

Week 9 Review

Memory Verse
Galatians 5:22

Catechism

Question 25: In the covenant of life, what did God require Adam to do?

Question 26: What did God promise in the covenant of life?

Question 27: What did God threaten in the covenant of life?

Question 73: Why do you need Christ as your prophet?

Question 74: Why do you need Christ as your priest?

To the Teacher :   The answers to catechism questions 25–27 are found on page 265.

Activity
Matching

For each group below, draw lines to match the descriptions to the people.

1. Became king of Israel when he was thirty	Asahel
2. A very fast runner	Uzzah
3. Killed by God for touching the ark of the covenant	David
4. Led some of David's army	Joab

5. Saul's general	Saul
6. Killed on Mount Gilboa with his sons	Abner
7. Made a covenant with David to protect his family	Mephibosheth
8. Jonathan's crippled son	Jonathan

Unit 10   *David's Sin Affects His Family*

LESSON 46

David's Sin

2 Samuel 11:1–12:25

In the spring, when kings went out to battle, David sent Joab out to command his army instead of going himself. While the army was gone, David did a very wicked thing.

One evening, he was up on the roof of his palace. All the roofs in Canaan were flat, with a railing around them. From his roof, David could see down into the court of a nearby house where a woman was washing herself. She was a very beautiful woman. David sent one of his servants to tell the woman to come to him.

The woman was named Bathsheba. She was the wife of Uriah, a mighty man in David's army. Bathsheba came to see the king, and David fell in love with her. However, David could not have her, for she was another man's wife.

David wanted Bathsheba so much that he allowed himself to think and act wickedly. He sent a letter to Joab and told him to put Uriah in the front lines of the battle. Then, Joab and the rest of the army were to pull back and leave Uriah alone at the front of the battle. David hoped that in this way, Uriah would be killed.

Joab obeyed David, and Uriah was killed. Bathsheba mourned for her husband for a little, and then David took her as his wife. Before long, they had a son. What David had done, however, greatly displeased the Lord.

God sent the prophet Nathan to David. This time, Nathan told David a story: Two men lived in one city. One man was rich and had many flocks of sheep. The other man was poor and had only one little lamb. Yet the poor man loved his lamb and took very good care of it. Now, a traveler came into the land and stopped to stay with the rich man. Instead of taking one of his own sheep to make a meal for the traveler, the rich man took the poor man's one lamb and killed it.

David was angry when he heard the story. He exclaimed,

"As the LORD lives, the man who has done this shall surely die!" (2 Samuel 12:5). Then Nathan answered, "You are the man!" (2 Samuel 12:7).

Nathan went on to explain that God was very angry. God had anointed David king over Israel and had given him many wonderful things. Yet he had taken Uriah's only wife and murdered Uriah. God promised to punish David for his sin.

David listened to Nathan's words and realized how wicked he had been. He repented before God and said, "I have sinned against the LORD" (2 Samuel 12:13). Nathan told David that because he had repented, the Lord would spare his life. He would not die for his sin, but the baby that he and Bathsheba had would die.

Nathan left, and the baby soon became very sick. David knew the baby was sick and dying because of his sin. He refused to eat anything. Instead, he lay on the ground and pleaded with God for his son. On the seventh day after the baby became sick, the baby died. David's servants were afraid of what David would do when he found out about the baby, and they did not want to tell him.

David saw his servants whispering and knew his baby was dead. Then he stood up, washed himself, and went to worship God. Then he went home to eat. His servants were amazed. David answered them, "While the child was alive, I fasted and wept; for I said, 'Who can tell whether the LORD will be gracious to me, that the child may live?' But now he is dead; why should I fast? Can I bring him back again? I shall go to him, but he shall not return to me" (2 Samuel 12:22–23).

The next year, David and Bathsheba had another son. They named him Solomon. God loved Solomon very much and even gave him a special name, Jedidiah, which means "Beloved of the LORD."

Questions

1. Who was Bathsheba's husband? _____

2. What happened to David's baby son? _____

3. Because God loved Solomon, what did He call David's new son? _____

Thought Question

Why was it so important for David to repent of his sin?

Catechism

Question 75: Why do you need Christ as your king?

Answer 75: Because I am weak and helpless

Memory Verse

Galatians 5:23

… gentleness, self-control. Against such there is no law.

LESSON 47

Absalom

2 Samuel 14:25–15:14

As David continued to rule, he had fewer and fewer enemies to fight. Some more giants like Goliath fought him; but, like Goliath, they were killed. Other than that, David began to enjoy a time of peace as he ruled his kingdom.

By this time, David's oldest sons were grown men. David's third son, Absalom, was especially handsome. He had long, thick hair that was very beautiful. Absalom was married and had four children. All the people of Israel liked Absalom. However, they did not know that, while he was handsome on the outside, he was very ugly and wicked on the inside.

Absalom lived in Jerusalem and rode in a fine chariot with fifty men who would run before him. He tried very hard to make the people of Israel like him. He stood in the gate of the city. When people came to bring their problems to the king, Absalom would talk to them first. He would tell the people that they were right to bring their problems to the king, only the king had no time to hear them. He told all the people that if he were king, then everyone would receive justice for any problem they brought before him. In this way, "Absalom stole the hearts of the men of Israel" (2 Samuel 15:6).

Soon, just as Absalom wanted, the men of Israel began to like Absalom a lot. Still, David was their king. David had a large kingdom, and he was not at war. He worshiped God and, during his reign, the people of Israel did not worship idols. The land and people were prosperous and happy.

However, David could not remain a young king forever. From the time Solomon was young, David had planned to make him the next king of Israel. Solomon was wise, and the Lord loved him.

This did not make Absalom happy, however, for he wanted to be king. He wanted to be king so badly that he did not wait for his father to die. One day, he asked David if he could go down to Hebron to fulfill a vow. David said yes.

Now Absalom had been planning to take the kingdom for some time. He had sent spies throughout the land and told them that when they heard the trumpets sound, they should shout to all the people, "Absalom reigns in Hebron" (2 Samuel 15:10). So Absalom rode to Hebron with 200 men from Jerusalem. He also called David's own wise advisor, Ahithophel, to come and counsel him.

Sure enough, when the trumpets sounded and people heard that Absalom was king, many of them flocked to his side. By the time David heard what had happened, Absalom had raised his own army. Someone who was still loyal to David ran to Jerusalem and told the king the news. David was very sad, for he loved his son Absalom. He had not imagined his own son would try to take the throne from him. David was not prepared for war. He told his servants, "Arise, and let us flee, or we shall not escape from Absalom" (2 Samuel 15:14). So David and his faithful servants ran away from Jerusalem before Absalom arrived.

Questions

1. David's son _____ wanted to be king.

2. Absalom stole the _____ of the Israelites.

3. When David heard the news about Absalom, he _____ from Jerusalem.

Thought Question

Why did David run from his son instead of stay to talk to him or fight him?

Catechism

Question 76: How many commandments did God give on Mount Sinai?
Answer 76: Ten commandments

Memory Verse

Galatians 5:23

… gentleness, self-control. Against such there is no law.

LESSON 48

David Runs Away

2 Samuel 15:15–16:14

David ran from Absalom, but he did not run alone. His 600 faithful warriors who had been with him since he ran from Saul went with him. So did the Levites, and they brought the ark with them. All the people wept as they crossed the Kidron River and went into the wilderness.

Then David told Zadok and Abiathar, the priests, to take the ark and go back to Jerusalem with their sons, Jonathan and Ahimaaz. He knew the Lord would bring him back to Jerusalem if He chose. He wanted the priests to keep an eye on the city and let him know what was happening. So the priests took the ark and returned to Jerusalem.

David and everyone with him went up the side of the Mount of Olives. The king was sad, for he knew that even this horrible thing was happening because of his sin with Bathsheba and Uriah.

Then someone came and told David that his own counselor, Ahithophel, was with Absalom. So David said, "O, Lord, I pray, turn the counsel of Ahithophel into foolishness!" (2 Samuel 15:31).

Soon another of David's counselors, Hushai, came to see David. His coat was torn, and earth was on his head, for he was mourning. Yet David did not want Hushai to come with him. Instead, he sent the counselor back to Jerusalem to be his spy. Hushai was to tell Absalom that he would serve him instead of David. Then he could work against Absalom. Anything that Hushai learned would be told to the two priests' sons. Then the young men would come out and find David to give him whatever news they had.

As David went along, Mephibosheth's servant, Ziba, came to him with donkeys and food. The donkeys were for the king's family, and the food was for anyone who was hungry. Ziba told David that Mephibosheth had not come because he thought the Israelites would make him king because he was Saul's grandson. David told Ziba that if that was true, then he could have all of Mephibosheth's land.

David continued his journey. Soon they saw a man who was related to Saul. This man, Shimei, threw stones at David and cursed him saying, "The Lord has brought upon you all the blood of the house of Saul" (2 Samuel 16:8).

Joab's brother Abishai wanted to kill Shimei; he did not want anyone to curse the king. David, however, would not let Shimei be killed. He knew Shimei could do nothing worse than what his own son was already doing.

Consequently, King David ran away from the son whom he loved.

Questions

1. David was running from _____.

2. David asked Hushai to be his _____.

3. Shimei threw _____ and _____ at David.

Thought Question

Why did David need a spy in Absalom's advisors?

Catechism

Question 76: How many commandments did God give on Mount Sinai?
Answer 76: Ten commandments

Memory Verse

Galatians 5:23

… gentleness, self-control. Against such there is no law.

LESSON 49

Cumulative Review 2

Job-David

Word Bank: ark   covenant   cursed   fell   God   Jonathan   king   mourned   Saul   Solomon   sword

1. Job _____ after losing everything, but he never _____ God.

2. _____, alone, is all-powerful.

3. The elders of Israel and Eli's sons wanted to bring the _____ of the _____ into battle.

4. _____ was the first human king of Israel.

5. David cut off Goliath's head with the giant's own _____.

6. David's best friend was _____, Saul's oldest son.

7. Saul knew that David would someday become _____ of Israel.

8. Saul died when he _____ on his own sword.

9. David's son, _____, would build God's house.

Catechism

Question 75: Why do you need Christ as your king?
Answer 75: Because I am weak and helpless

Memory Verse

Galatians 5:23
… gentleness, self-control. Against such there is no law.

LESSON 50

Week 10 Review

Memory Verse

Galatians 5:22–23

Catechism

Question 28: Did Adam keep the covenant of life?

Question 29: What is sin?

Question 30: What is meant by lack of conformity?

Question 75: Why do you need Christ as your king?

Question 76: How many commandments did God give on Mount Sinai?

To the Teacher :   The answers to catechism questions 28–30 are found on page 265.

Activity
Fill in the Blanks

Word Bank: Absalom   Bathsheba   David   Hushai   Jedidiah   Nathan   Solomon   Uriah

1. David fell in love with a woman named _____.

2. David had _____, Bathsheba's husband, killed.

3. _____ the prophet came and confronted David with his sin.

4. David and Bathsheba's second son was named _____.

5. _____ means "Beloved of the Lord."

6. David's son _____ wanted to be the king.

7. _____ fled from his own son.

8. _____ agreed to be David's spy in Absalom's camp.

Unit 11   *David Returns as King*

LESSON 51

Good Advice, Bad Advice

2 Samuel 16:15–17:29

Absalom soon arrived in Jerusalem with his army and his advisors, including Ahithophel. Hushai, David's spy, came to Absalom in the city and greeted him as king. Absalom was surprised that Hushai would abandon David, but Hushai convinced him that he would be loyal to any man chosen to be king of Israel.

When Absalom asked for advice, Ahithophel was quick to answer. Now Ahithophel was so wise that he seemed to speak from God. He said, "Now let me choose twelve thousand men, and I will arise and pursue David tonight" (2 Samuel 17:1). He knew David would be weary and sad from his flight and thought it would be best to defeat the old king right away.

Absalom was pleased with this advice. Yet, before he made any decisions, he asked for Hushai's advice, as well. Hushai knew that Ahithophel's counsel was wise, and he did not want Absalom to follow good advice. Instead, he said, "You know your father and his men, that they are mighty men, and they are enraged in their minds, like a bear robbed of her cubs in the field" (2 Samuel 17:8).

Hushai told Absalom that David was probably already hiding somewhere away from the people. If Absalom sent men up to fight that night, they would not find David. Besides, if any of Absalom's men were killed in the fight, the people might not believe that Absalom was strong any longer. Hushai counseled Absalom to wait until all of Israel was gathered into his army in order to fight an open battle against his father.

Absalom and the men of Israel thought Hushai's advice was better than Ahithophel's advice, "For the LORD had purposed to defeat the good advice of Ahithophel, to the intent that the LORD might bring disaster on Absalom" (2 Samuel 17:14).

When Ahithophel heard that Absalom preferred Hushai's advice to his own, he was very upset. He left Jerusalem and went to his own home. There, he hanged himself and died. This meant Hushai was left to counsel Absalom.

Meanwhile, Hushai went straight to the priests, Zadok and Abiathar. He told them what he had told Absalom. Then he told them to send their sons to tell David to cross over the Jordan River.

Zadok and Abiathar sent a young girl to the outskirts of the city where their sons, Jonathan and Ahimaaz, were hiding. A boy saw the young girl leave and told Absalom. Absalom sent men to search for Jonathan and Ahimaaz.

Jonathan and Ahimaaz had come to a house that had a well. When they realized they were being hunted, they went down into the well. The woman who lived in the house covered the well. When Absalom's men came, the woman told them that the two men had already crossed over the nearby brook.

When Absalom's men left, Jonathan and Ahimaaz came out of the well and ran to find David. They told the king everything Hushai had said. In the morning, David and all of his men were on the other side of the Jordan River. They continued traveling far from Jerusalem. On the way, many men who still loved David came to join him. Soon he had a large army. He was also given food and supplies.

Questions

1. God wanted Absalom to listen to _____ , and he did.

2. Jonathan and Ahimaaz hid in a _____.

Thought Question

Why would the Lord want to bring disaster on Absalom?

Catechism

Question 77: Why should we obey the Ten Commandments?
Answer 77: Because God is our Creator, Savior and King

Memory Verse

Exodus 20:1–2
And God spoke all these words, saying: "I am the LORD your God, who brought you out of the land of Egypt, out of the house of bondage."

LESSON 52

Absalom's Defeat

2 Samuel 18:1–18

David had thousands of soldiers in his army now. He broke them into three groups and set captains over them. His captains were Joab, Joab's brother Abishai, and a man named Ittai. David wanted to go out to battle with his men, but the people would not let him. They knew he would be more helpful if he was safe. David agreed, but he commanded his captains saying, "Deal gently for my sake with the young man Absalom" (2 Samuel 18:5).

Absalom had followed Hushai's advice. He had gathered a large army and then crossed over the Jordan River to hunt for his father.

The two armies met in a forest near the city where David was staying. There was a huge battle, and Absalom's army lost; 20,000 men were killed. Absalom tried to escape from David's men by galloping away on his mule. The mule went under a tree, and Absalom's thick, long hair caught on the tree branches. The mule galloped away, and Absalom was left hanging by his hair.

A young man saw what happened and ran to tell Joab, "I just saw Absalom hanging in a terebinth tree" (2 Samuel 18:10). Joab was a fierce soldier. He did not want to deal gently with Absalom, for he was a traitor. Joab asked the man why he had not killed Absalom. The man answered that he would not have killed Absalom for any reward because he had heard David's request that Absalom be treated gently. He knew he would have been killed for killing David's son.

Joab did not stay to hear more. He took three spears and went to find Absalom. Once there, he thrust all three spears into the prince's heart. Joab's ten armorbearers came close and killed Absalom. Then they threw his body in a pit. Joab blew his trumpet so that everyone would know the battle was over.

The soldiers stopped fighting and gathered around Joab. Each man picked up a stone and threw it into Absalom's grave until he was completely buried under a heap of stones.

Questions

1. How did David tell his captains to treat Absalom? _____

2. Absalom was captured after his _____ got caught in the branches of a tree.

3. Who thrust three spears into Absalom's heart? _____

Thought Question

Why did Joab ignore David's warning to treat Absalom gently?

Catechism

Question 77: Why should we obey the Ten Commandments?
Answer 77: Because God is our Creator, Savior and King

Memory Verse

Exodus 20:1–2
And God spoke all these words, saying: "I am the LORD your God, who brought you out of the land of Egypt, out of the house of bondage."

LESSON 53

David Hears of Absalom's Death

2 Samuel 18:19–19:8

Then Ahimaaz, one of the young men who warned David to cross the Jordan, asked Joab if he could run and bring the news to David. Joab said no and sent another man. Yet Ahimaaz insisted he wanted to run, so Joab let him. Ahimaaz was so fast that he soon overtook the other messenger.

King David was waiting for news at the gate of the city. A watchman looked out and saw a man running all alone, so he told the king. When he looked again, the watchman saw a second man running behind. He told the king this too. David knew both men brought news. Then the watchman recognized the running of the first man, for this was Ahimaaz. David answered, "He is a good man, and comes with good news" (2 Samuel 18:27).

Soon Ahimaaz arrived. He blessed God and told the king that the enemy had been defeated. David immediately asked if Absalom was alive. Ahimaaz said he had seen a great tumult when he was leaving but did not know what had happened. The second messenger was the one who told David his son was dead. He said, "May the enemies of my lord the king, and all who rise against you to do harm, be like that young man!" (2 Samuel 18:32).

Then David was full of grief. He went away into a little room and began to weep saying, "O my son Absalom—my son, my son Absalom—if only I had died in your place" (2 Samuel 18:33).

All the soldiers of David returned in joy, thanking God for their victory. However, when they heard that David was weeping for his son, their joy turned to mourning.

Then Joab went to David and told him that he was disgracing all his servants who had risked their lives to save him, his wives, and his children. He told David that he was showing love for his enemies and hatred for his friends and that if Absalom had lived while all of David's soldiers had died, then David might have been happy. Then Joab told David to go out and thank the people, or they would all leave him and he would be in even worse trouble than before.

So David listened to Joab and went down to speak with the people.

Questions

1. David _____ when he heard of Absalom's death.

2. Joab was upset with David's response because he _____ his people.

3. Did David listen to Joab? _____

Thought Question

Was David right to mourn for his son even though his son had tried to kill him?

Catechism

Question 78: What do the first four commandments teach?

Answer 78: What it means to love and serve God

Memory Verse

Exodus 20:1–2

And God spoke all these words, saying: "I am the LORD your God, who brought you out of the land of Egypt, out of the house of bondage."

LESSON 54

David's Triumphant Return

2 Samuel 19:9–39, 22:1–51

Soon the people of Israel wanted to bring their rightful king back into Jerusalem. So David and all the people with him started the journey home. The tribe of Judah was so happy to have their king back that the whole tribe went out to meet David at the Jordan River. A ferryboat brought the king across the river. The people rejoiced to have their king returned.

One man, however, met King David with fear instead of joy. This man was Shimei, the man who had thrown stones at David and cursed him when he fled from Absalom. Shimei threw himself on the ground and humbly begged the king to forgive him. He said, "I, your servant, know that I have sinned" (2 Samuel 19:20).

Abishai, David's general, thought Shimei should be killed for the way he had acted. King David, however, was merciful to Shimei and swore to him, "You shall not die" (2 Samuel 19:23).

Next, Jonathan's lame son Mephibosheth came to greet David. When David asked why Mephibosheth had not left Jerusalem with him, Mephibosheth said he had been tricked. He told David that everything his servant Ziba had told the king was a lie. Mephibosheth had not waited in the city because he was against David. However, David had already told Ziba that he could have Mephibosheth's land. So David divided the land between Ziba and Mephibosheth. Then Mephibosheth said he did not mind losing his land to Ziba as long as the king was back safely.

Finally, a man named Barzillai spoke with David. He was an old man who lived across the Jordan and had given David and his men supplies when they were fleeing Absalom. David invited Barzillai to come and live in Jerusalem with him.

Barzillai answered that he was too old to move so far from his home. He was honored that David had asked, but he did not want to go. Instead, he sent his son to Jerusalem with David. So David blessed the old man and, with Barzillai's son, went to Jerusalem. Barzillai returned to his own home.

After David returned, he fought several more battles. He and his mighty men defeated more giants. They put to death other rebels. They defeated the Philistines and brought peace to the land of Israel.

When David had defeated all his enemies, he praised God and sang, "The Lord is my rock and my fortress and my deliverer; the God of my strength, in whom I will trust; my shield and the horn of my salvation, my stronghold and my refuge; my Savior, You save me from violence" (2 Samuel 22:2–3).

Questions

_____

1. David showed _____ to Shimei.

   _____

2. David wanted Barzillai to live in _____.

   _____   _____

3. When David had defeated all his enemies, he _____ God and _____.

Thought Question

Why did Barzillai send his son instead of going to Jerusalem himself?

Catechism

Question 78: What do the first four commandments teach?
Answer 78: What it means to love and serve God

Memory Verse

Exodus 20:1–2
And God spoke all these words, saying: "I am the Lord your God, who brought you out of the land of Egypt, out of the house of bondage."

LESSON 55

Week 11 Review

Memory Verse

Exodus 20:1–2

Catechism

Question 31: What is meant by transgression?

Question 32: What does every sin deserve?

Question 33: What was the sin of our first parents?

Question 77: Why should we obey the Ten Commandments?

Question 78: What do the first four commandments teach?

To the Teacher :   The answers to catechism questions 31–33 are found on pages 265–266.

Activity

Dot-to-Dot

Complete the dot-to-dot to see where Jonathan and Ahimaaz hid from Absalom's soldiers.

Unit 12   *Solomon Becomes King*

LESSON 56

Solomon Anointed King

1 Kings 1:1–53

King David continued to rule and grew to be an old man. He became too old to attend to all the affairs of his kingdom. Another of his sons, Adonijah, thought that because his father was old, he could easily take over Israel and become king.

Adonijah was Absalom's full brother. Like his brother, he was very handsome and liked to impress people. He did not, however, try to kill his father as Absalom had. Instead, he thought his father simply would not hear that he was going to become king. David would soon die and, if he had not clearly established a new king, then Adonijah would not have to fight to become king.

Adonijah had a big feast and invited all his brothers except for Solomon. He knew that David intended for Solomon to be king, and he did not want Solomon to try to stop him from becoming king. Some of David's men, such as Joab, his general, and Abiathar the priest followed Adonijah and went to the feast. Yet Zadok the priest, David's mighty men, and Nathan the prophet did not go.

King David did not know what Adonijah was doing. So Nathan the prophet went to Solomon's mother, Bathsheba. He told her to go to the king and say, "Did you not, my lord, O king, swear to your maidservant, saying, 'Assuredly your son Solomon shall reign after me, and he shall sit on my throne'? Why then has Adonijah become king?" (1 Kings 1:13).

Bathsheba listened to Nathan and did all that he advised. She also mentioned that all of Israel was watching David, waiting to hear whom he had chosen as the next king. While she was still talking to David, Nathan also came to speak with the king. Nathan repeated everything Bathsheba had said.

Then David knew that Solomon must be made king before he himself died, or Solomon and Bathsheba might be killed when David died. He had Nathan and Zadok anoint Solomon with oil. Then they blew a trumpet, and all the people came running to see what had happened.

When the people saw Solomon riding King David's own mule and heard David's trusted men shouting that Solomon was king, they too began to shout, "Long live King Solomon!" (1 Kings 1:39).

Adonijah and all the people with him heard a great noise in the city. Jonathan, the son of Abiathar the priest, came to Adonijah and told him everything. The people were rejoicing that Solomon was king, all of David's most trusted men were rejoicing, and David himself was praising God for allowing him to have a son to sit on his throne.

Then Adonijah and all the people with him were afraid. Everyone went to his own home, and Adonijah ran to the tabernacle. He grabbed onto the horns of the altar, for he thought Solomon would not dare to kill him there.

Word was brought to Solomon that Adonijah would not leave the tabernacle unless Solomon swore not to kill him. Solomon agreed that if Adonijah would behave righteously then he would not be killed. However, if he acted wickedly, then he would be put to death. So Adonijah was brought from the tabernacle, and he bowed down before King Solomon.

Questions

1. David had promised _____ that her son Solomon would be the next king.

2. _____ tried to become king, but he became afraid and ran to the tabernacle for safety.

Thought Question

Why did Adonijah think the tabernacle was a safe place for him to stay?

Catechism

Question 79: What do the last six commandments teach?
Answer 79: What it means to love and serve my neighbor

Memory Verse

Exodus 20:3
You shall have no other gods before Me.

LESSON 57

Solomon's Wisdom

1 Kings 2:1–3:28; 1 Chronicles 28:2–29:30

Before David died, he called a meeting of all the chief men of Israel. When everyone was there, he stood up before them and told them that God had chosen Solomon as king and that Solomon was to build God's house.

Then David turned to Solomon and said, "Keep the charge of the LORD your God: to walk in His ways, to keep His statutes, His commandments, His judgments, and His testimonies, as it is written in the Law of Moses, that you may prosper in all that you do and wherever you turn" (1 Kings 2:3).

David also warned Solomon about several men in the kingdom who might not want him to be king. Finally, he gave him plans and many expensive materials for the building of the temple. Then the people of Israel also offered offerings to be used for building the temple. A lot of money and precious materials were given, and all the people were joyful.

So David praised God before all the people once more. Solomon was officially crowned king. Then the great and mighty King David died, full of days, riches, and honor. So his son Solomon reigned in his place.

One day, Solomon went to Gibeon to sacrifice to God. That night, the Lord appeared to Solomon in a dream and said, "Ask! What shall I give you?" (1 Kings. 3:5). Solomon knew that this was a great opportunity. He also knew that the Lord was blessing him greatly for the sake of his father. He also knew that he was not truly worthy to rule over Israel. So he asked, "Therefore give to Your servant an understanding heart to judge Your people, that I may discern between good and evil" (1 Kings 3:9).

The Lord was pleased that Solomon had asked for wisdom instead of riches, honor, or long life. So God promised that Solomon would have all of those things he had not asked for, as well as wisdom. God promises to make Solomon wiser than any other man on earth.

It soon became evident that God's promise was true, for Solomon was very rich, honored, and wise. He wisely dealt with the enemies of David who did not want him to be David's heir. He spoke 3,000 wise sayings and made 1,000 songs. People came from all over the world just to listen to the wisdom of Solomon. Great kings visited in order to hear him judge the people.

One day two women came before the king with a dispute to be settled. One woman had a living baby, but the other had a dead baby. One woman explained that the two women and their babies lived in the same house. One night, one woman's baby had died. Then that woman had taken her dead baby and switched it with the living baby so that she had the living baby. When the second woman woke up, her baby was dead. She looked closer and realized that the dead baby was not hers. The women were still fighting as they stood before Solomon and asked him which woman got to keep the living baby.

Solomon asked for a sword. When it arrived, he said, "Divide the living child in two, and give half to one, and half to the other" (1 Kings 3:25). Then one woman became upset and told Solomon to give the living baby to the other woman and not to kill him. The second woman wanted the child killed and divided.

So Solomon gave the living baby to the first woman. He knew that the real mother would rather give her baby to someone else than to have it killed. When Israel heard this story, they realized that "God gave Solomon wisdom and exceedingly great understanding, and largeness of heart like the sand on the seashore" (1 Kings. 4:29). So Solomon's reign was full of wisdom and prosperity.

Questions

1. Before David died, he gave Solomon plans, money, and materials for building the _____.

2. Solomon asked God for _____.

Thought Question

How did Solomon know how to judge the two women in the story so wisely?

Catechism

Question 79: What do the last six commandments teach?
Answer 79: What it means to love and serve my neighbor

Memory Verse

Exodus 20:3
You shall have no other gods before Me.

LESSON 58

The Temple

1 Kings 5:1–6:38, 7:15–9:9

In the fourth year of his reign as king of Israel, Solomon began to build a house for God as David had instructed him. On the northeastern seacoast of the Mediteranean Sea was the great city of Tyre. The king of Tyre, Hiram, had been a friend of David. Solomon sent a letter reminding Hiram of his friendship with David and asking for the wood of cedar trees to build a great house for God. Solomon would pay with barley, oil, and wine if Hiram would have his men cut down the trees and send the cedar wood to Israel.

Hiram rejoiced when he heard Solomon's message, for he knew that God had given David a wise son to rule after him. He agreed to send everything that Solomon needed for his building on rafts down the seacoast to Israel.

Then Solomon counted all the people of Canaan who were left from the heathen nations. He sent 30,000 men up to be workmen in the country of King Hiram—10,000 each month in shifts.

Finally, Solomon began the actual construction of God's house, which would be called the temple. The temple was covered inside and out with gold. The walls and doors were decorated with cherubim, palm trees, and open flowers.

Inside, there was a holy place and a Most Holy Place (or Holy of Holies) just as there had been in the tabernacle. These rooms were much larger and stronger than the rooms in the tabernacle had been. There were two cherubim for the Most Holy Place that were much larger than the two small ones that stood over the ark. They were fifteen feet tall, and their wings spread out so that one cherub's wing touched one wall while the other cherub's wing touched the other wall. The remaining two wings touched each other in the center of the room.

A beautiful curtain of blue, purple, and crimson linen was hung in front of the Most Holy Place. The curtain was also embroidered with cherubim.

There was also a brass bowl for the priests to wash in. The bowl, called a laver, was round and measured fifteen feet across the top. It was held up by twelve brass oxen figures. Then there were ten smaller lavers for washing the animals that were brought to be sacrificed. Ten golden candlesticks provided light. A hundred golden basins were made, as well as spoons, candle snuffers, censers, and many other wonderful instruments.

The people worked for seven years to build God's house. When they were done, the temple was the most beautiful building in the land. Solomon called all the important men of Israel to Jerusalem. Together, they brought the ark and the holy dishes from the tabernacle into the temple.

All the priests and Levites were dressed in white linen. Many of them played instruments and sang, praising the Lord when the ark was placed in the Most Holy Place. Then the temple was filled with a cloud, for the glory of the Lord shone brightly around.

Solomon stood on a platform before the people and prayed. He knew that no house on earth could contain God, but he asked that God would answer the prayers of His people and forgive them when they repented of their sins. After praying, Solomon blessed the Israelites and warned them to follow God all their lives. Finally, Solomon and all the people offered sacrifices to God.

That night, the Lord appeared to Solomon. He had heard his prayers and would answer them. As long as the people obeyed God and repented of their sins, God would hear their prayers. God also told Solomon that if he lived as his father had and obeyed God, then he would always have a son to rule Israel. However, if Solomon did not obey God, then Israel would be taken away from his family. If Israel turned away from God, then God would cast them off, too.

Questions

1. God's house was called the _____ .

2. God promised if the people _____ Him, then He would hear their prayer.

Thought Question

Why was it so important for God to remind Solomon that if the people began to disobey, then God would cast them off?

Catechism

Question 80: What do the Ten Commandments teach?
Answer 80: To love God with all my heart, and my neighbor as myself

Memory Verse

Exodus 20:3
You shall have no other gods before Me.

LESSON 59

Cumulative Review 3

Job-Solomon

Word Bank: Abigail   Absalom   God   Goliath   Hannah   Joab   Job   Jonathan   Samuel   Uriah's

1. Who was a wealthy man living in the land of Uz? _____

2. Who prayed earnestly for a son? _____

3. Who called to Samuel in the night? _____

4. Who anointed Saul as king? _____

5. Who was Saul's oldest son? _____

6. Whom did David kill with a sling and stone? _____

7. Who was married to Nabal and later to David? _____

8. Whose wife did David steal? _____

9. Who was the son who tried to kill David? _____

10. Who thrust spears through Absalom? _____

Catechism

Question 80: What do the Ten Commandments teach?
Answer 80: To love God with all my heart, and my neighbor as myself

Memory Verse

Exodus 20:3
You shall have no other gods before Me.

LESSON 60

Week 12 Review

Memory Verse

Exodus 20:3

Catechism

Question 34: Who tempted Adam and Eve to this sin?

Question 35: How did Adam and Eve change when they sinned?

Question 36: Did Adam act for himself alone in the covenant of life?

Question 79: What do the last six commandments teach?

Question 80: What do the Ten Commandments teach?

To the Teacher :   The answers to catechism questions 34–36 are found on page 266.

Activity
Matching

Match the people on the right to their actions on the left. Answers may be used more than once.

1. _____ supplied the cedar wood for the temple

2. _____ asked God to give him wisdom

3. _____ tried to become king without David's knowledge

4. _____ reminded David that her son was going to be king

5. _____ promised to bless His people if they obeyed Him

6. _____ fled to the tabernacle for safety

7. _____ built the temple as a house for the Lord

8. _____ was good friends with David and was happy to help Solomon

A. Adonijah

B. Hiram

C. God

D. Solomon

E. Bathsheba

Unit 13   *The Kingdom Is Divided*

LESSON 61

The Queen of Sheba

1 Kings 10:1–29

Besides being wise, Solomon was also very rich. Along with the temple, Solomon had built himself a splendid home and another palace for his wife, the princess of Egypt. Then he built some cities in the mountains of Lebanon and in the desert.

Solomon gathered a large army of chariots and horses to defend his kingdom. He kept a navy on the Red Sea. These ships sailed around Arabia to the land of Ophir and brought back much gold to King Solomon. They also brought back precious stones and rare woods. Solomon's ships went to India, as well, and brought back gold, silver, ivory, apes, and peacocks. Jerusalem became a rich and splendid city.

In the palace, Solomon made a throne of ivory and covered it with pure gold. Six steps led up to the throne, and each step had two carved lions on it. No one else had a throne like his.

Solomon also provided a lot of food for his court. He was wiser and richer than all the other kings of the earth. Men came from far countries to see King Solomon and hear the wisdom God had put in his heart. All these kings brought more presents for Solomon.

More than a million dollars in gold came to Solomon every year. All his cups and dishes were made of gold. None were made of silver. Solomon was so rich that silver became a common thing in his kingdom.

Solomon ruled over all the land from the Euphrates River to the border of Egypt, and he had peace on all sides.

Among the guests King Solomon entertained was a lady, who was queen of Sheba. Sheba was a rich country in Arabia. This queen had heard of Solomon's wisdom and of his God, and she wanted to come and speak with him.

The queen of Sheba traveled with a large train of camels and servants. When she met Solomon, she tested him. She asked him very hard questions, and he answered every one of them. No question was too hard for Solomon. Then the queen saw the city and everything Solomon had built, including the magnificence of the temple.

Then the queen of Sheba told Solomon that she had not believed what people had told her concerning him and his kingdom. Now she realized that they had not even told her half of the truth, for Solomon's kingdom was beyond what she imagined. She said, "Blessed be the LORD your God, who delighted in you, setting you on the throne of Israel!" (1 Kings 10:9).

Finally, the queen of Sheba gave Solomon gold, precious stones, and delicious spices from her country. In return, Solomon gave the queen a present of every beautiful thing she had admired in his palace. Loaded with gifts, the queen of Sheba and her mighty train of camels and servants returned home.

Questions

1. Besides the temple, Solomon built a splendid _____ and several _____.

2. The _____ of Sheba came to visit and test Solomon.

Thought Question

Why was it important that Solomon had peace in all his lands during his reign?

Catechism

Question 81: Who is your neighbor?
Answer 81: Everybody is my neighbor.

Memory Verse

Exodus 20:4

You shall not make for yourself a carved image—any likeness of anything that is in heaven above, or that is in the earth beneath, or that is in the water under the earth.

LESSON 62

The Kingdom of Israel Splits

1 Kings 11:1–12:24; 2 Chronicles 10:1–19

In spite of Solomon's wisdom, he did one very foolish and wicked thing. He married many heathen women. King Solomon had 700 wives, many of whom were daughters of wicked kings. His first wife was the daughter of Egypt's king. He had also married young women from among the wicked Canaanites.

You will remember that God strictly commanded the Israelites not to marry heathen wives. Solomon disobeyed God, and this became his downfall.

In Solomon's old age, his wives turned his heart away from the one true God, and he began to worship idols. Solomon built a place for his Moabite wives to worship their idol, a place for his Ammonite wives to worship their false god, and places for all of his wives to worship false gods.

God was very angry with Solomon for this. The king had shamefully deserted God after the Lord had spoken directly to him twice. Because Solomon had disobeyed God, the kingdom would be taken from him. For David's sake, the kingdom would not be taken during Solomon's lifetime. God had also promised that David's children would reign forever, so God would leave two tribes to be ruled by David's children. God told all of this to Solomon.

Then the Lord began to raise up enemies against Solomon. At the same time, God sent the prophet Ahijah to Solomon's servant Jeroboam. The prophet took the clothing he was wearing and tore it into twelve pieces. He told Jeroboam to take ten pieces of the cloth. This was a picture of how God was going to take the kingdom of Israel and divide it. Ten tribes would follow Jeroboam while two tribes would follow Solomon's son Rehoboam.

Solomon soon learned what the Lord had told Jeroboam. He tried to kill Jeroboam, but Jeroboam escaped and lived in Egypt until Solomon died.

Solomon reigned forty years over Jerusalem. When at last he died, his son Rehoboam ruled in his place. As soon as Jeroboam heard that Solomon was dead, he returned to Israel. The people of Israel sent him with some of their chief men to ask a favor of King Rehoboam.

The prophet Samuel had warned Israel that if they had an earthly king, then they would have to pay taxes. During Solomon's rule, this warning had come true. Now the people wanted to see if Rehoboam would make their lives easier and let them pay less money in taxes to the king.

Rehoboam did not have an answer ready. He told them to return in three days for his decision. Then he asked the old men who had advised his father what they thought. They answered, "If you will be a servant to these people today … and speak good words to them, then they will be your servants forever" (1 Kings 12:7). Rehoboam, however, did not like this advice. Instead, he listened to his own young advisors who told him to increase the taxes on the people.

When the people returned for Rehoboam's answer, he told them he was going to make their lives even harder than before. When the people heard these proud words, they said, "What share have we in David?" (1 Kings 12:16). This meant they no longer wanted to be ruled by David's descendants.

The people left Rehoboam and crowned Jeroboam king. Two tribes, Judah and Benjamin, remained loyal to Rehoboam, David's grandson. All the other tribes followed Jeroboam.

From then on there were two kingdoms: Israel, which was ten tribes, and Judah, which was two tribes. They were never joined together again. David's descendants ruled over Judah, but many different people ruled in Israel.

Questions

1. In his old age, Solomon turned from God and worshiped the _____ of his wives.

2. _____ became king of Israel.

3. Which two tribes became the kingdom of Judah and followed Rehoboam? _____

    and _____

Thought Question

Why did God take the kingdom away from Solomon?

Catechism

Question 81: Who is your neighbor?

Answer 81: Everybody is my neighbor.

Memory Verse

Exodus 20:4

You shall not make for yourself a carved image—any likeness of anything that is in heaven above, or that is in the earth beneath, or that is in the water under the earth.

LESSON 63

Sin in Israel and Judah

1 Kings 12:25–33, 14:21–15:8; 2 Chronicles 13:1–22

Jeroboam, the first king of Israel, was not a good king. He was afraid that the Israelites would not like him as king and return to Rehoboam. He was especially afraid that they would want to go to Jerusalem, where the temple was, to worship. The problem was that Rehoboam also lived in Jerusalem.

To stop the people from going to Jerusalem, Jeroboam decided to make new gods for Israel. He made two golden calves and set one in the north and one in the south. Then he made new priests and told all the people that the calves were the gods who had brought them out of Egypt. The wicked people of Israel turned their backs on God and began to worship golden calves instead of the one true God.

Meanwhile, Rehoboam ruled in Judah. Even though he was King David's grandson, he was not a good king. His mother had been an Ammonite princess, and her son learned to worship idols. Under Rehoboam, the people of Judah lived evil lives and did not follow God. Rehoboam fought against Jeroboam his whole life.

Rehoboam ruled seventeen years. When he died, his son Abijam (2 Chronicles calls him Abijah) became king of Judah. Abijam also fought against Jeroboam his entire life, even though he did not have nearly as many men as Jeroboam did.

Abijam gathered his men and went to war. He went to a high place in the land and called out to Jeroboam. He shouted across the land that Judah relied on the one true God and that Israel could not win if they were fighting against God. God's true priests were in Judah, sacrificing to God and blowing the trumpets against Jeroboam.

Instead of listening to the warning, Jeroboam tried to send men around behind Abijam's armies. He had twice as many soldiers as Judah, and he felt certain he could win. When Abijam finished talking, he turned and saw Jeroboam's men approaching from in front and behind.

The men of Judah shouted and began to fight. The soldiers of Judah trusted in God, and He fought with them that day. The soldiers of Israel ran away from Judah's army, and God gave Judah a great victory—500,000 soldiers of Israel were killed that day.

Abijam followed Jeroboam and captured several cities. That day, Abijam proved that trusting in God is more successful than trusting in large armies.

Sadly, even though Abijam seemed to follow God at this time, the Bible says that he "walked in all the sins of his father …; his heart was not loyal to the LORD his God" (1 Kings 15:3). Abijam reigned three years. Then, for the sake of David, God raised up a righteous king. Abijam's son, Asa, was the next king of Judah, and he followed and obeyed God.

Questions

1. Jeroboam made golden _____ for Israel to worship, instead of God.

2. Who would be the next good king of Judah? _____

Thought Question

What does the Bible mean when it says that Abijam "walked in all the sins of his father"?

Catechism

Question 82: Is God pleased with those who love and obey him?
Answer 82: Yes. God says, "I love them that love me."

Memory Verse

Exodus 20:4
You shall not make for yourself a carved image—any likeness of anything that is in heaven above, or that is in the earth beneath, or that is in the water under the earth.

LESSON 64

The Wicked Kings of Israel

1 Kings 13:1–10, 14:1–20, 15:25–34; 2 Chronicles 16:1

Jeroboam, the first king of the ten tribes of Israel, ruled for a long time. One day, as he stood by the heathen altar he had built to worship the golden calves, a prophet came to him from the Lord.

The prophet declared that one day, a king would be born to David's family whose name would be Josiah. This king would kill the priests of the altar Jeroboam had built and destroy the altar itself. This prophecy came true 300 years later when King Josiah went through the land and destroyed all the heathen altars.

A short time later, Jeroboam's son became very ill and close to death. Jeroboam did not go ask the golden calves for help. Instead, he sent his wife to ask the prophet Ahijah if his son would live. He told his wife to wear a disguise so that the prophet would not know she was Jeroboam's wife.

Ahijah was the prophet who had told Jeroboam he would be king. He was now old and blind. However, the Lord told him Jeroboam's wife would come to him and what he should say to her.

As soon as she entered, Ahijah called out, "Come in, wife of Jeroboam. Why do you pretend to be another person? For I have been sent to you with bad news" (1 Kings 14:6). Jeroboam's son would die, and the whole kingdom would be taken from Jeroboam because of all the wicked things he had done. The son who died would be the only member of the family who would be buried, "because in him there is found something good toward the LORD God of Israel in the house of Jeroboam" (1 Kings 14:13). Everyone else in Jeroboam's house was wicked and would die and be eaten by birds or dogs. All Israel would be punished.

Ahijah sent Jeroboam's wife home after telling her all this and adding that her son would die as soon as she reached her house. Sure enough, as soon as the woman came to her house, her son died. He was buried, and all Israel mourned.

Soon after his son's death, Jeroboam died, as well. His son Nadab became king. Nadab was also a wicked man. He ruled for two years. Then a man named Baasha killed Nadab and made himself king.

Baasha killed every man of the house of Jeroboam, just as Ahijah had prophesied. This was God's punishment on Jeroboam's house for the wickedness of Jeroboam.

Baasha was not a good king, either. He began his reign by murdering Jeroboam's family. Then he continued by worshiping idols and the golden calves. He built extra cities on the border of Judah and Israel so no one could come or go between the two nations. He was a very wicked king. Soon he died, and his son Elah ruled Israel in his place.

Questions

1. Josiah destroyed the _____ altars Jeroboam had built.

2. _____ knew who had come to see him because God told him.

3. When _____ became king, all of Jeroboam's family was killed.

Thought Question

Why did God let Jeroboam's son die? What does it mean that there was found something good in Jeroboam's son towards the Lord?

Catechism

Question 82: Is God pleased with those who love and obey him?
Answer 82: Yes. God says, "I love them that love me."

Memory Verse

Exodus 20:4
You shall not make for yourself a carved image—any likeness of anything that is in heaven above, or that is in the earth beneath, or that is in the water under the earth.

LESSON 65

Week 13 Review

Memory Verse

Exodus 20:4

Catechism

Question 37: What effect did the sin of Adam have on you and all people?

Question 38: How sinful are you by nature?

Question 39: What is the sinful nature that we inherit from Adam called?

Question 81: Who is your neighbor?

Question 82: Is God pleased with those who love and obey him?

To the Teacher : The answers to catechism questions 37–39 are found on page 266.

Activity

Number the Order of Events

Number the parts of the kings' story in order from one to five.

_____ Rehoboam, Solomon's son, becomes king of Israel.

_____ The queen of Sheba visits Israel.

_____ The kingdom of Israel splits into two kingdoms—Israel and Judah.

_____ Rehoboam increases the taxes against the advice of his wise older advisors.

_____ Jeroboam builds golden calves for Israel to worship.

Unit 14   *Righteous Elijah, Wicked Ahab*

LESSON 66

King Asa

1 Kings 15:9–16:28; 2 Chronicles 14:1–15:18

While wicked kings were ruling in Israel, the righteous king Asa was ruling in Judah. He destroyed all the idols he could find and commanded the people to worship God. He built stone walls around many of his cities to protect them. He trained a large army, too. Because Asa obeyed the Lord, God gave him peace in Judah for ten years.

After ten years of peace, a mighty Ethiopian army of a million men came to fight against Asa. Instead of relying on his own large army, Asa turned to God. He said, "LORD, it is nothing for You to help, whether with many or with those who have no power; help us, O LORD our God, for we rest on You, and in Your name we go against this multitude" (2 Chronicles 14:11).

God listened to Asa's prayer and gave Judah a great victory. The Ethiopians fled and left many wonderful things behind that the people of Judah took as their own. The people of Judah were rich, and their land had peace once more.

Then God sent a prophet to King Asa. God promised to be with Asa as long as he followed God. This word from God encouraged Asa, and he decided to do even more for the Lord.

Asa called all the people of Judah and Benjamin together for an outdoor meeting. Many people from Ephraim, Manasseh, and Simeon who lived in Judah also came to the meeting. The people offered a great sacrifice to the Lord and promised to serve God with all of their hearts.

The people decided that anyone who would not serve God would be put to death. Together, they shouted out their oath to serve God. Asa continued to take down idols and lead the people of Judah to serve only the Lord. So God continued to give the people of Judah peace.

Meanwhile, the kings of Israel were still wicked. King Baasha had killed all of Jeroboam's family. Yet he soon died; and when his son Elah began to rule, bad things continued to happen. Elah's servant Zimri murdered Elah while the king was drunk.

Zimri made himself king, but that only lasted a week. The people of Israel did not like Zimri. They chose Omri, the captain of Israel's soldiers, to be king. With his soldiers, Omri went to fight against the city where Zimri was staying. When Zimri heard that the city had been captured by Omri, he went into his palace and set it on fire. He was burned to death in his own palace.

Omri was the most wicked king yet. He ruled for twelve years, acting wickedly against God. When he died, his son Ahab began to rule over Israel.

Questions

1. One _____ men came from Ethiopia to fight Judah.

2. Whom did Asa ask for help? _____

3. The kings of Israel _____ God.

Thought Question

King Asa proved to everyone that when he listened to God, God answered. Why did so many kings still ignore God and disobey Him?

Catechism

Question 83: Is God displeased with those who do not love and obey him?
Question 83: Yes. "God is angry with the wicked every day."

Memory Verse

Exodus 20:5
You shall not bow down to them nor serve them. For I, the LORD your God, am a jealous God, visiting the iniquity of the fathers upon the children to the third and fourth generations, of those who hate Me.

LESSON 67

Wicked King Ahab

1 Kings 16:29–17:7

Ahab was even more wicked than his father. He was the most wicked king Israel ever had. His wife, Jezebel, was just as bad. She was the daughter of the wicked king of Sidon, who was a priest of the idol Baal.

Ahab built a temple for Baal in Samaria, the royal city, and he set up his own wicked idols, too. He also set up Asherah, more heathen idols. Jezebel had 400 priests for the Asherah while Ahab had 450 priests for the worship of Baal.

A few righteous priests still lived in Israel and tried to keep the people from worshiping idols. Jezebel tried to kill all the good priests. She hated anyone who loved and served the one true God. She wanted to destroy anyone and anything that loved God. She wanted Israel to be a completely wicked country, just like all the heathen nations around them.

With Ahab and Jezebel ruling, Israel had become a wicked place. In those days, when God was forgotten, a man named Hiel did something that God had forbidden over 500 years before.

When Joshua and the Israelites had crossed into Israel, they destroyed the city of Jericho. Joshua had commanded the people never to rebuild Jericho. Whoever rebuilt Jericho would have his oldest and youngest sons die.

For 500 years, Israel had listened to Joshua's words. Now, with God forgotten and Joshua's words ignored, Hiel decided to rebuild the city of Jericho. As Joshua had foretold, Hiel's oldest and youngest sons both died as he rebuilt the forbidden city.

Israel was in real trouble with Ahab and Jezebel ruling. Still, God did not leave His people entirely alone. He continued to send prophets to warn the people of God's promise to curse Israel if they stopped obeying God. One of the greatest prophets God ever sent was named Elijah.

God sent Elijah to Ahab to tell him that God was going to punish the king for his wickedness. When God gave him the message for Ahab, Elijah marched up the steps of the palace and into the presence of the king. Lifting his hands to the sky, Elijah said, "As the LORD God of Israel lives, before whom I stand, there shall not be dew nor rain these years, except at my word" (1 Kings 17:1).

Then the Lord sent Elijah away to a brook called Cherith. Elijah hid there by the brook, and the Lord sent ravens to him with bread and meat so that he would not starve.

The Lord protected Elijah, for there was a lot more work for the prophet. Elijah would have a lot more to tell King Ahab before Ahab's long reign was over.

Questions

1. What wicked couple ruled Israel? _____ and _____

2. Which city did Hiel rebuild? _____

3. God sent the prophet _____ to King Ahab.

Thought Question

Why would Hiel rebuild the city if he knew his sons would die?

Catechism

Question 83: Is God displeased with those who do not love and obey him?
Question 83: Yes. "God is angry with the wicked every day."

Memory Verse

Exodus 20:5

You shall not bow down to them nor serve them. For I, the LORD your God, am a jealous God, visiting the iniquity of the fathers upon the children to the third and fourth generations, of those who hate Me.

LESSON 68

Elijah and the Widow

1 Kings 17:1–24

Elijah continued to live by the brook for some time. God faithfully sent him ravens that brought food. Elijah drank water from the brook until the brook began to dry up because there had been no rain in the land. Then the Lord commanded Elijah to go north to the town of Zarephath.

Immediately, Elijah obeyed God. He traveled a long way on foot. When he finally reached the town, a widow was at the gate gathering sticks. God had commanded the widow to take care of Elijah.

When Elijah saw the woman, he asked her for a drink of water and some bread. The widow answered, "As the LORD your God lives, I do not have bread, only a handful of flour in a bin, and a little oil in a jar; and see, I am gathering a couple of sticks that I may go in and prepare it for myself and my son, that we may eat it, and die" (1 Kings 17:12).

Then Elijah told the woman not to worry. God had promised that the woman's oil and flour would last until God sent rain to the earth once more. So the woman made a little cake for Elijah. Then she and her son ate some, as well. There was only a little flour and oil to use, but when they had all eaten, there was plenty of both left over. This was a miracle, something only God could do.

Some time later, the widow's little boy became very sick. Then he died. The widow thought that her son's death was punishment for her sins. She became upset with Elijah, for she did not want him to bring up her sins or to kill her son; but Elijah had not killed the boy.

He commanded the widow to give him the boy's body. He carried the boy upstairs to his own room and laid him on the bed. Then Elijah cried out to God saying, "O LORD my God, I pray, let this child's soul come back to him" (1 Kings 17:21).

Elijah had faith that God could do what he had asked. After he prayed, Elijah lay down and stretched himself out over the boy's body three times.

God listened to Elijah's prayer. The child's soul returned to him, and the little boy breathed once more. Elijah carried him to his mother. The widow rejoiced to see her son alive once again. She turned to Elijah and said, "Now by this I know that you are a man of God, and that the word of the LORD in your mouth is the truth" (1 Kings 17:24).

Questions

1. God fed Elijah at the brook by sending _____ with food.

2. God did a miracle for the widow by not letting her _____ run out.

3. When Elijah called out for God to return the dead boy's soul, the boy _____ again.

Thought Question

Why would God let the little boy die, only to bring him back to life?

Catechism

Question 84: What is the first commandment?

Answer 84: The first commandment is "You shall have no other gods before Me."

Memory Verse

Exodus 20:5

You shall not bow down to them nor serve them. For I, the LORD your God, am a jealous God, visiting the iniquity of the fathers upon the children to the third and fourth generations, of those who hate Me.

LESSON 69

Who Shall be God?

1 Kings 18:1–24

Three years passed without rain. Day after day, the people scanned the sky looking for any sign of clouds that might bring rain. Rivers dried up, and people and animals began to starve for lack of food and water.

A man named Obadiah ruled King Ahab's house for him. He was a righteous man. When Jezebel tried to kill all God's prophets, Obadiah had taken 100 righteous men and hidden them in caves. He had kept them safe and fed them.

Now Ahab spoke to Obadiah. He said that they needed to go out and look for grass for their animals to eat. If they could find no grass, then they would have to kill their animals. Obadiah went one way and Ahab went the other, searching for food for their animals.

As Obadiah journeyed, he met Elijah. God had just told Elijah to leave the widow's house and show himself to Ahab. Obadiah recognized Elijah, and he was very surprised. Elijah said, "It is I. Go, tell your master, 'Elijah is here'" (1 Kings 18:8).

Obadiah was scared. King Ahab had searched everywhere for Elijah because he blamed him for the drought. Ahab wanted to kill Elijah. Obadiah thought that as soon as he told Ahab, the Spirit of God would take Elijah away. Then Ahab would be angry and kill Obadiah. Obadiah was a faithful servant of God. He did not want to be killed by Ahab because of Elijah.

Elijah reassured Obadiah and told him he would stay and present himself to the king. That way, Obadiah did not have to worry about his own life. So Obadiah ran to bring Ahab.

As soon as Ahab saw Elijah, he said, "Is that you, O troubler of Israel?" (1 Kings. 18:17).

Elijah answered, "I have not troubled Israel, but you and your father's house have, in that you have forsaken the commandments of the LORD and have followed the Baals" (verse 18). Then Elijah told Ahab to call together the prophets who served Baal.

So Ahab sent throughout the country and gathered the prophets of Baal. They came together to meet with Elijah on Mount Carmel. The people of Israel gathered around to see what would happen.

Elijah stood in front of the people and boldly cried out, "How long will you falter between two opinions? If the LORD is God, follow Him; but if Baal, follow him" (1 Kings 18:21).

The people did not answer. They knew they had pretended to follow God while they had really been worshiping Baal. So Elijah spoke again and suggested they have a test between God and Baal.

Two bulls were brought to Mount Carmel. Elijah would put one bull on an altar to God. The prophets of Baal would put the other bull on an altar to Baal. Neither side would light their altar. Instead, they would pray. Whichever god answered with fire and burned up the sacrifice, was the true God.

The people agreed that this was a good idea. So preparations began.

Questions

1. Obadiah saved God's prophets by hiding them in a _____.

2. Ahab called Elijah the "_____ of Israel."

3. Who was the true troubler of Israel? _____

Thought Question

What do you think was the reason for the test? Which god will answer?

Catechism

Question 84: What is the first commandment?
Answer 84: The first commandment is "You shall have no other gods before Me."

Memory Verse

Exodus 20:5

You shall not bow down to them nor serve them. For I, the LORD your God, am a jealous God, visiting the iniquity of the fathers upon the children to the third and fourth generations, of those who hate Me.

LESSON 70

Week 14 Review

Memory Verse

Exodus 20:1–5

Catechism

Question 40: Can anyone go to heaven with this sinful nature?

Question 41: What is this change of heart called?

Question 42: Who can change a sinner's heart?

Question 83: Is God displeased with those who do not love and obey him?

Question 84: What is the first commandment?

To the Teacher :   The answers to catechism questions 40–42 are found on page 266.

Activity

True or False

1.   God gave Asa peace in Israel because Asa was obedient. **True/False**

2.   Asa relied on his own army to defeat the Ethiopian army. **True/False**

3.   God listened to Asa's prayer and gave him the victory. **True/False**

4.   Ahab was the most wicked king of Israel. **True/False**

5.   Isabel was Ahab's wicked wife. **True/False**

6.   Elijah was a great prophet sent by God during the time of Ahab. **True/False**

7.   God sent ravens to feed Elijah so that he would not starve. **True/False**

8.   Elijah killed the widow's son because she was a sinner. **True/False**

Unit 15   The Prophets Elijah and Elisha

LESSON 71

Fire from Heaven

1 Kings 18:25–46

The wicked priests of Baal built up their altar. They took their bull and placed it on the altar. The people watched with excitement as the priests began to jump around, leap into the air, and cut themselves with knives. The priests screamed and shouted, "O Baal, hear us!" (1 Kings 18:26).

The priests shouted to their god all morning. There was no answer. After a while, Elijah began to mock the wicked priests. He said, "Cry aloud, for he is a god; either he is meditating, or he is busy, or he is on a journey, or perhaps he is sleeping and must be awakened" (1 Kings 18:27).

Then the priests began to shout even louder and run even faster. They screamed and howled. They called to Baal all day. Still there was no answer.

When evening came, the people had become tired of waiting and watching the priests call out to their god. Elijah called out to the people and told them to gather around.

On top of Mount Carmel was an old, broken-down altar of God. Elijah repaired the altar with twelve large stones. He cut his bull into pieces and laid them on the altar. Then he dug a ditch around the altar. Finally, he told the people to fill four large jars with water and to pour the water on the altar over the sacrifice. The water was quickly brought, and Elijah commanded the people to bring water two more times.

Everything was ready. God's altar was wet, and the ditch around the altar was filled with water. It would be almost impossible to light the sacrifice on fire when there was so much water around it.

Then Elijah lifted his face to heaven and began to pray. He said, "Lord God of Abraham, Isaac, and Israel, let it be known this day that You are God in Israel and I am Your servant, and that I have done all these things at Your word. Hear me, O Lord, hear me, that this people may know that You are the Lord God, and that You have turned their hearts back to You again" (1 Kings 18:36–37).

The fire of God blazed suddenly from heaven as Elijah prayed. Fire came down from heaven and consumed the bull and the wood. It was so hot that the water in the ditch boiled away. Even the stones of the altar and the ground around the altar began to burn.

The people of Israel were astonished and afraid. They fell on their faces and cried out, "The Lord, He is God!" (1 Kings 18:39).

Then Elijah ordered the people to seize the wicked prophets of Baal. The people obeyed and took the prophets down to the Brook Kishon and killed them all there.

Finally, Elijah told Ahab to return to his home and get something to eat and drink, for plenty of rain would be coming.

Elijah himself returned to the top of Mount Carmel. He threw himself on the ground and began to pray. He told his servant to go and look towards the sea. His servant obeyed, but came back saying nothing was there. Seven times, Elijah told his servant to look towards the sea. On the seventh time, the servant saw a little cloud. Elijah told his servant to go and tell Ahab to hurry in his chariot before the rains came and stopped him.

The sky became black with clouds and wind. A great rain came. Then the hand of God came upon Elijah so that he ran ahead of Ahab to the entrance of Jezreel.

Questions   _____

1. As Elijah prayed, _____ came down from heaven and consumed the bull and the wood.

2. Elijah ordered the people to seize the _____ prophets of _____.

Thought Question
Describe what happened between Elijah and the prophets of Baal.

Catechism
Question 85: What does the first commandment teach you?
Answer 85: To worship the true God, and him only

Memory Verse

Exodus 20:6
But showing mercy to thousands, to those who love Me and keep My commandments.

LESSON 72

A Still, Small Voice

1 Kings 19:1–18

Sadly, the people of Israel still had hard hearts that did not want to obey God, even after God showed His awesome power on Mount Carmel. Jezebel was especially upset. When Ahab told her that Elijah had had all the prophets of Baal killed, Jezebel was furious. She sent a messenger to Elijah to tell him that she was going to kill him.

Elijah left the royal city quickly. He ran for his life and traveled a long way. When he reached the country of Judah, he left his servant and kept traveling another day. Finally, he stopped and sat under a broom tree. Elijah was tired and discouraged, for he knew that the people of Israel had wicked hearts.

He was so tired that he told God, "It is enough! Now, LORD, take my life, for I am no better than my fathers!" (1 Kings 19:4). God, however, knew it was not time for Elijah to die. Instead, Elijah fell asleep. God was taking care of His tired servant who had served Him faithfully at Mount Carmel.

As the prophet slept, God sent an angel to him. The angel touched Elijah and said, "Arise and eat" (1 Kings 19:5). Elijah looked around and found some food and a jar of water waiting for him. So he ate and drank and then slept some more. Again the angel touched him and told him to get up and eat.

Rested and no longer hungry, Elijah began to travel again. Strengthened by the food the angel had given him, Elijah traveled for forty days and nights. At last, he came to Mount Sinai where God had given the Ten Commandments to the children of Israel.

At Mount Sinai, Elijah was safe from Jezebel. He found a cave and went inside to spend the night. Then the word of God came to him saying, "What are you doing here, Elijah?" (1 Kings 19:9). Elijah explained that he had been obedient and zealous for the Lord. He had done everything God had commanded. Yet he was discouraged because the Israelites had turned away from God and were worshiping Baal. Elijah was so discouraged he thought he was the only person left in Israel who loved and obeyed God. Moreover, all the wicked people were hunting him to kill him.

God was kind to Elijah. He told him to go outside the cave and stand on the mountain before the Lord. Then God sent a terrible wind that tore the mountain and broke rocks in pieces, but the Lord was not in the wind. Then God sent a dreadful earthquake, but the Lord was not in the earthquake. Next, God sent fire, but the Lord was not in the fire.

Finally, Elijah heard a still, small voice. He immediately knew that God was speaking to him. Once again, God asked what Elijah was doing there. Elijah gave the same answer. This time, God told Elijah to return to Israel and anoint a new king over Syria, as well as a new king, Jehu, over Israel. Last of all, Elijah needed to anoint a new prophet who would follow him and continue his work after he had died. At last, God told Elijah that he was not alone in following God. God had kept 7,000 righteous people for Himself, those who had not bowed to Baal.

Questions

1. _____ wanted to kill Elijah.

2. Elijah was so discouraged he thought he was the only one left who _____ and _____ God.

3. God had kept _____ people for Himself.

Thought Question

Why would God reveal Himself to Elijah in a still, small voice instead of in a great wind, earthquake, or fire?

Catechism

Question 85: What does the first commandment teach you?
Answer 85: To worship the true God, and him only

Memory Verse

Exodus 20:6
But showing mercy to thousands, to those who love Me and keep My commandments.

LESSON 73

Elisha

1 Kings 19:19–20:21

Elijah was encouraged to hear that he was not the only one who still worshiped God. He was also happy to know that he would not have to be a prophet much longer. In those days it was very hard to be a prophet of God and to stand alone when everyone else was worshiping idols. Elijah was brave and courageous. He had done everything God had told him to do. Still, Elijah was tired, and he did not want to continue living in such a wicked world.

As God had directed, Elijah left the cave and began to travel back. When he reached Israel, he saw a man named Elisha plowing a field with twelve yoke of oxen. Elijah did not stop to speak to him. Instead, he threw his mantle over Elisha's shoulders as he walked past.

Elisha knew what this meant. He had been chosen to follow the prophet Elijah and to become a prophet after him. From that time on, Elisha stayed with Elijah. Elijah finally had a companion who loved God, and Elisha had a wonderful teacher to show him how to become a prophet of God.

Now Syria was a country north of Israel. The current king was Ben-Hadad. He gathered his army and, with thirty-two other kings, made war against Israel. Their armies surrounded King Ahab's capital city.

Ahab was terrified. While the king of Judah had been building up his country's defenses, Ahab had done nothing. He had only 7,000 soldiers. Then Ben-Hadad sent a cruel message. He said, "Your silver and your gold are mine; your loveliest wives and children are mine" (1 Kings 20:3).

Ahab had almost no army, and he had torn down all of God's altars. He had nowhere to turn. So he submitted. He said, "My lord, O king, just as you say, I and all that I have are yours" (1 Kings 20:4).

Ben-Hadad was not satisfied with Ahab's answer. He sent another message announcing that he would send his servants the next day to search Ahab's house for anything he felt like taking.

So Ahab called the elders of Israel together. They told the king not to submit to Ben-Hadad's demands. So Ahab responded and told Ben-Hadad he would not let his servants come and search his house.

Ben-Hadad was pleased for an excuse to go to war. He wanted to crush Israel so that hardly anything was left. However, as Syria's king was making his plan to defeat Israel, a prophet appeared to King Ahab and told him God would defeat Syria.

Then Ahab asked who would fight, and the prophet told him to send the young princes out to fight. So Ahab counted 232 princes. Then he and the people went out to fight.

Ben-Hadad and his army's leaders were getting drunk when Israel came to fight them at noon. Ben-Hadad did not care that men were coming to fight him. He ordered his army to take the Israelites alive, whether they came to fight or to surrender.

God was helping Israel, however, and they would win the fight. Each of the young princes picked out a man of Syria and killed him. Then all of Israel chased the Syrians as they ran away. Ahab's men killed many Syrians, but Ben-Hadad escaped.

Questions

1. Who followed Elijah and would be the next prophet? _____

2. Ahab was ready to submit to _____ because Ahab had no army and no God.

Thought Question

Why would God help Israel when Ahab had turned his back on God and most of Israel had followed?

Catechism

Question 86: What is the second commandment?

Answer 86: The second commandment is "You shall not make for yourself a carved image—any likeness of anything that is in heaven above, or that is in the earth beneath, or that is in the water under the earth; you shall not bow down to them nor serve them. For I, the LORD your God, am a jealous God, visiting the iniquity of the fathers upon the children to the third and fourth generations of those who hate Me, but showing mercy to thousands, to those who love Me and keep My commandments."

Memory Verse

Exodus 20:6
But showing mercy to thousands, to those who love Me and keep My commandments.

LESSON 74

Cumulative Review 4

Job–Elijah

Word Bank: battle Samuel Saul Solomon

1. Who became judge after Eli died? _____

2. Samuel anointed _____ as the first king of Israel.

3. Samuel said that Saul and his sons would die in _____ .

4. Who built God's temple? _____

Oral Questions

1. What did Job not understand about God?

2. Why was Saul jealous of David?

3. How did God feed Elijah at the brook?

Catechism

Question 86: What is the second commandment?
Answer 86: The second commandment is "You shall not make for yourself a carved image—any likeness of anything that is in heaven above, or that is in the earth beneath, or that is in the water under the earth; you shall not bow down to them nor serve them. For I, the LORD your God, am a jealous God, visiting the iniquity of the fathers upon the children to the third and fourth generations of those who hate Me, but showing mercy to thousands, to those who love Me and keep My commandments."

Memory Verse

Exodus 20:6
But showing mercy to thousands, to those who love Me and keep My commandments.

LESSON 75

Week 15 Review

Memory Verse

Exodus 20:1-6

Catechism

Question 43: Can anyone be saved through the covenant of life?

Question 44: Why can't anyone be saved through the covenant of life?

Question 45: How did you break the covenant of life?

Question 85: What does the first commandment teach you?

Question 86: What is the second commandment?

To the Teacher :   The answers to catechism questions 43–45 are found on page 266.

Activity

Matching

Draw lines to match the correct word or name to each sentence.

1. could not answer the priests because he is an idol   water

2. sent fire from heaven to burn up Elijah's sacrifice   kill

3. Elijah soaked God's altar with this   Baal

4. Elijah ordered the people to do this to Baal's prophets   God

5. wanted to kill Elijah   Jezebel

6. became so tired that he wanted to die   voice

7. God spoke to Elijah in a still, small …   Elisha

8. was chosen to be prophet after Elijah   Elijah

Unit 16 — King Ahab and King Jehoshaphat

LESSON 76

How Ahab Treated God's Enemy

1 Kings 20:22–43

God had helped Israel defeat Syria because the Israelites were still His people. God loved them and did not want them to be utterly destroyed. The Syrians were a wicked people who needed judgment, and the Lord was teaching them that He alone is God of all the earth.

When Ahab returned from the battle, God's prophet warned him that the Syrians would come again in the spring. Israel needed to get ready for another battle.

Sure enough, when Ben-Hadad returned to his home, his servants said, "Their gods are gods of the hills. Therefore they were stronger than we; but if we fight against them in the plain, surely we will be stronger than they" (1 Kings 20:23). Ben-Hadad listened to his advisors and gathered another army.

The next year, Ben-Hadad returned to Israel. This time he did not go to the capital city, Samaria, for it was built on a hill. Instead, he set up his army in the lowlands east of the Sea of Galilee.

Ahab had gathered only a small army. But once again, the Lord sent a prophet. This time, the prophet said that God would help Israel because Syria had boasted that Israel's God was God of the hills only. God would show both Syria and Israel that He rules the entire world.

Once again, little Israel defeated the large Syrian army. That day, 100,000 Syrian soldiers were killed. The rest of the Syr- ians fled to a nearby city hoping they would be safe there. Instead, one of the city walls fell on the soldiers and killed 27,000 more men.

Meanwhile, Ben-Hadad had run away and hidden in an inner room of a house in the city. His servants came to him and told him the king of Israel might be merciful. So the servants put on sackcloth and went to meet King Ahab. They told Ahab that Ben-Hadad was alive and was asking for Ahab to spare his life.

Ahab answered, "Is he still alive? He is my brother" (1 Kings 20:32). He sent for Ben-Hadad and brought him into his own chariot. Ben-Hadad agreed to give back the land he had stolen from Israel, and Ahab made a treaty with the Syrian king, letting him live.

This was a foolish thing for Ahab to do. God had delivered Ben-Hadad into Ahab's hands and wanted him killed. God sent yet another prophet to Ahab who told him, "Because you have let slip out of your hand a man whom I appointed to utter destruction, therefore your life shall go for his life, and your people for his people" (1 Kings 20:42).

Then King Ahab returned to his home, angry and displeased. He had tried to keep God out of his kingdom, but he could not escape from God. The Lord was still in control of Israel and continually sent prophets to Ahab to remind him of the Lord's will.

Questions

1. The Syrians thought God was only God of the _____ .

2. The _____ _____ fell on the men of Syria and killed many of them.

3. Ahab called Ben-Hadad his _____ when he realized he was alive.

Thought Question

Why did God want Ben-Hadad to be killed?

Catechism

Question 87: What does the second commandment teach you?
Answer 87: To worship God only as he commands, and not to worship God by using statues or pictures

Memory Verse

Exodus 20:7
You shall not take the name of the LORD your God in vain, for the LORD will not hold him guiltless who takes His name in vain.

LESSON 77

Naboth's Vineyard

1 Kings 21:1–29

A man named Naboth owned a vineyard next to King Ahab's palace. This land had come down to Naboth from his fathers, as Moses had commanded. Naboth's family had owned the vineyard for many years.

King Ahab wanted Naboth's vineyard so that he could make a vegetable garden near his home. He offered Naboth money or even a different vineyard. Yet Naboth answered, "The LORD forbid that I should give the inheritance of my fathers to you!" (1 Kings 21:3).

Ahab was angry. When he heard this, he went into his house, lay down on his bed, turned his face to the wall, and would not come down for dinner. The king of Israel was sulking because he did not get what he wanted.

Soon Jezebel came to find out what was wrong. Ahab told her that Naboth would not give him the vineyard. So Jezebel said, "You now exercise authority over Israel! Arise, eat food, and let your heart be cheerful; I will give you the vineyard of Naboth the Jezreelite" (1 Kings 21:7).

Jezebel thought the king deserved whatever he wanted. If someone did not give him what he wanted, then he could take it. So Jezebel wrote letters to the elders of the city, signed them with the king's name, and sealed them with the king's seal. She commanded the elders to proclaim a fast within the city. They were to honor Naboth. Then they were to call in two wicked men who would lie and accuse Naboth of blaspheming God and the king. Then they were to stone Naboth until he was dead.

The elders of Israel were afraid to disobey Jezebel. They did everything that Jezebel had ordered. Naboth was falsely accused. The people carried him out of the city and stoned him. Dogs licked his blood which stained the stones of that place.

Word was sent to Jezebel that what she had commanded had been carried out. When she heard, she went to Ahab and told him to get up and take Naboth's vineyard as his own.

Then the word of the Lord came to the prophet Elijah telling him to go meet Ahab in Naboth's vineyard. So Elijah went to Ahab, who greeted him by saying, "Have you found me, O my enemy?" (1 Kings 21:20).

Elijah answered that he had come to find him because of the evil he had done. Elijah told Ahab that the Lord would destroy his house and his children as Jeroboam's had been destroyed. Indeed, Elijah said, "In the place where dogs licked the blood of Naboth, dogs shall lick your blood, even yours…. The dogs shall eat Jezebel by the wall of Jezreel" (1 Kings 21:19, 23).

There was never a king as wicked as Ahab. He had been stirred up by his wicked wife, and he had worshiped idols. Yet he was still an Israelite who understood God's laws. He had seen God's power.

After hearing Elijah's terrible prophecy, he tore his clothes and put on sackcloth. He ate no food and had no visitors. So the Lord told Elijah, "Because he has humbled himself before Me, I will not bring the calamity in his days. In the days of his son I will bring the calamity on his house" (1 Kings 21:29).

Questions

1. Ahab wanted the _____ that belonged to Naboth.

2. Naboth refused the king because it was against _____ _____.

3. Jezebel got the vineyard for Ahab by killing _____.

Thought Question

Why would Ahab kill Naboth for obeying God's commands?

Catechism

Question 87: What does the second commandment teach you?
Answer 87: To worship God only as he commands, and not to worship God by using statues or pictures

Memory Verse

Exodus 20:7
You shall not take the name of the LORD your God in vain, for the LORD will not hold him guiltless who takes His name in vain.

LESSON 78

Ahab and Jehoshaphat

1 Kings 22:1–12, 41–49

While evil King Ahab was ruling over Israel, good King Asa, after ruling Judah for forty-one years, died. His son Jehoshaphat became king. Jehoshaphat was also a good king, and Judah prospered under his reign.

The Lord was with Jehoshaphat and blessed him in all that he did. So Jehoshaphat built strong walls around his cities, gathered a large army of more than a million soldiers, and appointed men to teach the Law of Moses to all the people. Before this time, the people had not had much opportunity to hear God's Law. Under Jehoshaphat, all the people could learn what God had told them.

During this time, Judah also had peace in the land, for none of their enemies wanted to fight them. Instead, many other kings and nations brought gifts to King Jehoshaphat.

Despite all of the good things Jehoshaphat did, he also made one very bad mistake. He became friends with Ahab, king of Israel. God did not want a righteous king to be good friends with a king who despised God and had taught the people of Israel to worship idols.

One time, Jehoshaphat took many of his servants and soldiers and went to visit Ahab. A splendid feast was given in his honor, and all the nobles of the land were invited. During the feast, Ahab asked Jehoshaphat if he would help Israel fight against Syria so that they could regain some land that Syria had stolen.

Jehoshaphat was happy to agree, but he would not go to war without asking God first. Ahab had let his wife try to kill all the prophets of God, but he wanted Jehoshaphat to come with him. So Ahab gathered together 400 prophets. These men were not prophets of the true God. When Ahab asked them if he should go up to fight against Syria, the prophets received no word from God. They simply told the king that if he went to fight, he would win.

Now Jehoshaphat knew these men were not real prophets. He asked Ahab if there was not even one true prophet of God left in the land. Ahab answered, "There is still one man, Micaiah the son of Imlah, by whom we may inquire of the LORD; but I hate him, because he does not prophesy good concerning me, but evil" (1 Kings 22:8).

Jehoshaphat was appalled at Ahab's answer and asked to see the prophet. So Ahab sent a messenger to find Micaiah.

Meanwhile, the 400 prophets continued to tell Ahab to go out to war. One of them even made some horns out of iron. He told the kings that God had told him the kings would go out to war and push the Syrians with the horns until they were consumed. This too was a lie, for God had not yet spoken concerning the kings going out to battle.

Questions

1. Jehoshaphat's mistake was that he became ＿＿＿＿＿＿＿＿＿＿ with ＿＿＿＿＿.

2. ＿＿＿＿＿＿＿＿＿＿ wanted to ask for God's guidance before going to war.

3. Ahab did not like Micaiah because he prophesied ＿＿＿＿ ＿＿＿＿ for Ahab.

Thought Question

Why did Micaiah only prophesy evil concerning King Ahab?

Catechism

Question 88: What is the third commandment?
Answer 88: The third commandment is "You shall not take the name of the LORD your God in vain, for the LORD will not hold him guiltless who takes His name in vain."

Memory Verse

Exodus 20:7
You shall not take the name of the LORD your God in vain, for the LORD will not hold him guiltless who takes His name in vain.

LESSON 79

Micaiah, the Prophet Who Would Not Lie

1 Kings 22:13–40

Ahab's messenger soon found Micaiah the prophet. He told the prophet what was happening and what the other, false, prophets were saying. Then he asked Micaiah to agree with the other prophets and not to say anything bad. Micaiah answered, "As the LORD lives, whatever the LORD says to me, that I will speak" (1 Kings 22:14). Micaiah was a true prophet of God, and he would not lie.

Determined to speak the truth, Micaiah went before the kings. When Ahab asked if they should go to war, Micaiah answered mockingly, mimicking the 400 prophets who had lied, saying "go to war". Ahab could tell that Micaiah was making fun of him, so he angrily told Micaiah to tell him the truth of God.

Then Micaiah cried out, "I saw all Israel scattered on the mountains, as sheep that have no shepherd. And the LORD said, 'These have no master. Let each return to his house in peace'" (1 Kings 22:17). This meant that if Ahab went to war, he would be killed and Israel would have no king anymore. Ahab was very angry and told Jehoshaphat he had known Micaiah would not say anything good.

Micaiah, however, was not yet done. He told Ahab of another vision he had had. In this one, God was sitting on His throne in heaven. God asked who would persuade Ahab to go up and die in battle. Many spirits had different ideas until one suggested it become a lying spirit in the mouths of all Ahab's prophets. The Lord told this spirit it would succeed. So Micaiah told Ahab his prophets were lying.

However, King Ahab was determined to have his own way and go to war. He had beaten Syria twice and thought he could do it again. Four hundred prophets had told him to go to war, and only one had said not to go, so Ahab went. He also decided to punish Micaiah for his prophecy by sending him to prison.

Then Ahab and Jehoshaphat marched to war. Now Ahab did not believe Micaiah, but he was also a little afraid of what he had said. He thought that if he dressed like a common soldier instead of a king, then he would not die in the battle. Jehoshaphat, however, wore his kingly robes.

Now the king of Syria had commanded the captains of his chariots to fight no one except the king of Israel. When the captains saw Jehoshaphat's robes, they turned to fight him. Then Jehoshaphat cried out in terror, and the captains knew he was not the king of Israel, so they stopped trying to kill him.

Finally, a Syrian soldier drew his bow and fired an arrow randomly into the air. That arrow flew straight through King Ahab's disguise, as well as his armor, and wounded the king. Ahab told his chariot driver to turn around because he was wounded. Then King Ahab lay in a pool of his own blood at the bottom of a chariot. By evening, he died.

Ahab's men took his body to Samaria where he was buried. Then his servants took the chariot to a pool to wash it. There, the dogs licked up Ahab's blood just as Naboth's blood had been licked and just as God had foretold through Elijah.

Questions

1. God said that _____ would die if he went to war.

2. Ahab put Micaiah in _____ for his prophecy.

3. Ahab finally died when he was shot with an _____ in battle.

Thought Question

Do you think the arrow that the Syrian soldier fired was really random? Did Ahab's disguise really work?

Catechism

Question 88: What is the third commandment?

Answer 88: The third commandment is "You shall not take the name of the LORD your God in vain, for the LORD will not hold him guiltless who takes His name in vain."

Memory Verse

Exodus 20:7

You shall not take the name of the LORD your God in vain, for the LORD will not hold him guiltless who takes His name in vain.

LESSON 80

Week 16 Review

Memory Verse

Exodus 20:1–7

Catechism

Question 46: How, then, can you be saved?

Question 47: Whom did Christ represent in the covenant of grace?

Question 48: How did Christ fulfill the covenant of grace?

Question 87: What does the second commandment teach you?

Question 88: What is the third commandment?

To the Teacher: The answers to catechism questions 46–48 are found on page 266.

Activity

Fill in the Blank

Word Bank: blasphemy   brother   eat   hills   Law   lie   stone   vineyard

1. Ben-Hadad and the Syrians thought God was only God of the _____.

2. Ahab called Ben-Hadad his _____.

3. Naboth owned a _____ that Ahab wanted.

4. Jezebel plotted to have men accuse Naboth of _____.

5. The men who accused Naboth were then supposed to _____ him.

6. Elijah prophesied that dogs would _____ Jezebel.

7. Jehoshaphat appointed men to teach the _____ of Moses.

8. Micaiah would not _____ to Ahab. He spoke only God's truth.

Unit 17   Elijah's Final Days

LESSON 81

Fire from Heaven

1 Kings 22:51–2 Kings 1:18

Ahab was dead, but Jezebel was still alive. Their son Ahaziah had become king of Israel. Like his parents, Ahaziah was a wicked king who worshiped heathen idols.

Ahaziah was king for only two years. He fell out of an upstairs window in his palace and was hurt very badly. He wanted to know whether or not he would recover from his injuries. Ahaziah did not think of asking God, for he worshiped idols. He sent messages to one of the Philistine cities where an idol was kept and asked if he would get well or die.

God was angry with Ahaziah. Before the messengers had gone far on their journey, they were met by an austere old man. God had sent the prophet Elijah to talk to the messengers. Elijah told the messengers what God had said concerning King Ahaziah. God had said, "You shall not come down from the bed to which you have gone up, but you shall surely die" (2 Kings 1:4).

So the messengers returned to Ahaziah. He was surprised to see them and asked why they had returned so quickly. The messengers told the king they had met a man on the road who had asked why the king was inquiring of idols when there was a God in Israel. They explained that the man had sent them back with news that the king would die because he trusted in idols instead of God.

When the king heard the news, he asked what kind of man had stopped the messengers. They described him. Then Ahaziah knew that the man was Elijah, the prophet of God.

As his mother Jezebel had done, Ahaziah tried to kill Elijah. He sent a captain with fifty soldiers out to find Elijah and bring him to the palace so Ahaziah could punish him. The captain found Elijah sitting on a hill and called for him to come down. Elijah answered, "If I am a man of God, then let fire come down from heaven and consume you and your fifty men" (2 Kings 1:10). Then God sent fire down from heaven and consumed the men just as Elijah had said.

Instead of acknowledging God's power and bowing before him, Ahaziah sent another captain with another fifty men. These men also found Elijah and were also consumed by fire from heaven, for the Lord was protecting His faithful servant who dared to stand firmly for the Lord.

Then Ahaziah sent a third captain with fifty men. This time, however, the captain feared God. When he found Elijah, he fell down on his knees and begged the prophet to save his life and the lives of his soldiers. So the Lord told Elijah to go with this captain to see King Ahaziah.

Elijah boldly entered the king's room and told him that the Lord was angry with him for asking false gods for answers to his questions. "Therefore," Elijah said, "you shall not come down from the bed to which you have gone up, but you shall surely die" (2 Kings 1:16).

In a short time, the word of Elijah was fulfilled. Ahaziah died. This king had no son, so his brother Jehoram became king of Israel.

Questions

1. The king was injured when he fell out a _____.

2. The captains and their men who commanded Elijah were _____ up by _____.

3. The captain who asked Elijah to save his life was _____.

Thought Question

How might King Ahaziah have known that the man who stopped his messengers was Elijah, and why did he want to kill the prophet?

Catechism

Question 89: What does the third commandment teach you?
Answer 89: To treat God's name, word and works with reverence

Memory Verse

Exodus 20:8–9
Remember the Sabbath day, to keep it holy. Six days you shall labor and do all your work.

LESSON 82

A Victory without a Battle

2 Chronicles 20:1–21:20

Jehoshaphat was still ruling in Israel, even after Ahab died. He urged his people to serve the Lord. He appointed judges in the cities and warned them all to be just since they were judging for God and not for man.

After some time, messengers came to Jehoshaphat and told him of a great army of Moabites, Edomites, and Ammonites that was coming to fight against him. Jehoshaphat began to pray to the Lord for help. He proclaimed a fast day for all of Judah, and the people came to stand before the temple in Jerusalem. The king stood in the court of the temple and raised his hands to God in prayer.

God had done much for His people already, and He had promised to answer if they cried to Him for help. Jehoshaphat knew he could not hope to defeat such a great army without God's help. He prayed, and God heard Jehoshaphat's prayer.

While the people prayed, the Spirit of the Lord came upon a Levite so that he prophesied the Lord's words. God told the people, "Do not be afraid nor dismayed because of this great multitude, for the battle is not yours, but God's" (2 Chronicles 20:15). Then God told the people what to do.

The next day, in obedience to God's word, the people of Judah went into the wilderness to meet their enemies. At the front of the line was a choir that sang praises to God as they went along.

Three nations had come up to fight Judah. As the people began to sing, the Lord made two nations, the Ammonites and the Moabites, fight against the third nation, the Edomites. After they destroyed the Edomites, the Ammonites and Moabites began killing each other.

Now a watchtower was set up in the wilderness. When the men of Judah reached it, they climbed up to see where their enemy was. To their surprise, the whole country was covered with dead bodies. Not a living man could be found.

The people found many riches and jewels among the slain people. It took them three days to carry all of the spoils home. On the fourth day, the people came together to thank and praise God for the marvelous thing He had done. Their enemies had been destroyed, and they were much richer than they had been before.

News of Judah's victory was spread through all the surrounding countries. All the wicked nations were afraid when they heard how God had fought for His people. After that, God gave the land peace.

Jehoshaphat reigned for twenty-five years. He died, having ruled as a just and righteous man. His son, however, became a wicked king. This king was called Jehoram, just as the king of Israel was called.

Jehoram of Judah was a wicked man. He had married King Ahab's daughter, Athaliah. She was as wicked as her mother, and she influenced Jehoram to be wicked. Jehoram worshiped idols and told his people to worship idols, too.

The old prophet Elijah sent a letter to warn King Jehoram that God would punish him. Because Jehoram was worshiping idols, God allowed the wicked nations around Judah to make trouble for him. The Philistines and Arabians came into the land, all the way up to the temple. They stole all the nice things they found and took away Jehoram's wives and sons so that only his youngest son was left. Finally, Jehoram became ill. After two years of suffering, he died. He was buried in Jerusalem, but not in the grave of the kings.

Questions

1. The _____ led the army of Judah to fight.

2. God defeated Judah's enemies by making them _____ and _____ each other.

Thought Question

Why were the men of Judah surprised when they saw that their enemies were already dead? Had not God promised to help them?

Catechism

Question 90: What is the fourth commandment?
Answer 90: The fourth commandment is "Remember the Sabbath day, to keep it holy. Six days you shall labor and do all your work, but the seventh day is the Sabbath of the LORD your God. In it you shall do no work: you, nor your son, nor your daughter, nor your male servant, nor your female servant, nor your cattle, nor your stranger who is within your gates. For in six days the LORD made the heavens and the earth, the sea, and all that is in them, and rested the seventh day. Therefore the LORD blessed the Sabbath day and hallowed it."

Memory Verse

Exodus 20:8–9
Remember the Sabbath day, to keep it holy. Six days you shall labor and do all your work.

LESSON 83

Elijah's Farewell

2 Kings 2:1–18

We have talked quite a bit about the kings of Judah and Israel. Now we must return to Elijah and Elisha, the prophets.

Elijah lived in very evil days, full of wicked kings, queens, and people. Elijah's job had been to tell the idolatrous kings that the Lord was going to punish them. All the kings had hated him and tried to kill him. Only God's care had saved Elijah's life.

At last, Elijah's work was over. God was going to take him to heaven. Elijah and Elisha were living in Gilgal when the word of the Lord came and told Elijah to leave. Elijah told Elisha to stay in Gilgal, but Elisha said, "As the LORD lives, and as your soul lives, I will not leave you!" (2 Kings 2:2).

Together the men went to Bethel, where there were many prophets. The prophets came out and asked Elisha if he knew that God was going to take his master away that day. Elisha answered, "Yes, I know; keep silent!" (2 Kings 2:3).

Again Elijah asked Elisha to stay behind. And again Elisha refused to leave his master. So the men went on to Jericho where more prophets came to ask if Elisha knew his master would be taken by God. Once again, Elisha told the men he knew and that they should be silent.

Elijah asked again, but Elisha would not stay in Jericho either. He wanted to be with Elijah when he left the earth. They went on together to the River Jordan. Once there, Elijah rolled up his cloak and struck the water with it. The water parted, and the two men passed on dry ground.

On the other side of the Jordan, Elijah asked if Elisha wanted him to do anything for him before the Lord took him. Elisha answered, "Please let a double portion of your spirit be upon me" (2 Kings 2:9). Elijah knew that Elisha had asked a hard thing. However, he told Elisha that if he saw Elijah when he was taken away, then his wish would be given to him.

As the two men stood talking, a chariot of fire pulled by horses of fire appeared. Elijah got into the chariot, and it took him up into heaven. Elisha watched the whole time. He saw Elijah go up into heaven and cried out, "My father, my father, the chariot of Israel and its horsemen!" (2 Kings 2:12).

As Elijah disappeared, his cloak fell to the ground. Elisha picked up the cloak and returned to the Jordan. He rolled up the cloak and struck the water, just as Elijah had done, and the water rolled away just as it had for Elijah.

The prophets from Jericho met Elisha as he returned. They could tell that the spirit of Elijah was upon Elisha, for the Lord had chosen Elisha as His new prophet. They did not, however, understand that the Lord had taken Elijah.

Jericho's prophets wanted to search for Elijah to see what had happened to him. Elisha did not want to send anyone to look, for he knew Elijah was with God. Yet the prophets kept asking until he told them they could go. Fifty men searched the mountains for three days but could not find Elijah.

Questions

1. Elisha wanted a _____ _____ of Elijah's spirit.

2. A fiery _____ came to take Elijah.

3. Elijah had gone up to _____.

Thought Question

Elijah was one of only two men known not to have died but to have been taken directly to heaven by God. Why might God have allowed Elijah not to die?

Catechism

Question 90: What is the fourth commandment?

Answer 90: The fourth commandment is "Remember the Sabbath day, to keep it holy. Six days you shall labor and do all your work, but the seventh day is the Sabbath of the LORD your God. In it you shall do no work: you, nor your son, nor your daughter, nor your male servant, nor your female servant, nor your cattle, nor your stranger who is within your gates. For in six days the LORD made the heavens and the earth, the sea, and all that is in them, and rested the seventh day. Therefore the LORD blessed the Sabbath day and hallowed it."

Memory Verse

Exodus 20:8–9
Remember the Sabbath day, to keep it holy. Six days you shall labor and do all your work.

LESSON 84

Cumulative Review 5

David–Elijah

Word Bank: Absalom Ahab battle Benjamin Elisha Jezebel Judah Naboth's obeyed wisdom

1. Which of David's sons tried to kill him? _____

2. Solomon asked God to give him _____ .

3. Which two tribes became the kingdom of Judah and followed Rehoboam? _____

   and _____

4. What wicked royal couple ruled Israel? _____ and _____

5. Elijah was so discouraged he thought he was the only one left who loved and _____God.

6. Who followed Elijah and would be the next prophet? _____

7. Jezebel got _____ vineyard for Ahab by killing him.

8. Ahab finally died in _____ when he was shot by a random arrow.

Catechism

Question 89: What does the third commandment teach you?
Answer 89: To treat God's name, word and works with reverence

Memory Verse

Exodus 20:8–9
Remember the Sabbath day, to keep it holy. Six days you shall labor and do all your work.

LESSON 85

Week 17 Review

Memory Verse

Exodus 20:8–9

Catechism

Question 49: Did Jesus ever sin?

Question 50: How could Christ suffer?

Question 51: For whom did Christ obey and suffer?

Question 89: What does the third commandment teach you?

Question 90: What is the fourth commandment?

To the Teacher :   The answers to catechism questions 49–51 are found on page 266.

Activity

Maze

Help Elijah and Elisha reach the other side of the Jordan River.

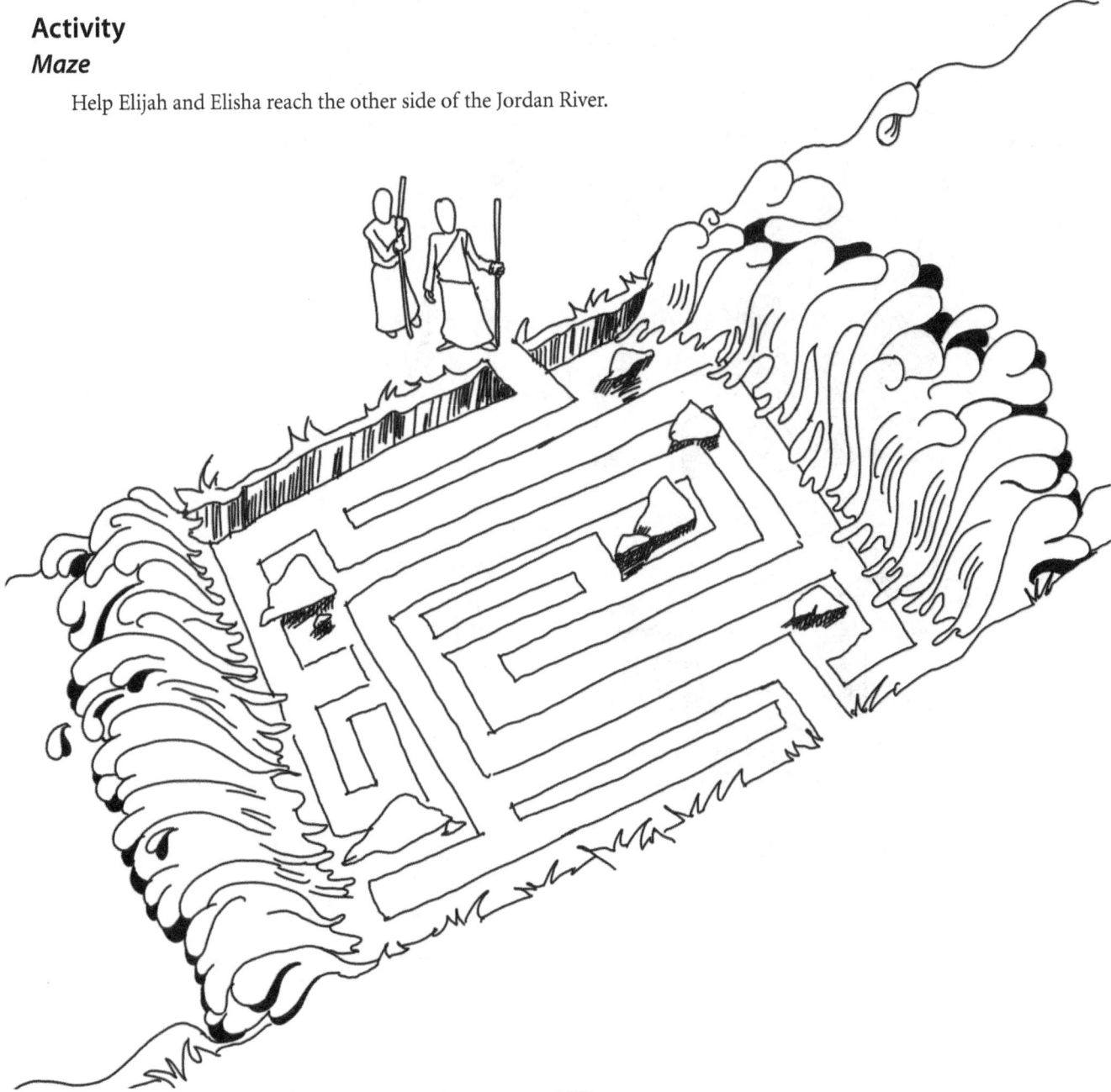

Unit 18   Elisha's Early Days

LESSON 86

Elisha's Miracles

2 Kings 2:19–25, 4:1–7

After the prophets returned from hunting, they had to admit that Elijah truly had gone to heaven. Then they asked Elisha for a favor. They told him that, while they had a nice city, their water was bad. Elisha told them to bring him a new bowl with salt in it. He took the bowl and went to the source of the water. He threw the salt into the water and told the men that the Lord had healed the water.

Finally, Elisha returned home. On the way, however, he met some disrespectful young men. These rude men ran after Elisha calling out, "Go up, you baldhead!" (2 Kings 2:23). They were mocking Elisha, which was wrong because the Lord had clearly told the people to respect their elders.

Elisha turned around and cursed the young men in the name of the Lord. Then God sent two bears that ran after the men and killed forty-two of them. Then Elisha returned home.

Now Elisha was a prophet of God like Elijah, but he was not exactly the same as Elijah. He had a different sort of work to do.

At this time, Ahaziah had fallen from his window and died. His brother Jehoram was ruling in Israel. Good King Jehoshaphat was still ruling in Judah. After Jehoshaphat, Judah's Jehoram would rule, and he would be a wicked king. It was in the days of these kings that Elisha lived.

Elisha worked among the people, teaching them. Among the people who came to him for help was a woman whose husband had been one of the sons of the prophets. Her husband was dead now, and his widow was very poor.

The woman had a large debt to pay, but she had no money with which to pay her debt. The man she owed money to wanted to come to her house and take away her two sons as payment for the debt. The two boys would become slaves. At the time, this was the custom for those who could not pay their debts, but the woman did not want her boys to become slaves.

She went to Elisha for help. He asked what kinds of things she had in her house. The poor woman answered that all she had was a jar of oil.

Elisha told the woman to go to all of her neighbors and borrow as many jars and pots as she could. Then she was to shut her door. Finally, Elisha told the woman to pour her little jar of oil into the borrowed pots and jars until they were all full. Then she could sell the oil to get enough money to pay her debt.

The woman listened to Elisha. She and her sons gathered pots and jars. They went into the house and closed the door. Then the woman began pouring her oil. Sure enough, the little jar did not run out of oil until every pot and jar was full. The woman sold the oil and had enough to pay her debt, as well as some left over for her and her sons to live on afterwards.

Questions

1. What did Elisha throw in the water to make it clean? _____

2. Two female _____ chased the young men when they mocked Elisha.

3. If the widow did not pay her debt, her sons would be sold as _____.

Thought Questions

Why did God send bears to punish boys who were disrespectful? How important is it for young people to respect those who are in authority over them?

Catechism

Question 91: What does the fourth commandment teach you?

Answer 91: To work six days and keep the Sabbath day holy

Memory Verse

Exodus 20:10

But the seventh day is the Sabbath of the Lord your God. In it you shall do no work; you, nor your son, nor your daughter, nor your male servant, nor your female servant, nor your cattle, nor your stranger who is within your gates.

LESSON 87

A Dead Child Raised to Life

2 Kings 4:8–37

At this time, a rich woman lived in Shunem, a town that Elisha often visited. Whenever Elisha came to the town, this woman offered him food, and the prophet accepted. She and her husband came to know Elisha well. The woman convinced her husband to set up a small upper room for Elisha. After that, whenever Elisha came to town, he stayed with the woman and her husband in the room set up for him.

Elisha was pleased with the woman's kindness. One day, when he had come to visit and was staying in his room, he called for the woman. His servant, Gehazi, called the woman, and she came.

Elisha explained that he wanted to repay the woman for her kindness. He asked what she wanted him to do, but the woman said that she did not need anything. Then Elisha asked Gehazi what he could do for the woman. Gehazi knew his master was a servant of God and could do mighty things through God's power. He answered, "Actually, she has no son, and her husband is old" (2 Kings 4:14).

When the woman returned, Elisha told her that the next year she would have a son. She was surprised and thought Elisha might be lying to her. Sure enough, however, the woman and her husband had a baby boy the following year.

The baby grew up and was soon a little boy, loved greatly by his parents. One day, when he was still quite young, the boy went out into the field where his father was working. He cried out, "My head, my head!" (2 Kings 4:19). His father had a servant carry the boy to his mother.

The woman held her son and tried to help him, but around noon, the little boy died. The woman carried him upstairs to Elisha's room and laid him on the bed. Then she asked her husband to send for a servant and her donkey so that she could ride to find Elisha, the man of God.

Elisha saw the woman as she came towards him. He sent Gehazi to ask if everything was all right. She answered that everything was fine, but when she reached Elisha she fell to her knees and grabbed onto his feet. Gehazi wanted to push her away, but Elisha said, "Let her alone; for her soul is in deep distress, and the LORD has hidden it from me, and has not told me" (2 Kings 4:27).

Finally, the woman reminded Elisha of their conversation several years ago when she had told him not to lie to her about having a son. Elisha understood what had happened. He gave Gehazi his staff and told him to go to the woman's house and lay the staff on the boy's face. Elisha and the woman came behind Gehazi.

Gehazi tucked his robe into his belt and ran. He reached the house and did as Elisha had said, but the boy was still dead. He turned around and went to meet Elisha as he came towards the house.

When Elisha reached the woman's house, he went to his room where the boy was lying. First, he prayed to God. Then he lay down on the bed on top of the boy. He put his mouth on the boy's mouth, his eyes over the boy's eyes, and his hands over the boy's hands. Soon the dead body of the boy began to warm up. Elisha got up and walked around a bit, then lay over the boy once more. This time, the boy sneezed seven times and opened his eyes.

Elisha called Gehazi and told him to bring the boy's mother. The woman was so joyful that she bowed to the ground in front of Elisha in thanks. Then she picked up her little boy and carried him out of Elisha's room.

Questions

1. The woman provided a _____ for Elisha when he came to town.

2. Who was Elisha's servant? _____

3. When Elisha prayed to God and then lay down over the boy, the boy _____ and woke up.

Thought Question

How did the woman know that she needed to find Elisha first thing after her son died?

Catechism

Question 91: What does the fourth commandment teach you?
Answer 91: To work six days and keep the Sabbath day holy

Memory Verse

Exodus 20:10
But the seventh day is the Sabbath of the LORD your God. In it you shall do no work; you, nor your son, nor your daughter, nor your male servant, nor your female servant, nor your cattle, nor your stranger who is within your gates.

LESSON 88

Naaman the Leper

2 Kings 5:1–14

Another person who needed Elisha's help was a man called Naaman. Naaman was the captain of the Syrian army, the army that had fought with Israel for so many years. The king of Syria liked Naaman a lot because he was a mighty man of valor. Naaman also, however, had the terrible disease of leprosy.

Some time before Naaman met Elisha, a band of Syrians had gone on a raid in the northern part of Israel. They had stolen many things, including a little girl. This girl became a servant in Naaman's house.

One day, the girl told her mistress, "If only my master were with the prophet who is in Samaria! For he would heal him of his leprosy" (2 Kings 5:3). Naaman heard the girl's words and went to tell the king of Syria what she had said. The king told Naaman to go straight to Israel, and he would send a letter to the king of Israel hoping his captain could be healed.

When Jehoram king of Israel received the letter, he was upset. He was not a godly man and did not know about Elisha. He did not know how to heal Naaman's leprosy. He thought the king of Syria was trying to create a war. Everyone in Israel heard what was happening. Even Elisha heard how upset the king was, and he sent to the king asking for the man who had upset the king to be sent to him, the prophet of God.

So it was that Naaman came to see Elisha. He came to Elisha's house, but Elisha did not come out to greet him. Instead, he sent a servant to tell Naaman to go wash himself in the Jordan River seven times and he would be cured.

Naaman was an important man. He was rich and honored. He had never been treated in such a way before. He became very angry and left Elisha's house. Naaman had hoped Elisha would come out and call on God's name to cure him. Besides, Naaman thought the rivers at home in Syria were all better than the Jordan, especially for washing in.

Naaman's servants tried to reason with him. They said, "My father, if the prophet had told you to do something great, would you not have done it? How much more then, when he says to you, 'Wash, and be clean'?" (2 Kings 5:13).

At last, Naaman agreed to try. He went down to the Jordan River and dipped himself in the water seven times. After the seventh time, he looked at his body and saw that his disease was gone. Naaman was no longer a leper!

Questions

1. Naaman learned of Elisha from an Israelite _____ girl.

2. Elisha told Naaman to wash seven times in the _____ _____.

3. When Naaman obeyed Elisha, he became _____.

Thought Question

Why did the Lord heal Naaman, the captain of the Syrian army, an enemy of Israel?

Catechism

Question 92: What day of the week is the Christian Sabbath?
Answer 92: The first day of the week, called the Lord's Day

Memory Verse

Exodus 20:10

But the seventh day is the Sabbath of the LORD your God. In it you shall do no work; you, nor your son, nor your daughter, nor your male servant, nor your female servant, nor your cattle, nor your stranger who is within your gates.

LESSON 89

Elisha's Disobedient Servant

2 Kings 5:15–27

Naaman rejoiced to be healthy again. He knew that Elisha's God had done a miracle for him. He returned to Elisha's house and offered to give the prophet a reward. Elisha refused, for he wanted Naaman to know that God had done the miracle.

Naaman promised to sacrifice only to the God of Israel from that day on, though he would still have to go to heathen temples with his master, the king of Syria. His heart would bow only to the true God. With that, Elisha said, "Go in peace" (2 Kings 5:19). So Naaman, the mighty soldier, departed.

Now Gehazi, Elisha's servant, had seen everything that had happened. He thought it was a shame to say no to the gifts Naaman had offered. He ran after the Syrian captain and told him a lie. He said that some travelers had just arrived at Elisha's home and Elisha needed some clothes and silver to give them as gifts.

Naaman happily gave Gehazi lots of silver and some very nice clothes. He even sent servants with Gehazi to carry the gifts.

Gehazi stopped the servants before they reached Elisha and hid the gifts in a house. He wanted to keep Naaman's nice gifts for himself, and he knew that Elisha would be very angry if he knew what he had done.

After Naaman's servants left, Gehazi went home. Elisha met him there and asked where he had been. Gehazi claimed he had not gone anywhere, but Elisha knew the truth. He told Gehazi that because of his sin, "the leprosy of Naaman shall cling to you and your descendants forever" (2 Kings 5:27). So Gehazi immediately became a leper and went out from Elisha's presence.

Questions

1. Naaman promised to sacrifice only to _____.

2. Who followed Naaman and asked for the gifts? _____

3. Gehazi was punished by receiving the _____ that Naaman had.

Thought Question

How did Elisha know what Gehazi had done?

Catechism

Question 92: What day of the week is the Christian Sabbath?
Answer 92: The first day of the week, called the Lord's Day

Memory Verse

Exodus 20:10

But the seventh day is the Sabbath of the Lord your God. In it you shall do no work; you, nor your son, nor your daughter, nor your male servant, nor your female servant, nor your cattle, nor your stranger who is within your gates.

LESSON 90

Week 18 Review

Exodus 20:1–10

Catechism

Question 52: What kind of life did Christ live on earth?

Question 53: What kind of death did Jesus die?

Question 54: What is meant by the atonement?

Question 91: What does the fourth commandment teach you?

Question 92: What day of the week is the Christian Sabbath?

To the Teacher: The answers to catechism questions 52–54 are found on page 266.

Activity
Matching

Match the names on the right to the descriptions on the left.

1. ___called Elisha "baldhead"	A. Gehazi
2. ___was so poor that her sons were almost made slaves	B. rude boys
3. ___Elisha's servant	C. a widow
4. ___cried out, "My head!" and soon died	D. an Israelite servant girl
5. ___captain of the Syrian army	E. Elisha
6. ___told the Syrian captain about Elisha	F. the Shunammite's son
7. ___the river in which Naaman washed his leprosy	G. Naaman
8. ___performed many miracles in God's name	H. Jordan

Unit 19   Elisha's Ministry Continues

LESSON 91

Elisha Fools the Syrians

2 Kings 6:8–23

Once again, the Syrians were at war with Israel. These two countries had been fighting off and on for many years. King Ahab of Israel had defeated Syria twice with God's help. The third time, he thought he did not need God's help and the Syrians beat him. That was the battle where Ahab was killed by a stray arrow.

Since then, there had been relative peace between Israel and Syria. Now Ben-Hadad, Syria's king, was planning another war against Israel. The Syrians carefully chose the place where they wanted to fight. When they set up camp, Elisha sent word to Jehoram, king of Israel, not to go anywhere near them. He told Jehoram exactly where the Syrians were camped. This happened several times, and so Jehoram and Israel avoided a war against Syria.

Ben-Hadad could not understand why Israel never came near his camp. He thought someone from his own army had turned against him and was warning Israel where Syria was camped. He called and asked his servants who the traitor was. Yet the servants answered, "None, my lord, O king; but Elisha, the prophet who is in Israel, tells the king of Israel the words that you speak in your bedroom" (2 Kings 6:12).

Then Ben-Hadad sent his men out to find Elisha, and they came back and told him Elisha was in Dothan. At night, Ben-Hadad sent a host of soldiers to surround the whole city.

In the morning, Elisha's servant went outside. He was terri-fied when he saw the whole city surrounded by the armies of Syria. He ran back inside and cried out in fear to Elisha, asking what they could possibly do.

Elisha answered his servant, "Do not fear, for those who are with us are more than those who are with them" (2 Kings 6:16). Then Elisha prayed for God to open his servant's eyes. God answered, and Elisha's servant could see what Elisha saw—the mountains surrounding the city were full of chariots and horses of fire sent from heaven to protect Elisha.

Soon the Syrians came up to fight. Elisha prayed for God to strike the army with blindness. Once again, God answered, and the entire army of Syria became blind.

Then Elisha went down to the army and told them they were in the wrong city. If the men followed him, Elisha said, then he would lead them to the man they were looking for. Yet, Elisha took the army to Samaria where King Jehoram lived. Elisha prayed again, and the Lord opened their eyes. Then the men saw they were in the middle of the wrong city.

King Jehoram was very excited when he saw the army. His enemies were trapped in his own city. He could easily kill them. He called down to Elisha and asked if he could kill the men.

Elisha told the king not to kill the men. He said it would be wrong to kill captured men. Instead, he told Jehoram to feed the men, give them water, and send them back to Ben-Hadad. Jehoram did exactly what Elisha told him to do.

Questions

1. Jehoram knew where Ben-Hadad was camped because _____ told him.

2. Elisha's servant saw God's _____ all around them when God opened his eyes.

3. When Elisha prayed, God struck the Syrian soldiers with _____.

Thought Question

Why would it have been wrong to kill the captured Syrians?

Catechism

Question 93: Why is it called the Lord's Day?

Answer 93: Because on that day the Lord Jesus Christ rose from the dead

Memory Verse

Exodus 20:11

For in six days the Lᴏʀᴅ made the heavens and the earth, the sea, and all that is in them, and rested the seventh day. Therefore the Lᴏʀᴅ blessed the Sabbath day and hallowed it.

LESSON 92

A City Escapes Starvation

2 Kings 6:24–7:20

For a little while, the Syrians were ashamed to come back to Israel. Yet peace did not last, and Ben-Hadad soon came to fight again. This time, he brought a huge army and surrounded the entire city of Samaria with his soldiers. No one could leave or come into the city. This type of warfare is called a siege, and it brings slow starvation to the people inside the city because they cannot get food.

Sure enough, the food in Samaria was soon gone. The last little bits of food were not very good to eat and were very expensive. The people began to starve.

King Jehoram took a walk on the wall of the city. Every direction he looked, he saw people suffering and distressed. People told him terrible stories about eating their own children because they were so hungry. Jehoram thought Elisha was to blame for the siege. He made up his mind to kill Elisha that very day.

Elisha was sitting in his house with the elders of Israel when Jehoram sent a messenger to him. Elisha knew the messenger was coming, so he shut the door and would not let him inside.

Jehoram had followed his servant and spoke to Elisha himself. Elisha told him that food would be sold very cheaply the next day. A man on whose arm Jehoram leaned did not believe the prophet, so Elisha told him that, while what he had said was true, that man would not get to eat any of the food himself.

On this same day, four lepers were sitting by the city gate. They debated amongst themselves. If they stayed in the city, they would starve. If they left the city, the Syrians might kill them, but they might also let them live. The lepers decided to leave the city and hoped that the Syrians would let them live.

When the lepers arrived in the Syrian camp, they were met with a great surprise. The camp was empty. Not a single person was there, but all the Syrians' food and supplies were there.

While the men of Israel were stuck in the city, the Lord had made the Syrians hear a noise like the coming of many chariots and horses and soldiers. The Syrians had become terrified. They thought a mighty army was coming to kill them; and they turned and ran, leaving everything behind.

The four lepers went through a couple of the tents. They ate and drank what they wanted and took gold, silver, and clothes and hid them. Then they decided that they should not keep such a great secret. It was a day of good news, and they wanted to share it.

By the time the lepers returned to the city, it was night and the gates were closed. They called up to the gatekeeper and told him what they had found in the Syrian camp. The gatekeeper sent some men to get the king out of bed. When the king heard the news, he did not believe it. He thought the Syrians were planning a trap to catch Israel.

Some of the king's servants convinced the king to let them take some horses and see if the news was true. They found everything in the Syrian camp just as the lepers had described. They followed the Syrians' trail all the way to the Jordan River to make sure the army was actually gone.

These men convinced the Israelites that it was safe to leave the city. People came pouring out of the city, frantic to get food. Just as Elisha had foretold, food was sold at a cheap price inside the city that day. And, just as Elisha had said, the man on whose arm the king leaned did not eat any. Jehoram appointed that man to have charge of the city gate. Many of the people were so hungry that they were not careful, and they trampled the man in the gate so that he died.

Questions

1. When an army traps another army in a city and waits for them to surrender, it is called a _____.

2. God frightened the Syrians away by a loud _____ like an army.

Thought Question

Why did Jehoram blame Elisha, and God, for the siege?

Catechism

Question 94: How should you keep the Lord's Day?
Answer 94: I should rest from my daily work and faithfully worship God.

Memory Verse

Exodus 20:11

For in six days the LORD made the heavens and the earth, the sea, and all that is in them, and rested the seventh day. Therefore the LORD blessed the Sabbath day and hallowed it.

LESSON 93

A King Is Murdered

2 Kings 8:7–15

Do you remember that when the Lord appeared to Elijah in the still, small voice on Mount Sinai, he told the prophet to anoint a new king over Syria? Well, Elijah did not finish this work. He passed it on to Elisha.

Elisha went up to Damascus in Syria. Ben-Hadad, the king, was an old man, and very sick. Ben-Hadad was a wicked king who worshiped idols. However, he must have learned something about the God of Israel through the years because when he heard that Elisha had come, he sent his servant Hazael to ask the prophet if he would recover from his sickness.

Hazael obeyed his master. When he met Elisha, he spoke respectfully and explained that he was there to find out if the king would get well. Elisha answered, "Go, say to him, 'You shall certainly recover.' However the LORD has shown me that he will really die" (2 Kings 8:10).

This message perplexed Hazael. He did not understand. He became even more confused when he realized that Elisha was staring at him very seriously and that the prophet of God was weeping.

Hazael asked why Elisha was weeping. Elisha said, "Because I know the evil that you will do to the children of Israel" (2 Kings 8:12). Then Elisha described some terrible things that Hazael would do to Israel, such as burning their cities and killing their children.

Hazael was astonished and upset. He did not understand why Elisha was saying such terrible things. Then Elisha told Hazael that he would indeed be the next king of Syria.

This information stayed with Hazael all the way back to the palace. When Ben-Hadad asked what Elisha had said, Hazael told him that he would get well. Yet he did not tell the king everything else Elisha had said. He kept that information to himself.

The next morning, Hazael took a thick cloth, dipped it in water, and spread it over Ben-Hadad's face. He held the cloth down tightly so the king could not breathe. Old Ben-Hadad suffocated at the hands of Hazael, who became king in his place.

This new king of Syria, who had begun his reign by murdering the old king, was a cruel man, killing many men, women, and children. In the course of time, he would do all the terrible things that Elisha had predicted, and all of Israel would suffer because of this Syrian king.

Questions

1. Ben-Hadad sent his servant _____ to find Elisha.

2. Elisha told Hazael he would be the next _____ of _____.

3. Hazael was a _____ and _____ man.

Thought Question

Why did Ben-Hadad, a pagan king, send to a prophet of God when he became sick?

Catechism

Question 94: How should you keep the Lord's Day?
Answer 94: I should rest from my daily work and faithfully worship God.

Memory Verse

Exodus 20:11

For in six days the LORD made the heavens and the earth, the sea, and all that is in them, and rested the seventh day. Therefore the LORD blessed the Sabbath day and hallowed it.

LESSON 94

Cumulative Review 6

Samuel–Elisha

Word Bank: chariot   God   Goliath   Hannah   Rehoboam   Saul   servant   vineyard

1. Who prayed so hard for a son that Eli thought she was drunk? _____

2. Who called to Samuel in the night? _____

3. Who was the first human king of Israel? _____

4. David killed the giant _____.

5. Under which king did Israel split into two kingdoms? _____

6. Naboth did not give his _____ to Ahab because it was against God's Law.

7. Elijah went up to heaven in a fiery _____.

8. Naaman learned about Elisha from his Israelite _____ girl.

Catechism

Question 93: Why is it called the Lord's Day?

Answer 93: Because on that day the Lord Jesus Christ rose from the dead.

Memory Verse

Exodus 20:11

For in six days the LORD made the heavens and the earth, the sea, and all that is in them, and rested the seventh day. Therefore the LORD blessed the Sabbath day and hallowed it.

LESSON 95

Week 19 Review

Memory Verse

Exodus 20:11

Catechism

Question 55: What does God the Father guarantee in the covenant of grace?

Question 56: How does God justify you?

Question 57: How does God sanctify you?

Question 93: Why is it called the Lord's Day?

Question 94: How should you keep the Lord's Day?

To the Teacher :   The answers to catechism questions 55–57 are found on page 266.

Activity

Number the Order of Events

Number the parts of the story in order from one to four.

_____ The four lepers go into the Syrian camp.

_____ Hazael kills Ben-Hadad.

_____The Lord made the Syrians hear a loud noise.

_____The hungry people trampled Jehoram's guard at the gate.

Unit 20   *Kings Jehu and Joash*

LESSON 96

Jehu, the Soldier King

2 Kings 8:16–9:16; 2Chronicles 21:1–22:7

We have not talked about Judah for quite some time. The last thing we learned about Judah was that Jehoram became king after his father, good King Jehoshaphat, died.

Jehoram was not a good king. He had married Athaliah, the wicked daughter of King Ahab and Jezebel. Athaliah convinced Jehoram to do wicked things such as murder his brothers, worship idols, and tell the people of Judah to worship false gods.

To punish Jehoram, God let the Philistines and Arabians come into the cities of Judah and carry away many treasures. They killed all except for the youngest of the king's sons. Then God sent Jehoram a sickness that soon killed him.

Then Ahaziah became king. He was wicked like his father. Soon after he became king, he went to visit his uncle, King Jehoram of Israel. The two kings decided to fight against Ramoth Gilead, a city the Syrians had taken from Israel.

Israel and Judah won the battle, but King Jehoram of Israel was wounded. The kings went back to Israel and left the army at Ramoth Gilead.

Both of these kings were members of Ahab's family. God had already punished Ahab for his wickedness and had said that every member of Ahab's family would die a bloody death. Ahab had already died, but Jezebel was still alive, and other members of Ahab's family were also still around.

So God sent a rough, violent man to carry out the rest of His punishment on Ahab's family. This man was named Jehu.

He was one of the captains of Jehoram's army.

At this time, Elisha was still living in Israel. He summoned a young prophet, gave him a jar of olive oil, and told him to go to Ramoth Gilead where the Israelite army was camped.

The young man found Israel's camp and called to Jehu. Jehu came to the young man. The young man poured the oil over Jehu's head and said, "Thus says the LORD God of Israel: 'I have anointed you king over the people of the LORD, over Israel. You shall strike down the house of Ahab your master, that I may avenge the blood of My servants the prophets, and the blood of all the servants of the LORD, at the hand of Jezebel'" (2 Kings 9:6–7). Then he told Jehu how Jezebel would die.

When the young man finished speaking, he left Jehu and ran away as fast as he could. Then Jehu came out from the house where they had been speaking. The other men asked what had happened. They thought the prophet was crazy, but they still wanted to know what he had said. At first, Jehu would tell them nothing. They kept asking until Jehu finally told the truth.

The men were happy. They blew their trumpets and cried, "Jehu is king!" (2 Kings 9:13). They did not like Ahab's family. Being a man of action, Jehu commanded all the gates of Ramoth Gilead to be shut. He did not want anyone to run and tell Jehoram that Jehu had been anointed king. Then he and his captains rode to Jezreel, where Ahaziah, Jehoram, and many other members of Ahab's family were staying.

Questions

1. Ahab's family would all be _____ because of Ahab's wickedness.

2. The young man told Jehu that he would be _____ of _____.

3. When they heard Jehu would be king, the men in the army blew their _____ and shouted, "Jehu is king!"

Thought Question

Why might the men in the army have been so happy to have a new king?

133

Catechism

Question 95: What is the fifth commandment?

Answer 95: The fifth commandment is "Honor your father and your mother, that your days may be long upon the land which the LORD your God is giving you."

Memory Verse

Exodus 20:12

Honor your father and your mother, that your days may be long upon the land which the LORD your God is giving you.

LESSON 97

The End of Ahab's Family

2 Kings 9:17–10:17; 2 Chronicles 22:8–9

A tower was built in Jezreel, and watchmen were posted in the tower night and day to make sure no enemies approached the city. As Jehu and his captains rode towards Jezreel, the watchman in the tower looked out and saw them coming. He did not know who was coming, but he sent word to the king.

King Jehoram sent a messenger out on a horse to greet the men who were coming and ask if they came in peace. When Jehu heard the messenger's question, he answered, "What have you to do with peace? Turn around and follow me" (2 Kings 9:18).

The watchman in the tower sent word to the king again. This time, he told the king that the messenger had gone out to the approaching horsemen but had not come back. So the king sent a second messenger. Jehu told this man the same thing as the first. Once again, the watchman had to tell the king that his messenger was not returning. Then he told the king he thought the coming horsemen belonged to Jehu, for they were driving their horses and chariots furiously.

King Jehoram made ready his chariot and went out to greet Jehu, the captain of his army. King Ahaziah of Judah went with him in his own chariot. When they came close to Jehu, Jehoram asked if Jehu was coming in peace. Jehu answered that there could never be peace while Jezebel and her wicked practices were allowed to live in Israel.

Then King Jehoram knew he was in trouble. He turned his chariot around and cried out to King Ahaziah, "Treachery, Ahaziah!" (2 Kings 9:23).

Jehu was a very strong man. When Jehoram turned to escape, Jehu drew his bow and shot King Jehoram through the heart. The king sank down dead in his chariot. Jehu told his men to throw the king's body into the field of Naboth to fulfill God's promise to Ahab that he and all his sons would be punished in Naboth's field.

When Ahaziah saw what was happening, he turned his chariot and fled. Jehu hurried after him and called for his captains to shoot the king of Judah, as well. The captains killed Ahaziah because he was part of Ahab's family, too. Then Ahaziah's servants took his body and brought him to Jerusalem, where he was buried with the kings in the city of David.

Meanwhile, Jehu and his men drove on until they reached the city of Jezreel, where Jezebel lived. Jezebel had heard what had happened to the kings, so she painted her face, combed her hair, and leaned out of an upstairs window.

As Jehu entered the palace, Jezebel called out to him. He ignored her. Instead, he called out, "Who is on my side? Who?" (2 Kings 9:32). Two or three men looked down at him, and he told them to throw Jezebel from the window. They obeyed, and Jezebel fell to the stones beneath and was killed. Her blood spattered on the wall and on Jehu's horses. Then Jehu trampled her body with his horse and chariot.

After he had eaten dinner, Jehu sent some men to bury Jezebel's body. When the men went out, however, they found that dogs had eaten Jezebel's body. Nothing was left except for her skull, feet, and the palms of her hands. This also was a fulfillment of God's prophecy concerning Jezebel.

After this, Jehu continued killing all the men of Ahab's family. He sent letters and commanded some men to cut off the heads of Ahab's sons. He met a company of Ahaziah's brothers, Ahab's grandsons, and killed them, too. Wherever he found any of Ahab's relatives, he killed them. He did not, however, go into Judah. So Athaliah, the wicked daughter of Ahab, survived.

Questions

1. Jehu killed _____ by shooting an arrow through his heart.

2. _____ was thrown out a window and trampled under horses.

Thought Question

Why had God promised to kill all of Ahab's family?

Catechism

Question 95: What is the fifth commandment?
Answer 95: The fifth commandment is "Honor your father and your mother, that your days may be long upon the land which the LORD your God is giving you."

LESSON 98

Jehu's Work in Israel

2 Kings 10:18–31

After Jehu killed Ahab's family, he had the important task of ridding the land of idol worship. In Samaria, almost all the people worshiped idols. Jehu wanted to gather all the prophets and priests of Baal together so that he could kill every one of them.

In order to get the wicked men all in one place, Jehu played a trick on them. He announced to the people of Samaria that he would serve Baal more than Ahab had ever done. He would make a great sacrifice, and all the prophets and priests of Baal should attend. If any Baal worshiper did not come to the sacrifice, he would be killed.

From all over the country, worshipers of Baal came to the sacrifice. The temple of Baal was full of people. Jehu told the people to make sure no worshipers of God were there with them. Then he brought out special clothes for the Baal worshipers to wear.

Now Jehu was smart. He had picked eighty men and set them up around the temple with weapons. He told them that if any worshiper of Baal escaped, the man who let him escape would be killed instead. When Jehu finished his sacrifice, the eighty men came into the temple of Baal and killed all the idolaters. Then they tore down the temple of Baal and destroyed it.

God had sent Jehu, a rough soldier, to do a hard job. Jehu had killed Ahab's family and gotten rid of the worship of Baal. These things were necessary, for God had commanded them. Jehu was a great soldier.

He was not, however, a great king. The people of Israel still thought they needed to worship idols. When Jeroboam, the first king of Israel, had split from Judah, he had built two golden calves for the people to worship. Jehu still allowed people to worship those calves.

God was pleased with Jehu for destroying Ahab's family and the Baal worshipers as He had commanded. But He was not pleased with how Jehu ignored God's Law. God promised to let Jehu's sons rule Israel for four generations because of the good Jehu had done. However, He also allowed Israel to be punished during the reign of Jehu because of the wicked things he had done.

During Jehu's reign, God began to punish Israel for forgetting Him. He let Hazael, the king of Syria, come fight against Israel and destroy many of Israel's towns.

Hazael was cruel in his victories. Elisha had wept when he saw how Hazael would burn Israel's cities and kill their children. All of these things came to pass during the reign of Jehu.

Questions

1. Jehu tricked the Baal worshipers by telling them there would be a great _____ to Baal; then he killed them.

2. Jehu displeased God by ignoring _____ _____.

3. How many generations of Jehu's family would rule Israel? _____

Thought Question

Why might God have chosen to use Jehu, a violent man who did not care for God's Law, to do His work?

Catechism

Question 96: What does the fifth commandment teach you?
Answer 96: To love and obey my parents and all others that God appoints over me

Memory Verse

Exodus 20:12
Honor your father and your mother, that your days may be long upon the land which the LORD your God is giving you.

LESSON 99

Joash Is Kept Safe

2 Kings 11:1–21; 2 Chronicles 22:10–24:1

While Jehu reigned in Israel, Judah needed a new king because Ahaziah, part of Ahab's family, had been killed. Ahaziah had only reigned for a year, but in that short time he had done many wicked things.

After Ahaziah died, Athaliah, the daughter of Ahab and the mother of Ahaziah, became a monster of wickedness. She killed Ahaziah's children, her own grandchildren. She did not want any of them to become king, for she wanted to rule over Judah.

Only Ahaziah's baby son, Joash, was saved. When Ahaziah's sister saw what was happening to the king's sons, she took baby Joash and hid him and his nurse in a bedroom. She kept the baby close by and never let his grandmother know he was alive. For six years, Joash's aunt kept him hidden.

Joash's aunt was married to Jehoiada, a very good man who was the high priest of God. He helped hide Joash in the temple.

When the prince turned seven years old, Jehoiada sent for all the captains of the army to come to Jerusalem. He showed them that Joash had been kept alive and made them swear to be true to the prince. The captains agreed to be true to Joash and to protect him from Athaliah.

Jehoiada commanded the captains to surround Joash and to keep him safe. Anyone who tried to get too close to the little boy would be killed. Then the priest placed the crown on Joash's head. So Joash became king, and the people began to shout, "Long live the king!" (2 Kings 11:12).

Queen Athaliah heard the people clapping their hands and shouting. She came out to the temple and saw the little king standing by the pillar surrounded by armed soldiers. She tore her clothes and cried out, "Treason! Treason!" (2 Kings 11:14).

Jehoiada commanded the guards to take Athaliah outside the city and kill her. He also told them to kill anyone who followed her outside. So the soldiers took the queen outside of the holy temple and killed her.

Then Jehoiada made all the people promise to serve and love the Lord and to be obedient to the king. Joash also promised to serve the Lord. Then all the people went to the temple of Baal and destroyed it.

Forming a great procession, the people brought the king into the palace. They lifted him up and set him on the kings' throne. All the people of the land rejoiced to have a new king. Even though Joash was only seven years old, he had good men like Jehoiada to guide him as he ruled the people. God allowed Joash to rule Judah for forty years.

Questions

1. Athaliah _____ all her grandchildren but one.

2. Joash was saved when his _____ hid him.

3. Who was the good priest who taught Joash? _____

Thought Question

Why was it important to keep Joash away from his grandmother and to teach him about God?

Catechism

Question 96: What does the fifth commandment teach you?
Answer 96: To love and obey my parents and all others that God appoints over me

Memory Verse

Exodus 20:12

Honor your father and your mother, that your days may be long upon the land which the LORD your God is giving you.

LESSON 100

Week 20 Review

Memory Verse

Exodus 20:1–12

Catechism

Question 58: What must you do to be saved?

Question 59: How do you repent of your sin?

Question 60: Why must you hate and forsake your sin?

Question 95: What is the fifth commandment?

Question 96: What does the fifth commandment teach you?

Activity

True or False

1. Jehu was a peaceful man. **True/False**

2. Israel's people liked Ahab's sons as kings. **True/False**

3. King Jehoram's own messengers sided with Jehu. **True/False**

4. Jehoram shot Jehu through the heart. **True/False**

5. Dogs ate Jezebel, just as God once promised. **True/False**

6. Jehu wanted the people to worship Baal. **True/False**

7. God was pleased with Jehu for destroying Ahab's family. **True/False**

8. Athaliah was a wicked woman who killed her own grandchildren. **True/False**

9. Only baby Joash was saved from Athaliah. **True/False**

10. Jehoiada was a king who helped protect Joash. **True/False**

Unit 21   Elisha's Final Days

LESSON 101

Joash Forgets God

2 Kings 12:1–16; 2 Chronicles 24:15–27

As Joash grew up, he followed God as Jehoiada told him to, but he did not tear down all the high places of the false gods. Still, when he was a man, he decided he wanted to repair the temple of God because parts of it had become old and were falling apart. Even some wicked kings had taken gold from the temple to be used for Baal worship.

Joash told Jehoiada to take the people's offerings and use the money to pay the workmen. The people of Judah placed money in a special chest. When the chest was full, the priest took the money and counted it. Eventually, they had enough money to repair the temple.

The money was used to pay workers and to buy stone and timber to repair the temple walls. The leftover money was used to buy gold and silver dishes for the temple. Finally, the temple was once again beautiful and splendid.

As long as the good priest Jehoiada lived, Joash remained faithful to God and was a good ruler. Jehoiada was an old man, however, and he died when Joash was still fairly young. The people had loved the priest very much, and so they buried him with the kings in the City of David.

After Jehoiada died, some very sad things happened. The princes of Judah came to Joash and told him that they were tired of worshiping God and wanted to worship idols instead. Joash listened to the princes and began to worship idols.

God was displeased with Joash and with Judah. He sent prophets to them, but they did not listen. Then the Spirit of God came upon Zechariah, the son of the good priest

Jehoiada. Zechariah went and told the people that they could not prosper if they did not worship God.

Joash and the people refused to listen. Joash commanded Zechariah be stoned until he died. Joash commanded the death of the son of the man who had saved him when he was a baby and raised him and taught him about God. This was a terrible thing, and it was made worse by the fact that Zechariah was killed in the court of the temple of God.

Right before he died, Zechariah called out, "The LORD look on it, and repay" (2 Chronicles 24:22). The Lord did indeed answer Zechariah and repay Joash and the people of Judah for their wickedness.

Hazael, the wicked king of Syria, came to fight against Israel. Though the son of Jehu, who was ruling Israel by then, was not a good king, he did pray to God when Hazael came to fight. God heard the king and turned Hazael towards Judah instead of Israel. Hazael did not have a large army, but God allowed him to kill all the princes of Judah because they had forgotten the God of their fathers. Joash himself was wounded in the battle, but not killed.

Two of Joash's servants thought he deserved to die for killing Zechariah, the son of Jehoiada. They went into the king's bedroom and murdered him. The people buried their king in the City of David, but not in the graves of the kings.

King Joash had begun to reign when he was seven. He ruled for forty years, but died because he had disobeyed God. Joash's son, Amaziah, ruled in his place.

Questions

1. Joash remained faithful to God until _____ died.

2. Joash had _____ killed by stoning.

3. Joash died when his _____ killed him.

Thought Question

Why did Joash remain faithful as long as Jehoiada lived but left God as soon as the old priest died?

Catechism

Question 97: What is the sixth commandment?

Answer 97: The sixth commandment is "You shall not murder."

Memory Verse

Exodus 20:13
You shall not murder.

LESSON 102

Elisha's Last Prophecy

2 Kings 13:1–25

Although Joash was only forty-seven when he died, he had reigned forty years in Judah. During that time, three different kings had reigned in Israel.

First was Jehu, the warrior king who destroyed Ahab's family. He was king when Joash was crowned, and he reigned for twenty-one more years. While he did some good things for Israel, he did not stop worshiping the golden calves, and this displeased God.

Second was Jehu's son, Jehoahaz. He also worshiped the golden calves. God punished Jehoahaz and Israel by allowing Hazael, the king of Syria, to come fight against them. Yet Jehoahaz called upon God, and God listened. He turned Hazael away from Israel, even though Israel had only a very small army. Even after God saved them, however, Jehoahaz and Israel continued worshiping idols.

The third king was Jehoahaz's son, Jehoash. He was not as bad as Ahab had been, but he worshiped the golden calves just like his father and grandfather.

In the days of Jehoash, the old prophet Elisha, who had lived in Israel all these years, became very ill. The king was sad to realize he was going to lose Elisha as a friend and advisor. He went to Elisha and wept, crying out, "O my father, my father, the chariots of Israel and their horsemen!" (2 Kings 13:14).

Although Elisha was sick, he still spoke to the king and told him to take a bow and arrows. The king obeyed. Elisha told him to put his hand on the bow. Again, the king obeyed.

Then Elisha put his own hands over the king's hand on the bow. Elisha had the king open the east window of the room and shoot an arrow out of it. As the king shot the arrow, Elisha said, "The arrow of the LORD's deliverance and the arrow of deliverance from Syria; for you must strike the Syrians at Aphek till you have destroyed them" (2 Kings 13:17).

Then Elisha told Jehoash to take the arrows and strike the ground with them. Jehoash took the arrows and struck the ground three times with them. Then he stopped.

Elisha was angry at this, for he said that if Jehoash had struck the ground more times, then he would have struck Syria until Syria was completely destroyed. Instead, Israel would only strike Syria three times. Soon after this, Elisha died and the people buried him.

Some time after Elisha's death, bands of raiding Syrians began invading Israel. The people were afraid of them. One group of Israelites was out burying a man who had died. Suddenly, they saw a band of Syrians. They became afraid and quickly put the man's body in the closest grave they could find. This grave happened to be Elisha's. As soon as the body of the dead man touched Elisha's bones, he came back to life and stood up on his feet.

Elisha's last prophecy soon came to be. Hazael, king of Syria, died. His son, Ben-Hadad, became king. Ben-Hadad fought against Israel constantly. Three times Jehoash and his army defeated Syria.

Questions

1. Elisha was angry with _____ for striking the ground only three times because he would have defeated Syria for good if he had struck the ground three more times.

2. The man who was buried in Elisha's grave _____ again.

Thought Question

Why do you think the man who was buried in Elisha's grave became alive again when he touched Elisha's bones?

Catechism

Question 98: What does the sixth commandment teach you?
Answer 98: Not to take anyone's life unjustly and not to sin when I am angry

Memory Verse

Exodus 20:13
You shall not murder.

LESSON 103

A Proud King Is Defeated

2 Kings 14:1–21; 2 Chronicles 25:1–28

While Israel was fighting Syria, Joash's son, Amaziah, was ruling in Judah. Like his father, Amaziah was a good king early in his life but did some wicked things at the end of his life.

First, Amaziah killed the men who had murdered his father. Then he tried to make a strong army to defend his kingdom. He counted all the able-bodied men who were able to go to war, and there were 300,000 of them. Then Amaziah hired 100,000 men from Israel with 100 talents of silver. The king thought that such a large army could win many wars.

A prophet of God came to Amaziah and warned him not to take the men of Israel into war with him. God would not help the Israelites in battle, and Judah would lose the war, "for God has power to help and to overthrow" (2 Chronicles 25:8). Amaziah did not want to listen. He had already paid the soldiers! The prophet answered that God was able to give Amaziah much more money than what he had paid the soldiers. So Amaziah sent the Israelite soldiers home.

The men of Israel were angry that they had not been able to fight. Instead of going home happy with their money, they stopped at some cities of Judah and killed 3,000 people and took all their possessions.

Even without the Israelites, Amaziah still had his strong men of war. He took his army down to the Valley of Salt where the Edomites lived. In battle, he and his army killed 10,000 wicked Edomites.

Then Amaziah did a wicked thing. He took the idols and gods of the Edomites and brought them home with him and set them up in his house. Then God became very angry. He sent a prophet to the king and told him he would be punished for his wickedness. God promised to destroy Amaziah.

Even though he had angered God, Amaziah did not repent. Instead, he took credit for beating the Edomites and decided he wanted to win some more battles. He sent to the king of Israel, Jehoash, and told him he wanted to fight.

Jehoash had just come from fighting and beating the Syrians. He did not want to fight against Judah and be responsible for killing many soldiers and destroying Judah. He sent Amaziah a message, warning him not to fight.

Amaziah would not listen. So the king of Israel fought the king of Judah. The Lord was not with Judah, and Jehoash won the battle, killing many of Judah's soldiers and capturing Amaziah. Then he went to Jerusalem, to the temple, and took all the gold and silver he could find. He marched into Amaziah's palace and took all the treasure he could find.

Soon after this, Jehoash died. His son, Jeroboam, became king. Amaziah, meanwhile, lived for fifteen more sad years. The people blamed him for their defeat and conspired against him. Amaziah ran away to Lachish, but some of his soldiers followed him there and killed him. They brought his body back on horses and buried him with his fathers in Jerusalem. His son, Azariah, was made king.

Questions

1. The prophet told _____ not to bring Israelite soldiers to war because God would not fight for Israel.

2. The king of Judah became arrogant and insisted on fighting against _____, even though King Jehoash warned him not to.

3. Amaziah died when his soldiers followed him to _____ and killed him.

Thought Question

If God did not want Judah to fight with Israel, then why did Israel eventually win the battle between Judah and Israel?

Catechism

Question 98: What does the sixth commandment teach you?
Answer 98: Not to take anyone's life unjustly and not to sin when I am angry

Memory Verse

Exodus 20:13
You shall not murder.

LESSON 104

Cumulative Review 7

David–Joash

Word Bank: Elijah Jezebel Jonathan Sheba wept

1. Who was David's best friend? _____

2. David _____ when he heard his son Absalom had been killed.

3. The queen of _____ came to visit King Solomon.

4. Who was Ahab's wicked wife? _____

5. What prophet did God send to Ahab? _____

Oral Questions

1. Describe what happened between Elijah and the prophets of Baal.

2. What did Elisha's servant see when God opened his eyes?

3. How was Joash saved?

Catechism

Question 97: What is the sixth commandment?
Answer 97: The sixth commandment is "You shall not murder."

Memory Verse

Exodus 20:13
You shall not murder.

LESSON 105

Week 21 Review

Exodus 20:1–13

Catechism

Question 61: What does it mean to believe in Christ?

Question 62: Can you repent and believe in Christ by your own power?

Question 63: How can you get the help of the Holy Spirit?

Question 97: What is the sixth commandment?

Question 98: What does the sixth commandment teach you?

Activity

Matching

Draw lines to match the people with the correct description.

1. Joash had this righteous man killed	Joash
2. killed all Judah's princes in battle	Jehoiada
3. raised Joash and helped rebuild the temple	Zechariah
4. turned away from God when Jehoiada died	Hazael
5. murdered King Joash	Jehoash
6. prophesied that Israel would not destroy Syria	two servants
7. wept when he heard Elisha was dying	Amaziah
8. worshiped the gods of the Edomites	Elisha

Unit 22   The Prophet Jonah and King Azariah

LESSON 106

Jonah Tries to Run from God

Jonah 1:1–2:10

During the reign of Jeroboam II, a prophet named Jonah was living in Israel. The Lord spoke to Jonah and told him to go the great city of Nineveh. Jonah was to tell the people of Nineveh that unless they turned away from their wickedness, God was going to destroy their city.

Nineveh was 500 miles away from Judah. It was the capital of Assyria, one of the greatest countries in the world. Nineveh was a very large, splendid city with more than 120,000 people. However, Nineveh was also a very wicked city full of idols and evil practices.

Even though Jonah was a prophet of God, he did not want to preach to his enemies. Instead of obeying God and going to Nineveh, Jonah turned and ran the other way. He went to Joppa on the seacoast. There, he found a ship sailing for Tarshish, that is, a faraway place. He paid to get on board the ship. He thought that if he got far enough away, God could not reach him.

After the ship began to sail, Jonah went down into the hold. He lay down and fell asleep. The sailors kept sailing out onto the deep sea.

Jonah was foolish to think that he could run away from God. God saw Jonah get onto the ship. He saw the ship sail away. And He sent a great storm to catch the ship. Wind began to roar, and great waves came to toss the ship across the sea.

The sailors were terrified. They thought their ship was going to sink and they were all going to drown. They threw all the extra things they were carrying out of the ship to make the ship lighter. They called on their gods to save them.

However, the storm still raged, and their ship still tossed on the waves.

Jonah was still sleeping below the deck. The sailors found him and woke him up. They told him to pray to his God to save them. When Jonah realized what was happening, he knew that the storm had been sent by God for him.

The sailors decided that someone on the ship had angered his god, and so the whole ship was being punished. They cast lots to see who was guilty. The lot fell on Jonah. The sailors asked what Jonah had done. He admitted, "I am a Hebrew; and I fear the LORD, the God of heaven, who made the sea and the dry land" (Jonah 1:9).

The sailors did not know what to do with Jonah. They did not know how to make the storm stop. They asked Jonah what to do, and he told them they needed to throw him out of the ship into the sea, but the sailors did not want to. So they tried to row out of the storm, but the storm was too strong. Consequently, the sailors took Jonah and threw him into the sea, asking God not to punish them for doing so. Immediately, the storm stopped. The sailors feared God and made sacrifices to Him.

Meanwhile, God sent a great fish to swallow Jonah. Jonah was in the fish's belly for three days and three nights. During those three days and nights, Jonah had plenty of time. He spent much of that time praying to God. He ended his prayer by saying, "I will pay what I have vowed. Salvation is of the LORD" (Jonah 2:9).

At the end of three days and three nights, the Lord spoke to the fish, and the fish vomited Jonah up onto the dry land.

Questions

1. God want Jonah to preach in _____.

2. God sent a huge _____ to catch the ship.

3. What did Jonah do while he was inside the fish? _____

Thought Question

Why was it foolish for Jonah to think he could run away from God?

147

Catechism

Question 99: What is the seventh commandment?
Answer 99: The seventh commandment is "You shall not commit adultery."

Memory Verse

Exodus 20:14
You shall not commit adultery.

LESSON 107

Nineveh

Jonah 3:1–4:11

Again the word of the Lord came to Jonah and told him to go to Nineveh and preach to the people there. This time, Jonah obeyed God immediately.

When Jonah reached Nineveh after a long journey, he walked through the streets of the city shouting out, "Yet forty days, and Nineveh shall be overthrown!" (Jonah 3:4).

The people of Nineveh stopped to listen to Jonah and asked each other who he was and what he was saying. As they listened to Jonah, they believed God. They proclaimed a fast so that everyone in the city did not eat. Everyone, rich and poor, put away their nice clothes and put on sackcloth. The king of Nineveh himself sat in ashes instead of on his throne.

The king sent messages throughout the whole city which said, "Let neither man nor beast, herd nor flock, taste anything; do not let them eat, or drink water. But let man and beast be covered with sackcloth, and cry mightily to God; yes, let every one turn from his evil way and from the violence that is in his hands. Who can tell if God will turn and relent, and turn away from His fierce anger, so that we may not perish?" (Jonah 3:7–9).

When God saw the people of Nineveh turn from their sin, He turned back from destroying their city.

Jonah was displeased with God. Assyria was an enemy of Israel, and Jonah did not want God to have mercy on Israel's enemy. He was even so bold as to pray to God and complain that he had known God would have mercy and that was why he had tried to run away. Then he asked God to let him die, for he did not want to live if the people of Nineveh were going to be forgiven.

Then Jonah went out of the city and made himself a little shelter on the east side of the city. God prepared a plant to come up over Jonah to shade him from the hot sun. Jonah was very grateful for the shade. Yet the next morning, God prepared a worm to come and eat the plant so that the plant died.

When the sun came up, the plant withered under the heat. Jonah was miserable. Once again, he asked God to let him die. God asked if it was right for Jonah to be angry about the plant. Jonah said yes.

Then God told Jonah, "You have had pity on the plant for which you have not labored, nor made it grow, which came up in a night and perished in a night. And should I not pity Nineveh, that great city, in which are more than one hundred and twenty thousand persons who cannot discern between their right hand and their left—and much livestock?" (Jonah 4:10–11).

So God taught Jonah the lesson of mercy.

Questions

1. When Jonah told the people of Nineveh that God would destroy the city, the people _____ God.

2. The plant God had given Jonah _____ in the sun.

3. Jonah was angry because God had _____ on Nineveh.

Thought Question

Why was it right for God to show mercy to the people of Nineveh?

Catechism

Question 99: What is the seventh commandment?
Answer 99: The seventh commandment is "You shall not commit adultery."

Memory Verse

Exodus 20:14
You shall not commit adultery.

LESSON 108

Six Wicked Kings

2 Kings 14:23–15:31, Amos, Hosea

Jeroboam II was reigning in Israel. He ruled for forty-one years. Even though he was not a good man, the Lord allowed him to win battles against Syria, the country that had oppressed Israel for many years. Israel regained some of the cities Syria had taken away, and they became a large, prosperous nation again.

For all of his wealth though, Jeroboam worshiped the golden calves just as his fathers had. The people of Israel were living in luxury, and they were forgetting God. They began to act very wickedly and did not obey God's commandments.

During this time, God sent the prophets Amos and Hosea to bring the people back to God. Amos told Israel that God would punish them for their sins and idolatry. Their king Jeroboam would be killed, and the people would be carried away into captivity.

A false prophet told Jeroboam what Amos was saying. Then the false prophet told Amos that he should leave Israel and go to Judah where his prophecies might be more welcome. Amos answered and told the false prophet that God had sent him to prophesy to Israel. Then he told the false prophet about some terrible things that would happen in Israel. Amos said, "Israel shall surely be led away captive from his own land" (Amos 7:17).

Long before Amos was born, Moses had warned the people of Israel that if they disobeyed God, then God would take them away from the land He had given them. Now, because Israel had forgotten God, God would fulfill that promise.

Amos prophesied during the reign of Jeroboam II. That king was wicked, but the kings who came after him were even more wicked.

When Jeroboam died, his son Zechariah became king. He reigned only half a year before his servant, Shallum, killed him. As God had promised, four generations of Jehu's family had ruled Israel. Now Jehu's family was gone, and Shallum became king.

Shallum ruled for only one month before a man named Menahem killed him and began to rule Israel. Menahem was a savagely cruel king. He raided Syria and killed his prisoners with cruel torture.

While Shallum reigned in Israel, the country of Assyria had grown to be the greatest country in the world, much bigger than Israel or Syria. The king of Assyria came to fight against Israel. If Menahem had been a good king, he would have prayed to God for help. Instead, he paid Assyria 1,000 talents of silver so that he would not have to fight.

God had been almost entirely forgotten in Israel. The people lived in drunkenness and sin. They worshiped idols and even sacrificed their children to false gods. One king after another seized the throne and then was killed. There was no goodness or peace in the land. The people of Israel had become like the heathen nations that surrounded them.

After ten years, Menahem died. His son Pekahiah became king. Pekahiah was also a wicked, cruel man. He reigned only two years before Pekah, one of his generals, killed him. Then Pekah reigned for twenty years.

Questions

1. Who were the prophets who warned Israel during the reign of Jeroboam II?

   _____ _____

   _____ and _____

   _____

2. God promised that if Israel disobeyed Him, they would be sent into _____.

Thought Question

Why might most of the kings from this time in Israel have been murdered instead of died naturally?

Catechism

Question 100: What does the seventh commandment teach you?

Answer 100: To be pure in heart, language and conduct, and to be faithful in marriage

Memory Verse

Exodus 20:14
You shall not commit adultery.

LESSON 109

A Leper King

2 Kings 15:1–7, 32–38; 2 Chronicles 26:1–23

While Israel was running through many different kings, only one king, Azariah (also called Uzziah), was ruling in Judah. He was only sixteen when he became king, and he reigned for fifty-two years. Azariah did what was right before the Lord, and God gave him a long, fairly prosperous reign.

Azariah went to fight against the Philistines. The Lord helped him conquer Philistine cities and break down their walls. Then Azariah subdued the Arabians, as well, and the Ammonites had to bring him tribute.

He built strong, fortified towers at the gates of Jerusalem. He repaired the city wall and built watch towers in the desert that could house soldiers. Azariah trained a large army, more than 300,000 soldiers with shields, spears, and helmets. The army also had bows and slings.

Azariah had large devices for shooting arrows and stones placed on the towers in Jerusalem. Wise men in the city helped invent these towers. He was strong, and his army was well prepared for anything that came their way. Azariah became famous throughout many nations.

King Azariah also had vineyards and large flocks of sheep and cattle. He ordered many wells to be dug so that his sheep and cattle had plenty of water.

All of these things were considered wonderful in those days. Azariah had a very strong kingdom. Sadly, however, his strength made him proud. He thought he could go into the temple and burn incense on the altar of incense, just as the priests did.

Some of the priests saw Azariah enter the temple with a censer to burn incense. Eighty of the priests followed him and said, "It is not for you, Uzziah, to burn incense to the LORD…. Get out of the sanctuary, for you have trespassed!" (2 Chronicles 26:18).

The king was angry with the priests for stopping him. Yet while he was standing there, the Lord punished him. The terrible disease of leprosy appeared on his forehead. The priests realized what had happened and tried to get the king out of the temple. As soon as he saw and felt that he was a leper, Azariah hurried out.

All the rest of his life, Azariah had to live alone in a house. He could never go to the temple again. Although he was still technically king of Judah, his son Jotham had to rule for him.

At last, Azariah died, and Jotham officially began to rule. For sixteen years, Jotham ruled in Judah. As his father had done, he did what was right in the eyes of the Lord. He conquered his enemies and built impressive towers. The people of Judah were happy and prosperous when their kings feared the Lord. Yet for all this, Jotham still did not remove the high places where the people worshiped idols.

After reigning for sixteen years, Jotham died. His son, Ahaz, ruled in his place.

Questions

1. Azariah went into the temple and burned _____, which displeased God.

2. God punished Azariah by causing him to become a _____.

3. The kings of Judah did not take down the _____ _____ where the people worshiped idols.

Thought Question

How did King Azariah's pride lead to his downfall?

Catechism

Question 100: What does the seventh commandment teach you?

Answer 100: To be pure in heart, language and conduct, and to be faithful in marriage

Memory Verse

Exodus 20:14
You shall not commit adultery.

LESSON 110

Week 22 Review

Memory Verse

Exodus 20:1–14

Catechism

Question 64: How long ago did Christ die?

Question 65: How were sinners saved before Christ came?

Question 66: Before Christ came, how did believers show their faith?

Question 99: What is the seventh commandment?

Question 100: What does the seventh commandment teach you?

Activity

Fill in the Blank

Word Bank: angry   fish   mercy   Nineveh   overboard   repented   ship   storm   three   worm

1. Jonah did not want to go preach in the city of _____.

2. Jonah tried to run away by getting on a _____.

3. While Jonah was at sea, a great _____ came up.

4. The sailors threw Jonah _____ and the storm stopped.

5. God sent a great _____ to swallow Jonah.

6. Jonah prayed inside the fish for _____ days.

7. When Jonah went to Nineveh, the people _____ from their sin.

8. Jonah was _____ with God for saving the people of Nineveh.

9. God sent a _____ to eat the plant that was giving Jonah shade.

10. God taught Jonah the lesson of _____.

Unit 23 — The Prophet Isaiah's Early Days

LESSON 111

Here Am I—Send Me

Isaiah

In these days, one of the greatest prophets the world has ever known was living in Judah. His name was Isaiah.

Isaiah was born in the last part of King Azariah's reign. He prophesied through the reigns of the next three kings of Judah. His prophecies are combined into a book in the Bible known as Isaiah.

In the year of King Azariah's death, Isaiah had a wonderful vision. He saw God Almighty sitting upon a throne, high and lifted up, and surrounded by angelic beings called seraphs or seraphim.

Each seraph had six wings. With two wings, he covered his face, with two he covered his feet, and with two he flew. All the seraphim cried out, "Holy, holy, holy is the LORD of hosts; the whole earth is full of His glory" (Isaiah 6:3). When the seraphim cried out, the foundation of the temple shook and the whole place was filled with smoke.

Isaiah was terrified of these things. He thought he would die because he, a terrible sinner, had seen the Lord God.

Then one of the seraphim took a live coal from the altar and flew with it to Isaiah. He placed the coal upon Isaiah's mouth and said, "Behold, this has touched your lips; your iniquity is taken away, and your sin purged" (Isaiah 6:7).

After that, Isaiah heard the Lord speak, saying, "Whom shall I send, and who will go for Us?"

So Isaiah answered, "Here am I! Send me" (Isaiah 6:8).

The Lord gave Isaiah many messages to the children of Israel. The book of Isaiah is filled with these wonderful prophecies.

Isaiah even told what was going to happen to Judah in the future.

The most wonderful of Isaiah's prophecies, however, were the ones that foretold the coming of Christ. Isaiah gave these prophecies 700 years before Christ was even born.

As you remember, God had promised Eve that through one of her children, He would bring back goodness and everlasting life to mankind (Genesis 3:15). God had promised Abraham that in one of his descendants, all the world would be blessed (Genesis 12:1–3). God had given promises to other people, as well, that someday a child would be born who would be the Savior of the world.

Isaiah spoke many of the most wonderful promises God ever gave to His people. Isaiah said, "Behold, the virgin shall conceive and bear a Son, and shall call His name Immanuel" (Isaiah 7:14).

Later, Isaiah added, "For unto us a Child is born, unto us a Son is given; and the government will be upon His shoulder. And His name will be called Wonderful, Counselor, Mighty God, Everlasting Father, Prince of Peace" (Isaiah 9:6).

Isaiah also prophesied about Christ's suffering. He wrote: "He is despised and rejected by men, a Man of sorrows and acquainted with grief" (Isaiah 53:3).

Isaiah understood that Christ would suffer because of our sins, for he said, "He was wounded for our transgressions, He was bruised for our iniquities" (Isaiah 53:5). All these things, and more, Isaiah spoke to the people of Judah, warning and encouraging them of what was to come.

Questions

1. When God asked for someone to send, Isaiah said, "Here am I—_____ _____."

2. The most important thing Isaiah prophesied about was the coming of _____ as Savior of His people.

Thought Question

Why was it important for the people of Israel to be told that God would send them a Savior when the Savior would not come for 700 more years?

Catechism

Question 101: What is the eighth commandment?
Answer 101: The eighth commandment is "You shall not steal."

Memory Verse

Exodus 20:15
You shall not steal.

LESSON 112

Judgment of Judah

2 Kings 16:1–19; 2 Chronicles 28:1–21

Sadly, even with Isaiah's prophecies, the next king of Judah was not a good man. Ahaz was the son of Jotham, and he was one of the worst kings Judah ever had. He undid all the good things his father and grandfather had done. He made idols for Baal and burned his own children as sacrifices to heathen gods.

When Ahaz turned to worship idols, many of the people in Judah did the same thing. So God sent an army against the people of Judah to punish them for their sin. This army was made up of Syrians under their king and of Israelites under King Pekah.

The Syrians fought against Judah, and God allowed the Syrians to win. They took much spoil. Then Israel fought against Judah and won. Israel killed 120,000 men and carried away 200,000 women and children to Samaria, to make them slaves.

A prophet of the Lord lived in Samaria, and he was greatly horrified when he heard what had happened. Israel ought not make slaves of their brothers in Judah. The prophet went out to meet the Israelite soldiers. He told them that the Lord had blessed them with victory, but that they were dishonoring God by keeping the people of Judah as slaves.

Then some of the heads of Israel came out to the soldiers and said, "You shall not bring the captives here, for we already have offended the LORD" (2 Chronicles 28:13). So the people of Judah were allowed to return to their homes after they were clothed and fed.

Yet what a sad homecoming! Many of the men were dead, and many other people had been captured by the Syrians. This was a severe punishment for the idol worshipers.

Still, Judah had not learned. Instead of seeking the Lord's saving hand of strength, King Ahaz sent to the king of Assyria and begged him for help. Ahaz had to give the Assyrians a lot of money for their help.

So the king of Assyria came and fought against the city of Damascus, where he won and killed the king of Damascus. Ahaz went up to help in the battle. While he was there, he saw a heathen altar that he liked. Ahaz sent the pattern of the altar back to the priest in Jerusalem. A wicked priest made a copy of the heathen altar and put it up in Jerusalem.

In Damascus, Ahaz offered sacrifices to heathen gods. Then he closed the doors of the temple in Jerusalem and cut up the gold and silver dishes that belonged in the temple. He had heathen altars built on every corner in Jerusalem and in every city of Judah.

Ahaz had made a mistake in asking the king of Assyria for help, for at this time Assyria was trying to conquer many nations. Never before had Assyria been able to defeat Damascus. As long as Damascus had been untouched, Assyria had not been able to reach Israel, for Damascus was between Assyria and Israel.

Now Damascus belonged to the Assyrians, and nothing stood between them and Israel. Assyria was ready to fight Israel.

Questions

1. God's prophet was horrified with the army of Israel for taking women and children of Judah as _____.

2. The wicked priest set up a _____ _____ in the temple.

3. Which important city did Assyria conquer? _____

Thought Question

Why was it so foolish for Ahaz to ask the king of Assyria for help?

Catechism

Question 102: What does the eighth commandment teach you?

Answer 102: Not to take anything that belongs to someone else

Memory Verse

Exodus 20:15
You shall not steal.

LESSON 113

The Ten Lost Tribes

2 Kings 17:1–41

Despite all the prophets that God sent to warn of punishment, Israel refused to obey God. The Northern Kingdom had never had a truly righteous king who followed God with his whole heart since the kingdom split from Judah. The time had come for God to punish the men and women who were supposed to be His people but were just as sinful and wicked as the nations that surrounded them.

The Israelites ignored God's prophets and insisted on worshiping idols, the sun, the moon, or the stars. They burned their children in sacrifice to heathen gods. The Lord's anger burned against Israel.

After reigning for twenty years, King Pekah was killed by Hoshea, who became the next king. He ruled for nine years and did evil in the sight of the Lord.

During Hoshea's reign, another great Assyrian king named Shalmaneser arose and came against Israel. The Assyrians quickly captured Samaria, Israel's capital city. Shalmaneser made Hoshea his servant. After a while, Hoshea rebelled. He did not send the tribute Shalmaneser asked for, and he sent to the king of Egypt for help in fighting Assyria.

When Shalmaneser discovered what Hoshea had done, he marched his army back to Samaria and besieged the city for three years. Finally, he overcame it and took the king prisoner. The people of Israel were taken captive and carried off to the land of Assyria. Because of their unfaithfulness, God no longer allowed these people to live in the land as His people. Hoshea was the last king of the ten tribes.

The Israelites were carried far away into the distant lands of Assyria. Once there, the people were scattered among the heathen nations. After many years they became mixed with the heathen nations and virtually disappeared.

These ten tribes of Israel were no longer God's people because they had been disobedient. They are not written of again in the Bible. The rest of the story of God's chosen people is about the men and women of Judah.

Some time after the Israelites had been carried away, people from Babylon were brought to live in the land. These were heathen people who did not know or worship God. Because they did not fear God, He sent lions among them to kill many of them.

News of what was happening reached Assyria. The king of Assyria commanded one of the priests of Israel to return to the land and teach the Babylonians about God. This teaching did little good, for the Babylonians kept worshiping idols and simply began to worship God right along with their idols.

The Babylonians' children and grandchildren followed their example. They claimed to serve both the Lord and idols, though this is not possible. In later years, these people came to be called Samaritans. They were despised by the people of Judah, for they were not true Israelites.

Questions

1. Which country conquered Israel and carried the people away? _____

2. The ten tribes were no longer considered to be God's people because they _____ God and were unrepentant.

3. When Babylonians first settled in Israel's land, _____ killed many of them because they did not worship God.

Thought Question

Why is it impossible to worship both God and idols?

Catechism

Question 102: What does the eighth commandment teach you?
Answer 102: Not to take anything that belongs to someone else

Memory Verse

Exodus 20:15
You shall not steal.

LESSON 114

Cumulative Review 8

Job through Isaiah

Word Bank: Christ David Eli Elihu Elijah Elisha Joash Jonah Jonathan Solomon

1. Which of Job's friends spoke wisely? _____

2. Who raised Samuel in the tabernacle of God? _____

3. Which of Jesse's sons was anointed as king? _____

4. Who took his armorbearer and fought the Philistines? _____

5. Who was the wisest man on earth? _____

6. _____ knew God was not in the storm or fire but in a still, small voice.

7. _____ saw Elijah go up to heaven in a fiery chariot.

8. Queen Athaliah killed all her grandchildren except for _____.

9. Who tried to run away from God and got swallowed by a fish? _____

10. Isaiah prophesied that _____ would come and suffer for our sins.

Catechism

Question 101: What is the eighth commandment?
Answer 101: The eighth commandment is "You shall not steal."

Memory Verse

Exodus 20:15
You shall not steal.

LESSON 115

Week 23 Review

Memory Verse

Exodus 20:1–15

Catechism

Question 67: What did these sacrifices represent?

Question 68: How many offices does Christ fulfill as the promised Messiah?

Question 69: What are they?

Question 101: What is the eighth commandment?

Question 102: What does the eighth commandment teach you?

Activity
Dot-to-Dot

Connect the dots to see what kind of animal God sent against the wicked people who wanted to live in Israel but were not God's people.

Unit 24　　　　　　　　King Hezekiah's Reign

LESSON 116

Hezekiah, Servant of God

2 Kings 18:1–12; 2 Chronicles 29:1–31:21

It was very sad to see the ten tribes of Israel in such a sad condition. They had not obeyed God, they had ignored God's warnings through the prophets, and they had been punished. Now Judah was coming close to a similar end. Few people were left in Judah, and they were unhappy because so many of their friends and family were dead or captured.

One good thing did happen, however, when King Ahaz died. His son Hezekiah became king after him. Although Hezekiah's father was wicked, his mother was a good woman, the daughter of a prophet. She taught her son to serve the Lord. Hezekiah became one of the best kings Judah ever had.

From the beginning of his reign, Hezekiah sought the Lord as the great King David had done. God was with Hezekiah because of this, and prospered him in all that he did.

During Ahaz's reign, the Levites had been scattered because the temple had been shut up. No sacrifices had been made, and the temple was dirty and full of rubbish. In the very first year of his reign, Hezekiah opened the doors of the temple. He gathered the Levites and priests and told them to clean the temple. He knew that the people of Judah had been forsaken by God because their fathers had forsaken God.

The Levites went into the temple and cleaned the entire thing very well. This work took eight days. When the Levites finished, they went to Hezekiah and told him all they had accomplished.

The service of God had been forgotten for so many years that it was hard for anyone to know just how to worship God in the right way. This earnest young king did his very best to bring the people back again to the true worship of the Lord.

He gathered the rulers of the city. Together, they went to the temple and offered a sin offering to atone for the great sin of Judah in turning away from God.

Hezekiah formed a choir of Levites, as David had done, to praise God with song. He invited anyone and everyone to bring thank offerings to the Lord. Many people responded generously.

Then Hezekiah began to reinstate the feast of Passover. He sent letters inviting the people to come to Jerusalem to keep the Passover. These letters passed all throughout Judah and into Israel.

In Israel, a few of the poorest people had been left behind by Assyria. Now Hezekiah offered to let them come celebrate Passover with Judah in Jerusalem. A few of the people from Israel, and all of the people from Judah, answered Hezekiah and came to Jerusalem for Passover.

The many people who gathered in Jerusalem were so happy to be celebrating Passover that, when the seven days of the feast ended, they decided to continue celebrating for another week. There had not been such a celebration in Jerusalem since the time of Solomon.

Finally, Hezekiah also commanded the people to bring a tenth of their corn, wine, oil, and whatever else they raised to the temple. God had commanded the priests to care for the temple and not to have farms of their own. When the people forgot God, the priests had a hard time surviving. Now those hard days were over. Hezekiah made sure the temple and God's priests were well cared for.

Questions _____

1. Hezekiah's _____ taught him to love God.

2. Hezekiah commanded the priests to clean the _____.

3. Which feast did Judah celebrate in Jerusalem? _____

Thought Question

Why was it important for the temple to be cleaned and Passover to be celebrated?

Catechism

Question 103: What is the ninth commandment?
Answer 103: The ninth commandment is "You shall not bear false witness against your neighbor."

Memory Verse

Exodus 20:16
You shall not bear false witness against your neighbor.

LESSON 117

Jerusalem in Danger

2 Kings 18:13–37; 2 Chronicles 32:1–19; Isaiah 36:1–22

After Hezekiah had been king for fourteen years, King Sennacherib of Assyria came to Judah with his army. Sennacherib had already captured Israel, and the people of Judah were very afraid.

Hezekiah was afraid, too. He sent a message to Sennacherib and told him that if he would leave Judah, then Hezekiah would pay him whatever he asked. Sennacherib asked for so much money that Hezekiah took all the silver and gold out of God's temple and sent it to the king of Assyria.

Sennacherib, however, was not done. He had conquered many nations by now and thought that it would be easy to conquer Judah. He left for a while, but Judah soon heard that he was returning with his huge army.

Judah was afraid because the Assyrians were cruel to the nations they conquered. They left ruin wherever they went. Towns became smoking heaps of ashes. Princes were tortured to death, and anyone who fought back was killed without mercy.

When Hezekiah realized that Sennacherib meant to make war, he met with the leaders of his cities. Together, they stopped up the rivers outside the city so when the Assyrians came they would have nothing to drink. Judah rebuilt its old walls and built new walls. Hezekiah encouraged the people to trust God for salvation from Assyria.

King Sennacherib did not go straight to Jerusalem. Instead, he went to a Philistine city nearby because he wanted to conquer that city, too. While he was there, he sent some of his generals and a host of soldiers to Jerusalem with a message to the Jews and King Hezekiah.

Sennacherib's messengers came as close to Jerusalem as they could get and called out loudly. Some of Hezekiah's officers came out to see what they wanted.

The messengers said, "Thus says Sennacherib king of Assyria: 'In what do you trust, that you remain under siege in Jerusalem? Does not Hezekiah persuade you to give yourselves over to die by famine and by thirst, saying, "The LORD our God will deliver us from the hand of the Assyrians?"'" (2 Chronicles 32:10–11).

They went on to explain what the Assyrians had done to all the countries they had already defeated. They said that no other god had been able to stop them and that the God of Judah could not stop them, either. They thought Judah's God was the same as other nations' gods, but they were wrong.

The Assyrian messengers shouted their message in the Jewish language so that the common people in the city could understand. They wanted the people to be afraid, and not to trust Hezekiah.

The people in the city heard the Assyrian message, and they were afraid. Nevertheless, they did not answer Sennacherib's messengers.

Questions

1. Hezekiah encouraged the people to trust _____ for salvation.

2. Sennacherib's messengers claim God could not defeat _____.

3. The messengers spoke in the common Jewish tongue to make the people _____.

Thought Question

Do you think God will let the Assyrians keep thinking that He cannot defeat them?

Catechism

Question 103: What is the ninth commandment?
Answer 103: The ninth commandment is "You shall not bear false witness against your neighbor."

Memory Verse

Exodus 20:16
You shall not bear false witness against your neighbor.

LESSON 118

The Angel of Death

2 Kings 19:1–20:21; 2 Chronicles 32:20–33; Isaiah 37:1–39:8

When Hezekiah heard Sennacherib's threat, he tore his clothes and went into the house of the Lord. Then he sent a messenger to the prophet Isaiah. He asked Isaiah to pray to God for Judah. Isaiah answered and told Hezekiah not to be afraid, for the Lord said He would "send a spirit upon him [Sennacherib], and he shall hear a rumor and return to his own land; and I will cause him to fall by the sword in his own land" (2 Kings 19:7).

Hezekiah was encouraged. Soon, however, Sennacherib sent a letter that repeated all the earlier threats he had made. Hezekiah was deeply upset. He took the letter into the house of the Lord and spread the letter out before the Lord. Then he began to pray, asking God to destroy Assyria so that all nations of the earth would know that the Lord is God.

Now the Assyrians had not defeated so many countries because of their own strength. God had given them strength and allowed them to win many battles. Now God promised that Sennacherib would not fire so much as one arrow against Judah. God would defend Judah for His own sake and for the sake of King David.

This message must have been a comfort to Hezekiah, who had trusted so long in the Lord. That night, the angel of the Lord went out and struck down 185,000 soldiers in the Assyrian camp. In the morning, thousands of dead bodies lay on the ground. Sennacherib's power was completely gone in a single night.

Shamed and humbled, Sennacherib turned towards his home, a king without an army. Sometime after he returned, his own sons took swords and stabbed him to death. Of course, the nations around Assyria heard what the Lord had done for Israel. Many of them brought presents to the temple and to Hezekiah.

Not long after this, Hezekiah became very ill. Isaiah came to him and said, "Thus says the LORD: 'Set your house in order, for you shall die, and not live'" (2 Kings 20:1).

When Hezekiah heard this news, he was very sad. He did not want to die. He turned his face to the wall and began to weep. He cried out to God, reminding Him of how he had lived according to God's word. He prayed for God to let him live.

The Lord answered Hezekiah's prayer before Isaiah left the city. He told the prophet to turn around and go back to tell Hezekiah that God had heard his prayer. God promised that Hezekiah would be well in three days and that he would live for fifteen more years.

Hezekiah enjoyed the final fifteen years of his life and continued to obey God. He did, however, do one wicked thing. Some men of Babylon came to visit him, and he was so proud of everything he owned that he showed the Babylonians every treasure in the entire city. Isaiah came to Hezekiah one more time and told Hezekiah that one day, all the treasures of Jerusalem would be taken away to Babylon. Yet this would not happen until after Hezekiah died.

At last, the fifteen years God had promised Hezekiah were ended. Hezekiah slept with his fathers and was buried in the tombs of the sons of David. All Judah and Jerusalem honored this good king. Then Hezekiah's son Manasseh reigned.

Questions

1. Hezekiah spread Sennacherib's _____ before the Lord in the temple and prayed.

2. Sennacherib died when his sons _____ him.

3. When Hezekiah was sick, he _____ and _____. God answered his prayer, promising him fifteen more years of life.

Thought Question

Why was it wrong for Hezekiah to show off his treasures to Babylon?

Catechism

Question 104: What does the ninth commandment teach you?
Answer 104: Never to lie, but to tell the truth at all times

Memory Verse

Exodus 20:16
You shall not bear false witness against your neighbor.

LESSON 119

Cumulative Review 9

David–Hezekiah

Word Bank: Ahab   Assyria   Israel   Judah   Rehoboam   temple   Zechariah

1. What did Solomon build for God? _____

2. Who was king when Israel split into two different countries? _____

3. The ten tribes were called _____ and were ruled by many wicked men.

4. The two tribes were called _____ and were ruled by David's sons.

5. Jezebel killed Naboth so that her husband King _____ could have a vineyard.

6. Which righteous prophet did Joash kill? _____

7. What country carried Israel into captivity? _____

Oral Questions

1. How did Jonathan save David from Saul?

2. How did Absalom die?

3. What did Hezekiah do with the letter from Sennacherib?

Catechism

Question 104: What does the ninth commandment teach you?
Answer 104: Never to lie, but to tell the truth at all times

Memory Verse

Exodus 20:16
You shall not bear false witness against your neighbor.

LESSON 120

Week 24 Review

Memory Verse

Exodus 20:1–16

Catechism

Question 70: How is Christ your prophet?

Question 71: How is Christ your priest?

Question 72: How is Christ your king?

Question 103: What is the ninth commandment?

Question 104: What does the ninth commandment teach you?

Activity

Matching

Match the items on the right to their descriptions on the left.

1. ___ a young, righteous king of Judah   A. Isaiah

2. ___ cleaned out the temple   B. God

3. ___ came with his army to capture Judah   C. Fifteen

4. ___ told Hezekiah not to be afraid of Sennacherib   D. Hezekiah

5. ___ promised to defend Judah   E. Sennacherib

6. ___ struck down 185,000 Assyrian soldiers   F. Angel of the Lord

7. ___ Hezekiah spread this before the Lord and prayed   G. Levites

8. ___ God added this many years to Hezekiah's life   H. Letter

Unit 25   King Josiah and the Prophet Jeremiah

LESSON 121

A Wicked King Who Repented

2 Kings 21:1–26; 2 Chronicles 33:1–25

After Hezekiah died, his son Manasseh reigned in his place. Manasseh had the longest rule of any king from Judah or Israel. He became king when he was twelve, and he ruled for fifty-five years.

Sadly, Manasseh was not a good king like his father. Instead, he was one of the worst kings Judah ever had. He undid all the good things his father Hezekiah had done. He rebuilt idols that Hezekiah had torn down. He built altars to Baal. He worshiped the sun, moon, and stars. He built altars for idols in the court of God's own temple. He even sacrificed his own children to heathen gods.

Manasseh lived just like the nations around him, and he convinced the people of Judah to live wickedly, as well. The Lord sent prophets to Judah and to Manasseh, but they refused to listen.

A new generation of people had grown up since Hezekiah ruled. With a godly king, the people had followed God for a little while. However, as soon as the godly king died, the people returned to their wickedness.

Though God is very loving and merciful, He is also just. He cannot let wickedness go unpunished. Because of what Manasseh did in Jerusalem, God decided to cause the people of Judah to be taken far away into foreign kingdoms of the earth. God would deliver the people of Judah into the hands of their enemies because they had done evil in His sight since He brought them out of Egypt.

God brought the captains of the Assyrian army against Judah. Assyria defeated Judah and took Manasseh captive. They bound the king in chains and carried him away to Babylon.

During his imprisonment in Babylon, Manasseh began to change his ways. He remembered the God of his father. He prayed earnestly to God. The Lord heard Manasseh's prayer and mercifully brought him back to Jerusalem to be king again.

Manasseh had learned that the Lord is the only God. He was a truly changed man. He spent the rest of his life trying to undo the wickedness he had done. He took away idols and broke down wicked altars. He sacrificed to God and commanded the people to serve the Lord. Yet many of the people still worshiped idols instead of the one true God.

Soon after his return to Judah, Manasseh died. His son Amon ruled after him. Amon was another wicked king who worshiped idols. Instead of repenting as his father had done, Amon became more and more wicked as he ruled. After only two years, his servants killed him in his own house.

The people of Judah took Amon's murderers and put them to death. Then they made Amon's son, Josiah, king in his place.

Questions

1. Manasseh ruled Judah for _____ years.

2. Manasseh repented of his sin after he was _____.

3. Amon died when his _____ killed him.

Thought Question

Why is it important to remember that God is just and cannot let sin go unpunished?

Catechism

Question 105: What is the tenth commandment?
Answer 105: The tenth commandment is "You shall not covet your neighbor's house; you shall not covet your neighbor's wife, nor his male servant, nor his female servant, nor his ox, nor his donkey, nor anything that is your neighbor's."

Memory Verse

Exodus 20:17
You shall not covet your neighbor's house; you shall not covet your neighbor's wife, nor his male servant, nor his female servant, nor his ox, nor his donkey, nor anything that is your neighbor's.

LESSON 122

The Boy King and the Discovery of God's Law

2 Kings 22:1–23:3 ; 2 Chronicles 34:1–32

Josiah was only eight years old when he became king. Although he was very young, Josiah proved that even a child can serve the Lord. He did what was right before the Lord from the time he was very young.

When Josiah was sixteen, he began to pray and seek after God. A few years later, he began to clean all the idols out of Jerusalem. He directed his men to break down the metal and carved images of Baal and grind them into little pieces. Then they were to take the dust and scatter it on the graves of the people who had worshiped them.

Josiah even went through the cities of Israel and cleaned out idols and altars to heathen gods. There had been no king in Israel since the people had been carried away, but Josiah knew that Israel had been a part of God's kingdom, as well. He took men with axes and hammers. Whenever they found idols, Josiah commanded his men to smash them into powder.

After all the idols were gone, Josiah commanded men to repair the temple. It had been neglected for many years and needed a lot of work. While they were cleaning and repairing the temple, Hilkiah the high priest found an old book hidden away in a corner. He showed it to the scribe, who read part of it and realized that they had found the book of the Law of Moses.

The two men brought the book to King Josiah. The scribe read the book to the king. Moses had commanded the people to read the Law every year, but it had been so many years since the Law had been read that the people had forgotten it even existed. The people had sinned because they did not know God's Law.

Josiah had never heard God's Law read. For the first time, he heard the terrible curses that would come on Judah if they did not obey God. He was so distressed that he tore his clothes and cried out. He knew that his people were not obeying God and that God would punish them if they did not change their ways. He sent Hilkiah to inquire of the Lord concerning the curses saying, "for great is the wrath of the LORD that is aroused against us, because our fathers have not obeyed the words of this book, to do according to all that is written concerning us" (2 Kings 22:13).

Isaiah had been dead for a while now, so Hilkiah and the scribe and a few other men went to see Huldah, a prophetess in Judah. They told her what had happened and asked whether or not the curses of God would come upon Judah. Huldah answered that all the curses from the Law of Moses would come upon Judah because the people had not obeyed God.

Then Huldah added, "'Because your [Josiah's] heart was tender, and you humbled yourself before the LORD…. I also have heard you,' says the Lord…. 'Your eyes shall not see all the calamity which I will bring on this place'" (2 Kings 22:19–20). God blessed Josiah for his contrite heart and recognition of Judah's sin by waiting until Josiah died to fulfill the promised curses.

After Josiah heard what Huldah had said, he called a meeting of all the people, young and old. He read to them the words of the book that had been found in the temple. Then he stood and made a solemn promise to serve the Lord, and he made all the people promise that they too would serve the Lord.

Questions

1. How old was Josiah when he became king? _____

2. Hilkiah found the Book of _____ _____ in the temple.

3. When Josiah read the book, he became sad because of the terrible _____ that would come upon Judah if they disobeyed God.

Thought Question

If Josiah knew God would fulfill His curses, why did he bother reading the Law of Moses to all the people?

Catechism

Question 105: What is the tenth commandment?

Answer 105: The tenth commandment is "You shall not covet your neighbor's house; you shall not covet your neighbor's wife, nor his male servant, nor his female servant, nor his ox, nor his donkey, nor anything that is your neighbor's."

Memory Verse

Exodus 20:17

You shall not covet your neighbor's house; you shall not covet your neighbor's wife, nor his male servant, nor his female servant, nor his ox, nor his donkey, nor anything that is your neighbor's.

LESSON 123

Josiah Picks a Fight

2 Kings 23:4–30, 2 Chronicles 34:1–35:27

King Josiah started out to destroy all the idols in the land, even more completely than he had done before. He made the priests burn all the dishes that had been used in worshiping false idols. Josiah had all the houses of witches pulled down, for God had commanded that no witches should be allowed to live.

Then Josiah went to a terrible place called Topheth. This was a valley where people burned their children as sacrifices to heathen gods. Josiah filled the valley with filth and garbage so that no one would ever want to worship there again.

Several fine horses were stabled near the temple of God. When Judah was full of idolatry, these horses had been dedicated to the sun god. Josiah took away all those horses and burned the chariots with fire.

On the Mount of Olives, across from Jerusalem, there were still some altars from when Solomon built them for his foreign wives. Josiah broke down all the old images. Then he burned the bones of dead men on the altars so that no one would want to sacrifice on them again.

Josiah went to Bethel where one of the golden calves, which Jeroboam had built 300 years before, was still standing. As Josiah stood in the graveyard at Bethel and directed his people to dig up bones to burn on the altars, he saw a grave on the hillside with some writing on it. He asked what was written on the stone. The men of the city said, "It is the tomb of the man of God who came from Judah and proclaimed these things which you have done against the altar of Bethel" (2 Kings 23:17).

Indeed, a prophet had lived 300 years before and prophesied that a king of David's line named Josiah would destroy the altar of the golden calf (I Kings 13:1–2). So Josiah and his men left the prophet's grave undisturbed.

At the end of Josiah's life, Pharaoh Necho, king of Egypt, passed through Judah to join the king of Assyria. Josiah wanted to fight against the Egyptian army. He called his army together and readied himself for battle.

Pharaoh Necho sent word to Josiah saying that he did not want to fight Judah. He was only passing through the land, and God had commanded him to go quickly.

Instead of listening, Josiah disguised himself and went out to fight Pharaoh Necho. In the battle, archers shot and wounded King Josiah. His servants took him back to Jerusalem, where he died.

All Judah and Jerusalem mourned for good King Josiah. Men and women sang songs of mourning for their beloved king. Jeremiah the prophet mourned with sad lamentations over him.

Even though the people anointed Jehoahaz, Josiah's son, to be king, the time of Judah's reign was coming to an end. Josiah was the last true king of Judah.

Questions

1. Josiah left the grave of a _____ from Judah undisturbed.

2. The prophet prophesied all that Josiah would do against the altar of _____ .

3. Josiah died when he was _____ in battle.

Thought Question

What could Josiah have done to avoid dying in battle? (2 Chronicles 35:20–21)

Catechism

Question 106: What does the tenth commandment teach you?

Answer 106: To be content with whatever God chooses to give me

Memory Verse

Exodus 20:17

You shall not covet your neighbor's house; you shall not covet your neighbor's wife, nor his male servant, nor his female servant, nor his ox, nor his donkey, nor anything that is your neighbor's.

LESSON 124

Jeremiah, the Prophet Who Had to Prophesy

Jeremiah 1–34

During Josiah's reign, a child was born who would grow up to be a very important man. He was the son of a priest, and his name was Jeremiah.

When he was scarcely more than a boy, God spoke to Jeremiah saying, "Before I formed you in the womb I knew you; before you were born I sanctified you; I ordained you a prophet to the nations" (Jeremiah 1:5).

Jeremiah was frightened by these words. He thought he could not be a prophet because he was too young. Yet the Lord told Jeremiah that he was to go where the Lord told him and do what the Lord said. Jeremiah was not to be afraid of anyone, for the Lord would keep him safe from harm.

During Josiah's reign, the people of Judah worshiped God. When his son Jehoahaz began to reign, the people turned back to worshiping false idols. God sent Jeremiah to warn the people that the Lord would not ignore their sins. Great punishment was coming.

Over and over again God sent Jeremiah to proclaim to the people of Judah their wickedness in worshiping idols and turning against God. Some people from Judah had already been taken into captivity. God told Jeremiah to stand in the gate of the city and proclaim to anyone who was left that unless they turned from their wickedness, God would severely punish them. If they repented, God would let them stay in their own land.

The people refused to listen to Jeremiah. The rulers of Judah were angry with Jeremiah because he prophesied evil against them and their nation. They warned him they would kill him if he did not stop prophesying evil.

Nonetheless, God had promised to protect Jeremiah, and He was stronger than all the rulers of Judah. God told Jeremiah to repeat his prophecy. The rulers were angry that Jeremiah had not obeyed, so they put him in the stocks, a wooden frame that held the prophet's feet so he could not move. Jeremiah was left in the stocks for a whole day.

When he was released, Jeremiah thought he should stop prophesying the word of the Lord, but he found that he could not stop. God's word was in his heart like a burning fire. He could not help but prophesy.

Soon Jeremiah's prophecies began to come true about Jehoahaz, who was not a God-fearing king. Jehoahaz built himself a wonderful palace, but made his laborers work without pay because he did not care about his people.

The soldiers of Pharaoh Necho, who had killed Josiah, came into the land and captured Jehoahaz. They carried him off to Egypt, where he lived in prison for the rest of his life.

Pharaoh Necho made Jehoahaz's brother, Jehoiakim, king instead. He also made the people of Judah pay him large amounts of money every year. This was only the beginning of the prophecies that were about to come true.

Questions

1. Which prophet warned Judah of God's coming judgment? _____

2. Jeremiah thought he was too _____ to prophesy.

3. The rulers of Judah put Jeremiah in _____ when he refused to stop prophesying.

Thought Question

Why could Jeremiah not stop prophesying, even after he had been punished?

Catechism

Question 106: What does the tenth commandment teach you?
Answer 106: To be content with whatever God chooses to give me

Memory Verse

Exodus 20:17
You shall not covet your neighbor's house; you shall not covet your neighbor's wife, nor his male servant, nor his female servant, nor his ox, nor his donkey, nor anything that is your neighbor's.

LESSON 125

Week 25 Review

Memory Verse

Exodus 20:1–17

Catechism

Question 73: Why do you need Christ as your prophet?

Question 74: Why do you need Christ as your priest?

Question 75: Why do you need Christ as your king?

Question 105: What is the tenth commandment?

Question 106: What does the tenth commandment teach you?

Activity
Number the Order of Events

Number the parts of the story in order from one to five.

_____ Josiah commands his men to destroy the idols.

_____ Josiah is shot by the archers of Egypt.

_____ Hilkiah finds the Law of Moses.

_____ Josiah has the Law read out loud to all the people.

_____ Josiah becomes king at age eight.

Unit 26   *The Ministry of Jeremiah*

LESSON 126

A Scroll is Burned

Jeremiah 35–36

Jehoiakim reigned for eleven years. He did what was wicked before the Lord, worshiping idols and murdering people without remorse. To punish Judah, God warned that the army of Babylon was going to come and take over all the land of Judah.

When Jeremiah brought this message to the king, Jehoiakim had the prophet shut up in prison so that he could not prophesy to the people.

So the Lord commanded Jeremiah to take a scroll, something like a book, and write down all the prophecies the Lord had spoken to him. Since Jeremiah could not leave the prison and go to the people, he sent for a scribe named Baruch. Jeremiah spoke the prophecies the Lord had given him, and Baruch wrote them all down.

After it was written down, Jeremiah told Baruch, "You go, therefore, and read from the scroll which you have written at my instruction, the words of the LORD, in the hearing of the people in the LORD's house on the day of fasting" (Jeremiah 36:6). The two men hoped that Judah would repent if they heard God's words.

It was not long before a day of fasting approached. On that day, Baruch took the scroll that he had written on and read it to all the people. A man named Micaiah became very interested in what Baruch was reading. He sent for some of the princes of the land. When the princes arrived, Micaiah asked Baruch to read again.

The princes were dismayed when they heard the dark prophecies Baruch was reading. They were certain God would punish Judah unless the people repented. They wanted to tell the king, but they knew the king would probably not be happy. Before they went to the king, they told Baruch to get Jeremiah. Both of them were to hide so the king could not find them if he became angry and wanted to kill them.

Leaving the scroll safely hidden, the princes went and told the king about the punishment Judah would receive if they did not repent. The king had a scribe go and fetch the scroll Baruch had written. The king's father Josiah had torn his clothes and mourned when he heard of Judah's upcoming judgment, but Jehoiakim did not fear God. After a few pages had been read, he scornfully took the book, cut out the parts that had been read with his knife, and threw the whole book into the fire. Then he burned each of the torn pages until not one page of the scroll was left.

Then the king commanded his servants to arrest Jeremiah and Baruch. However, the Lord had hidden His men so they could not be found. God said to Jeremiah, "Take yet another scroll, and write on it all the former words that were in the first scroll which Jehoiakim the king of Judah has burned" (Jeremiah 36:28). Jehoiakim was warned that because he had burned the scroll and ignored its warning, he would have no son to reign in Judah after him. Instead, he would soon die, and his body would not be buried.

Questions

1. The king put Jeremiah in _____ when he prophesied.

2. Who was Jeremiah's scribe? _____

3. The king cut up and burned the _____ of _____.

Thought Question

Why did Jeremiah and Baruch rewrite the prophecies when they knew the king and the people of Judah were just going to ignore them?

Catechism

Question 107: Can you keep the Ten Commandments perfectly?
Answer 107: No. Since the fall of Adam, the only One who has been able to do this is Jesus.

Memory Verse

Psalm 1:1
Blessed is the man who walks not in the counsel of the ungodly, nor stands in the path of sinners, nor sits in the seat of the scornful;

LESSON 127

Jeremiah Is Rescued

2 Kings 24:1–25:3; Jeremiah 37:11–38:13

At last, God sent His punishment to Judah. By this time, Assyria and Egypt had both been conquered by the great kingdom of Babylon. The king of Babylon was the great Nebuchadnezzar. He had fought many battles and conquered much land throughout the entire world.

Now he had brought his army up against Judah. As Jeremiah had prophesied, Jehoiakim died, and his body was not buried but was left to the heat of the day and the frost of the night.

Jehoiakim's son Jehoiachin reigned for three months before Nebuchadnezzar conquered him and put him in chains. In all the lands he conquered, Nebuchadnezzar took the kings as prisoners and carried them home to Babylon. At this time, Nebuchadnezzar carried away all of the finest people of the land. All the princes, soldiers, and men of skill were taken. He also carried away the fine gold and silver treasures that he found in the temple of the Lord.

The people of Judah were no longer free. Only a few of the poorest people were allowed to stay in the land. The others were all turned into slaves and servants in Babylon.

Josiah's third son, Zedekiah, was made king of the people left in Judah. Nebuchadnezzar made Zedekiah swear to the Lord that he would not rebel against him. During his reign, Zedekiah turned away from God. He did not listen to Jeremiah's prophecies or cries for repentance.

After nine years, Zedekiah rebelled against Nebuchadnezzar, even though he had sworn not to and Jeremiah had warned him against it. Once again, the king of Babylon came to Judah. He besieged Jerusalem for two years.

This was a very hard time for the people inside the city. They could not get food and began to starve. Jeremiah urged Zedekiah to surrender to Babylon, but the king and his princes would not listen. God warned that if Zedekiah would yield, his life and the lives of his princes would be spared; but if they did not surrender, they would all die and the city would be burned.

The princes of Judah became so angry with Jeremiah that they shut him up in the prison in the house of Jonathan the scribe. Jeremiah was in this prison for a long time.

Finally, Zedekiah sent for the prophet and asked if there was any word from the Lord. Jeremiah answered that God was going to give Zedekiah into the hands of the Babylonians.

This was not what the king wanted to hear. Jeremiah begged not to be sent back into the prison. So the king allowed him to be kept in the court of the prison instead. Jeremiah was also given one piece of bread each day until the bread in the city was gone.

Jeremiah continued to warn the people that Nebuchadnezzar would win this war. If they fought him, they would die by disease or the sword. The princes of Judah did not like what Jeremiah was saying. They came and told King Zedekiah that Jeremiah should be killed for disheartening the people.

Zedekiah was weak. He told the princes that they could kill Jeremiah. So the princes took Jeremiah and cast him into a dungeon. In the dungeon was a great pit. They lowered Jeremiah into the pit by tying ropes around his arms. There was no water in the pit, but the sides and bottom were made of mud and slime. Jeremiah sank into the mud at the bottom of the pit.

In the king's court, an Ethiopian man served the king. When he discovered what had happened to Jeremiah, he went to the king and warned him that Jeremiah was going to die. Once more, Zedekiah changed his mind and commanded his servants to pull Jeremiah up from the pit.

Zedekiah's servants sent down rags to Jeremiah. He placed the rags under his arms with the ropes on top of them. Then the men pulled Jeremiah out of the pit. Although he was not freed, Jeremiah was allowed to move around.

Questions

1. Who invaded Judah and took the people captive? _____

2. The princes threw Jeremiah into a _____ in a _____ when they disliked his prophecies.

Thought Question

How did God care for Jeremiah through this difficult time?

Catechism

Question 107: Can you keep the Ten Commandments perfectly?

Answer 107: No. Since the fall of Adam, the only One who has been able to do this is Jesus.

Memory Verse

Psalm 1:1
Blessed is the man who walks not in the counsel of the ungodly, nor stands in the path of sinners, nor sits in the seat of the scornful;

LESSON 128

The Fall of Jerusalem

Jeremiah 38:14–28, 51:1–52:34; 2 Kings 25:1–21; 2 Chronicles 36:11–21

While Jeremiah was in prison, the Babylonian siege was continuing. Almost all the food in Jerusalem was gone, and the people were starving. After Jeremiah was taken out of the dungeon, Zedekiah sent for him and asked what he should do.

Jeremiah told the king that if he surrendered, then his life would be saved and the city would not be burned. "But," he warned, "if you do not surrender to the king of Babylon's princes, then this city shall be given into the hand of the Chaldeans [Babylonians]; they shall burn it with fire, and you shall not escape from their hand" (Jeremiah 38:18).

Zedekiah was too proud to listen. He refused to give in to the Babylonians. So the siege continued until Babylon's soldiers finally broke through Jerusalem's walls. Soldiers poured into Jerusalem. When Zedekiah and the princes realized what had happened, they fled secretly at night.

By this time, it was too late. Babylonian soldiers saw them leaving. They chased the men and soon caught them and brought them before Nebuchadnezzar. Then the Babylonian king did a cruel thing. He killed the king's sons right in front of Zedekiah's eyes. This dreadful sight was the last Zedekiah ever saw, for when his children were dead, Nebuchadnezzar had his soldiers put out Zedekiah's eyes. The blind king was taken to Babylon, where he lived in prison for the rest of his life. Zedekiah was the last king of the two tribes of Judah.

The Babylonian soldiers continued moving through Jerusalem, stealing and destroying as they went. They took everything they could out of God's house and then burned the beautiful temple that Solomon had built for the Lord.

The soldiers burned all the magnificent houses in the city. They broke down the wall that surrounded the city. As a final measure, King Nebuchadnezzar carried away most of the people who still lived in the city. Only the poorest were left.

At last, God's terrible judgment had come. The once splendid city lay in ruins. The houses were burned, and the temple was a heap of ash. The city lay desolate and deserted.

Jeremiah was still in prison when the Babylonians came. They put the prophet in chains to take him away with the other captives, but the king commanded them to leave him behind, unharmed.

So Jeremiah remained free and lamented for his people and his city. He also encouraged the captives, telling them that God would not leave them in captivity forever. After seventy years, the Lord would bring them back to their own land.

Although the people had forgotten God for a while, they were still God's chosen people, and He loved them. He would bring them home.

Jeremiah also prophesied about the coming of Christ, who would be a blessing to the whole world. And he prophesied about the destruction of the nation of Babylon, which would come as a punishment for their cruelty and evil. These prophecies were written in a book which was brought to Babylon by one of the Judean princes. When he reached Babylon, he read all the words in the book before tying it to a rock and throwing it into a river. As the book sank, the prince warned that, just as the book was sinking, so Babylon would fall and not rise.

Questions

1. When Zedekiah tried to run from the Babylonians, he was captured, his sons were _____,

   and his _____ were put out.

2. How many years would pass before God would let His people return home? _____

3. According to Jeremiah's prophecies, God would eventually _____ Babylon.

Thought Question

Why was it important that Jeremiah prophesy about the coming of Christ and not just the destruction of Babylon and the return of the Israelites?

Catechism

Question 108: Of what use are the Ten Commandments to you?

Answer 108: They teach me what is pleasing to God, and how much I need a Savior.

Memory Verse

Psalm 1:1

Blessed is the man who walks not in the counsel of the ungodly, nor stands in the path of sinners, nor sits in the seat of the scornful;

LESSON 129

Cumulative Review 10

The Prophets

Word Bank: Baruch Elisha Isaiah Jeremiah Micaiah

1. Two bears chased the boys who mocked _____,

2. Who was the prophet who could not lie? _____

3. When God asked who he should send, _____ answered, "Here am I—Send me."

4. _____ could not stop prophesying.

5. Who was Jeremiah's scribe? _____

Oral Questions

1. Why did Elijah feel like he was all alone?

2. Describe the battle between Elijah and the prophets of Baal.

Catechism

Question 108: Of what use are the Ten Commandments to you?
Answer 108: They teach me what is pleasing to God, and how much I need a Savior.

Memory Verse

Psalm 1:1

Blessed is the man who walks not in the counsel of the ungodly, nor stands in the path of sinners, nor sits in the seat of the scornful;

LESSON 130

Week 26 Review

Memory Verse

Psalm 1:1

Catechism

Question 76: How many commandments did God give on Mount Sinai?

Question 77: Why should we obey the Ten Commandments?

Question 78: What do the first four commandments teach?

Question 107: Can you keep the Ten Commandments perfectly?

Question 108: Of what use are the Ten Commandments to you?

Activity

True or False

1. Jehoiakim listened to Jeremiah's warning from God. **True/False**

2. Jeremiah's scribe was named Baruch. **True/False**

3. Jehoiakim ate Jeremiah's scroll. **True/False**

4. Jeremiah gave up after Jehoiakim destroyed the first scroll. **True/False**

5. God gave Zedekiah over to the Babylonians because he disobeyed. **True/False**

6. The princes of Judah threw Jeremiah in a pit of mud and slime. **True/False**

7. A Babylonian man pulled Jeremiah out of the pit. **True/False**

8. The Babylonians put out Zedekiah's eyes. **True/False**

Unit 27   *Godly Men Take a Stand*

LESSON 131

The Boys Who Trusted God

Daniel 1:1–21

When King Nebuchadnezzar came to Judah for the first time, he commanded the master of his servants to bring some Jewish boys back to Babylon. These boys were to be handsome and intelligent, the best that Judah had to offer. They also needed to be able to learn the Babylonian language. Eventually, Nebuchadnezzar wanted these young Jewish men to serve in the king's palace.

Soon the young men of Judah arrived in the Babylonian court. Among the young men were four boys named Daniel, Hananiah, Mishael, and Azariah. The king did not want the boys to keep their Jewish names, so he gave them Babylonian names. Daniel was called Belteshazzar, Hananiah was called Shadrach, Mishael was called Meshach, and Azariah was called Abed-Nego.

King Nebuchadnezzar wanted the boys to be healthy as well as educated. He commanded his servants to feed the boys the same food that was placed on his own table, and wine that he himself drank.

This command worried Daniel and his three friends. Long ago, Moses had told Israel about God's laws for what the Israelites could eat and drink. They were only allowed to eat animals that were called clean. Even those animals had to be killed in a certain way so that no blood would be left in them. If the young Jewish boys ate the king's meat, they would surely be breaking God's Law. Daniel and his three friends were very young, and they had just been taken from their home and brought to a strange nation. Yet they had

been taught when they were children, and they knew they ought to do what the Lord commanded. These four young men decided that they would not eat the king's meat, because they did not want to disobey God.

So Daniel went to the master of the servants and asked if he and his friends could eat food that would not defile them before the Lord. The servant master was afraid that the king would not be pleased with that idea. He thought Daniel and his friends would be weaker and paler than the other boys because they were not eating the best food the land had to offer. However, Daniel said, "Please test your servants for ten days, and let them give us vegetables to eat and water to drink" (Daniel 1:12).

The master of the servants agreed. At the end of the ten days, Daniel and his friends looked healthier than any of the other young men who had eaten the king's food. God rewarded the four boys who were faithful to Him. Not only did He keep them healthy, but He gave them wisdom and knowledge and skill, as well.

After some time, the master of the servants prepared the boys to go before the king. When all the boys had been presented, King Nebuchadnezzar chose Daniel, Shadrach, Meshach, and Abed-Nego to serve him in his palace. He found these four young men to be better than all the rest. They were even ten times wiser and better than all the magicians and astrologers in the land. So God blessed the boys who trusted in Him.

Questions

1. The king wanted to serve the young men from Judah _____ and _____ from his table.

2. Daniel and his friends did not want to eat the king's food because it was against _____ _____.

3. The Lord blessed Daniel and his friends with _____ and _____.

Thought Question

Why did not all the Jewish boys refuse to eat the king's food?

Catechism

Question 1: Who made you?

Answer 1: God

Memory Verse

Psalm 1:2

But his delight is in the law of the Lord, and in His law he meditates day and night.

187

LESSON 132

Nebuchadnezzar's First Dream

Daniel 2:1–28

One night, Nebuchadnezzar had a strange dream. Like many heathens, the king was superstitious. He was afraid of dreams and signs. Many magicians and astrologers lived in Babylon and claimed to be able to interpret dreams and signs.

Nebuchadnezzar called all those men together and told them he had had a dream. The interpretation of the dream was bothering him. The magicians said, "O king, live forever! Tell your servants the dream, and we will give the interpretation" (Daniel 2:4).

Nebuchadnezzar, however, wanted the magicians to tell him the dream. He told the men that if they were real magicians they would be able to reveal the dream and interpret it without hearing it. If the magicians told the king his dream and its interpretation, he would reward them with wonderful gifts. If they could not tell the king his dream, however, then Nebuchadnezzar would cut all the magicians into pieces and burn down all their houses.

The magicians were afraid. They told the king that no man on earth could possibly know what the king had dreamed without being told by the king. Nebuchadnezzar was furious and ordered his servants to go through the land and begin to kill all the magicians and wise men in the land.

Daniel and his friends were known throughout the land as wise men. That meant that they were going to be killed, as well. Some of the king's servants warned Daniel what was about to happen, and Daniel asked them why the king was angry. When he heard what had happened, Daniel went before the king and asked for time. Before all the wise men were killed, Daniel wanted time to discover what the king's dream was.

When the king accepted Daniel's request, Daniel went home. As soon as he got home, he told his three friends what had happened. Then all four men began to pray to God, that He would make the king's dream known to them.

God revealed the king's dream to Daniel in a night vision. Daniel blessed God saying, "Blessed be the name of God forever and ever, for wisdom and might are His" (Daniel 2:20). Then Daniel hurried to the captain of the king's guard and told him not to destroy the wise men of Babylon, but to take Daniel to the king.

The captain was glad to hear Daniel's words, and he hurried and told the king that one of the captives from Judah could tell the king the interpretation of his dream. So Nebuchadnezzar called Daniel to speak before him.

Questions

1. The king wanted his _____ to tell him his dream and the dream's

   interpretation.

2. When the wise men could not tell him his dream, the king wanted to _____ them.

3. When Daniel got home after talking to the king, he told his friends and then _____ with them.

Thought Question

Why were all the magicians and wise men afraid except for Daniel and his friends?

Catechism

Question 2: What else did God make?
Answer 2: God made all things.

Memory Verse

Psalm 1:2
But his delight is in the law of the Lord, and in His law he meditates day and night.

LESSON 133

The Dream's Interpretation

Daniel 2:28–49

As soon as Daniel appeared, the king demanded to know whether or not Daniel could tell what the dream and its interpretation were. Daniel answered, "The secret which the king has demanded, the wise men, the astrologers, the magicians, and the soothsayers cannot declare to the king. But there is a God in heaven who reveals secrets, and He has made known to King Nebuchadnezzar what will be in the latter days" (Daniel 2:27–28).

In other words, only God could interpret dreams. The dream God had given Nebuchadnezzar would tell what was going to soon happen in the kingdom. And now, God had told Daniel the dream and given him the dream's meaning.

In his dream, the king saw a great and wonderful image. The image's head was made of gold. Its breast and arms were made of silver. Its belly and thighs were made of bronze. Its legs were made of iron. And its feet were made of mixed iron and clay.

Then in his dream, the king watched as a stone cut without hands came and crashed into the image's feet. The feet crumbled. Then the rest of the image, the iron, bronze, silver, and gold all crumbled into dust and blew away in the wind. Only the stone cut without hands was left, and that stone soon grew into the size of a mountain and filled the whole earth.

Once Daniel had told the king what his dream was, he went on to explain what the dream meant. Each metal of the image represented the coming of a new kingdom to rule the earth.

Daniel said, "You, O king, are a king of kings. For the God of heaven has given you a kingdom, power, strength, and glory; and wherever the children of men dwell, or the beasts of the field and the birds of the heaven, He has given them into your hand, and has made you ruler over them all—you are this head of gold" (Daniel 2:37–38).

However, the king and his golden kingdom would not last. Before long, a new kingdom would come and take over from Nebuchadnezzar. This would be the silver kingdom. After that, a bronze kingdom would come and rule over the earth. The next kingdom would be as strong as iron, but it would also be mixed with the weakness of clay.

Finally, God was telling Nebuchadnezzar that He would send a new kind of kingdom, represented by the stone cut without hands. This Kingdom would grow to be very big and strong, and it would crush the other kingdoms, for God would establish it. God's Kingdom would last forever.

Nebuchadnezzar was amazed when he heard Daniel tell his dream and its interpretation. He offered gifts and offerings to Daniel and exclaimed, "Truly your God is the God of gods, the Lord of kings, and a revealer of secrets, since you could reveal this secret" (Daniel 2:47).

Then Nebuchadnezzar made Daniel a ruler over all of Babylon and the chief of Babylon's wise men. Of course, Daniel did not forget his friends. He asked the king to make Shadrach, Meshach, and Abed-Nego rulers over different affairs within Babylon. The king agreed, but he kept Daniel near his own home so that Daniel could advise him with wisdom.

The dream that Nebuchadnezzar had would indeed come true. After Babylon rose the kingdom of the Medes and Persians. Then came the kingdom of Greece and, finally, the Roman Empire. During the days of Rome, the Father sent His Son Jesus Christ, the long promised Savior of the world, to earth. Christ began God's Kingdom, which has spread over the entire world and will never end.

Questions

1. The stone cut without hands represents God's _____ that Christ began.

2. Nebuchadnezzar was _____ when Daniel interpreted his dream and made Daniel and his friends rulers in the land.

Thought Question

Why would the Lord send a dream about His coming Kingdom to a heathen king?

Catechism

Question 3: Why did God make you and all things?
Answer 3: For his own glory

Memory Verse

Psalm 1:2
But his delight is in the law of the Lord, and in His law he meditates day and night.

LESSON 134

The Huge Golden Image

Daniel 3:1–12

In the time of Nebuchadnezzar of Babylon, the king could force the people in his kingdom to do what he told them. He could even force them to worship whatever idol he told them to worship. He had no respect for the one true God, even though Daniel had made it clear that God was the One who had shown Daniel the interpretation of the king's dream.

At one time, Nebuchadnezzar had a huge golden image built in Babylon. He called for all the governors and leaders in his land to come before the golden image. He wanted all the people of the land to worship his new golden idol.

He had his servant proclaim, "To you it is commanded, O peoples, nations, and languages, that at the time you hear the sound of the horn, flute, harp, lyre, and psaltery, in symphony with all kinds of music, you shall fall down and worship the gold image that King Nebuchadnezzar has set up; and whoever does not fall down and worship shall be cast immediately into the midst of a burning fiery furnace" (Daniel 3:4–6).

Babylon had captured many different nations, and most of these people worshiped different gods and idols. They did not care so much about changing which idol they worshiped. They would rather worship a new idol than be burned in a fiery furnace.

God's people, however, had been commanded never to bow to an idol, no matter what. Daniel's friends, Shadrach, Meshach, and Abed-Nego had been made governors in the land. They had been called to worship the king's idol, but they knew that they could not. They would rather die than bow down and worship before a fake, wicked idol.

All of the people knew that Nebuchadnezzar would not hesitate to do as he had said and kill the men who did not bow. Yet Shadrach, Meshach, and Abed-Nego knew that they could not disobey their God.

Soon the music began to play. Everyone heard the instruments. The people all around began to bow down before the idol. Yet three brave men stood straight amongst all the bowing people, trusting that obeying God would be better for them than obeying the king's command.

Questions

1. The king commanded the people to bow down and worship the _____ when they heard the _____ begin to play.

2. _____, _____, and _____ disobeyed the king and refused to bow down to the idol.

Thought Question

When obeying an earthly king means disobeying God, why is better to obey God, especially when the earthly king is threatening to kill you?

Catechism

Question 4: How can you glorify God?
Answer 4: By loving him and doing what he commands

Memory Verse

Psalm 1:2
But his delight is in the law of the Lord, and in His law he meditates day and night.

LESSON 135

Week 27 Review

Memory Verse

Psalm 1:1–2

Catechism

Question 1: Who made you?

Question 2: What else did God make?

Question 3: Why did God make you and all things?

Question 4: How can you glorify God?

Question 79: What do the last six commandments teach?

Question 80: What do the Ten Commandments teach?

Activity

Matching

Draw lines to match the descriptions on the left to the items on the right.

1. took young Jewish men to serve in his court   God

2. asked if he and his friends could not eat the defiled meat   wise men

3. gave Daniel and his friends knowledge, wisdom, and skill   Nebuchadnezzar

4. Nebuchadnezzar threatened to kill all of these   his and future kingdoms

5. Nebuchadnezzar dreamed of this   Daniel

6. Nebuchadnezzar's dream was really about these   fiery furnace

7. Shadrach, Meshach, and Abed-Nego refused to bow to this   image (statue)

8. the penalty for not bowing was being thrown into this   golden idol

Unit 28   *King Nebuchadnezzar's Reign*

LESSON 136

The Fiery Furnace

Daniel 3:8–30

Some of the king's wise men saw that Shadrach, Meshach, and Abed-Nego had not obeyed the king's command. They went to the king and told him what they had seen: three Jewish men had disobeyed the king and not worshiped the idol.

Nebuchadnezzar was furious. He had the men called before him and accused them of not bowing before the golden image. He decided to let them have a second chance. He would play the music again and, if the three men bowed, then they would be saved. "But," the king said, "if you do not worship, you shall be cast immediately into the midst of a burning fiery furnace. And who is the god who will deliver you from my hands?" (Daniel 3:15).

Bravely, the three men told the king that they were not afraid and had no need to even answer the king. For, they said, "If that is the case, our God whom we serve is able to deliver us from the burning fiery furnace, and He will deliver us from your hand, O king. But if not, let it be known to you, O king, that we do not serve your gods, nor will we worship the gold image which you have set up" (Daniel 3:17–18).

This answer made the king so angry that his face began to change with his anger. He ordered his men to heat the furnace seven times hotter than it had been before. Then he commanded his own mighty men of valor to tie Shadrach, Meshach, and Abed-Nego and throw them, bound, into the fiery furnace. The furnace was so hot that it killed the men who threw Shadrach, Meshach, and Abed-Nego into the fire. Consequently, the three brave men fell into the flames.

Suddenly, Nebuchadnezzar stood up and shouted in astonishment. He asked if only three men had been thrown into the fire. His servants assured him that only three men had been thrown in. Then Nebuchadnezzar said, "I see four men loose, walking in the midst of the fire; and they are not hurt, and the form of the fourth is like the Son of God" (Daniel 3:25).

The king went to the door of the furnace and shouted for Shadrach, Meshach, and Abed-Nego to come out. So the three men came out of the fire. They were not hurt. Even their clothes did not smell like fire.

Nebuchadnezzar exclaimed, "Blessed be the God of Shadrach, Meshach, and Abed-Nego, who sent His Angel and delivered His servants who trusted in Him, and they have frustrated the king's word, and yielded their bodies, that they should not serve nor worship any god except their own God!" (Daniel 3:28).

Finally, the king decreed that anyone who spoke against the God of Israel would be cut into pieces and have his house burned to ashes. He knew there was no god like the one true God.

Questions

1. The three men told the king they would _____ bow down to an idol.

2. The soldiers who threw the men into the fire were _____ by the heat of the fiery furnace.

3. The king was astonished when he saw a _____ _____ in the fire like the Son of God.

Thought Question

Why was it important for Shadrach, Meshach, and Abed-Nego to say they would not worship the idol even if God chose to let them die in the fiery furnace?

Catechism

Question 5: Why are you to glorify God?
Answer 5: Because he made me and takes care of me

Memory Verse

Psalm 1:3
He shall be like a tree planted by the rivers of water, that brings forth its fruit in its season, whose leaf also shall not wither; and whatever he does shall prosper.

LESSON 137

Nebuchadnezzar's Second Dream

Daniel 4:1–18

The next chapter of Daniel's story is written by King Nebuchadnezzar himself. This king of Babylon experienced such a strange thing in his life that he "thought it good to declare the signs and wonders that the Most High God has worked for me" (Daniel 4:2).

After the things that had happened with Daniel and his three friends, Nebuchadnezzar was at peace in his house. He was comfortable in his own palace until another dream came to disturb him.

Once again, the dream bothered the king so much that he called for all the wise men and magicians in the land. He wanted them to tell him what the dream meant, but none of them could. At last, Daniel came to stand before the king. Nebuchadnezzar knew that the Spirit of the one true God was in Daniel, and he hoped the man from Israel could tell him the meaning of his dream.

In the dream, Nebuchadnezzar had seen a tall tree in the middle of the earth. The tree grew tall and strong, all the way up to the sky. It could be seen from anywhere on the earth, and it provided good food for all with its green leaves and abundant fruit. The animals came to rest in the tree's shade, and birds lived among the tree's branches.

Then Nebuchadnezzar saw a watcher, a holy one, come down from heaven and cried out for the great tree to be chopped down. The tree's branches were chopped off, its leaves were stripped off, and the animals and birds were driven from the tree's side. Only the stump and roots were left in the ground. Then the watcher cried out, "Let his heart be changed from that of a man, let him be given the heart of a beast, and let seven times pass over him" (Daniel 4:16).

Nebuchadnezzar had no idea what his dream meant. When he told Daniel his dream, Daniel was astonished and troubled. He knew what the dream meant, but he remained silent before the king.

The king told Daniel not to let the dream trouble him. So Daniel told the king that he wished the dream were meant for the king's enemies. Then Daniel explained the dream.

Questions

1. The king dreamed of a great _____ that filled the earth but was then chopped down; only the _____ and roots were left.

2. When he heard the king's dream, Daniel was troubled and remained _____.

Thought Question

Why might God have chosen to communicate with many of the wicked kings through dreams?

Catechism

Question 7: In how many Persons does this one God exist?
Answer 7: In three Persons

Memory Verse

Psalm 1:3
He shall be like a tree planted by the rivers of water, that brings forth its fruit in its season, whose leaf also shall not wither; and whatever he does shall prosper.

LESSON 138

The Animal King

Daniel 4:19–37

The tree from the dream was Nebuchadnezzar. He was a great king, mighty in all the earth. Nevertheless, Nebuchadnezzar would be cut down, just like the tree. The Lord would drive the king away from men. Nebuchadnezzar would have to live with the animals of the field. For seven years, he would eat grass like the ox and be wet with dew. He would stay that way until he knew that God alone rules the earth and gives the kingdoms of men to whomever He chooses.

Because the stump and roots of the tree were left, Nebuchadnezzar would be able to return to his kingdom after the seven years. Then Daniel advised the king to turn away from his wickedness so the dream might not come true.

The king did not listen, however. A year after his dream, Nebuchadnezzar was walking in his palace and said, "Is not this great Babylon, that I have built for a royal dwelling by my mighty power and for the honor of my majesty?" (Daniel 4:30). As he spoke, a voice came from heaven and warned the king that his kingdom was being taken away from him.

In that very hour, the Lord made the king's dream come true. Nebuchadnezzar was driven away from men. For seven years, he roamed around like a wild animal, eating grass. His hair and fingernails grew long.

At the end of seven years, God gave back the king's understanding. Nebuchadnezzar blessed God and praised and honored Him. The king ruled for another year in his kingdom after his seven years of exile. Instead of lifting up himself, he praised God. He wrote his letter, the fourth chapter of Daniel, to all the people of the earth, in order to proclaim the greatness of God.

Questions

1. The tree represented _____.

2. When God made the dream come true, Nebuchadnezzar was praising his own _____.

3. For seven years, the king became like an _____.

Thought Question

Nebuchadnezzar had seen God's power, but still needed another lesson. What was it that the king did not seem to understand about God?

Catechism

Question 8: Name these three Persons.
Answer 8: The Father, the Son, and the Holy Spirit

Memory Verse

Psalm 1:3
He shall be like a tree planted by the rivers of water, that brings forth its fruit in its season, whose leaf also shall not wither; and whatever he does shall prosper.

LESSON 139

Cumulative Review 11

The Kings

Word Bank: Ahab   David   Hezekiah   Hoshea   Jeroboam   Joash   Josiah   Manasseh

Rehoboam   Saul   Solomon

1. Who was the first human king of Israel? _____

2. Which king was known as a man after God's own heart? _____

3. Who built the temple for God? _____

4. Under which king did Israel split into two nations? _____

5. Who was the first king of the ten tribes? _____

6. Which wicked king was married to Jezebel? _____

7. Who begged the Lord not to let him die and was answered? _____

8. Who was saved from Queen Athaliah? _____

9. Who repented and cried out to God from captivity? _____

10. Who was the boy king who honored God? _____

11. Who was the last king of the ten tribes? _____

Catechism

Question 6: Is there more than one true God?
Answer 6: No. There is only one true God.

Memory Verse

Psalm 1:3
He shall be like a tree planted by the rivers of water, that brings forth its fruit in its season, whose leaf also shall not wither; and whatever he does shall prosper.

LESSON 140

Week 28 Review

Memory Verse

Psalm 1:1–3

Catechism

Question 5: Why are you to glorify God?

Question 6: Is there more than one true God?

Question 7: In how many Persons does this one God exist?

Question 8: Name these three Persons.

Question 81: Who is your neighbor?

Question 82: Is God pleased with those who love and obey him?

Activity

Fill in the blank

Word Bank: animal dream fire four God killed music seven

1. When the _____ played, everyone was to bow to the idol.

2. Nebuchadnezzar heated the furnace _____ times hotter than usual.

3. The men who threw the righteous men into the furnace were _____.

4. Nebuchadnezzar saw _____ men in the fiery furnace.

5. The last man had the appearance of the Son of _____.

6. Shadrach, Meshach, and Abed-Nego's clothes did not smell like _____.

7. Daniel came to Nebuchadnezzar to interpret the king's _____.

8. Nebuchadnezzar would live like an _____ the fields.

Unit 29 — Daniel, Belshazzar, and Cyrus

LESSON 141

Writing on the Wall

Daniel 5:1–29

After Nebuchadnezzar died, his son Belshazzar ruled in Babylon. This king did not serve God. He also did not respect Daniel as much as Nebuchadnezzar had. He did not even really know who Daniel was.

Belshazzar gave a feast for 1,000 of his lords in his palace. He was trying to impress these men, so he called for the gold and silver dishes that had been stolen from the temple in Jerusalem to be brought out. He wanted to impress his guests by having everyone eat and drink from the temple's treasure.

The guests were impressed. They ate food, drank wine, and praised the gods of gold and silver. As they were celebrating, however, the fingers of a man's hand appeared on a wall in the feast hall.

Belshazzar saw the hand appear and write on the wall. He was terrified. His knees began to knock together, and his face became pale. He could see the hand, and he could see the words, but he did not know what the words said, for they were in a foreign language.

Belshazzar called for all his wise men and astrologers to come and read the words. He told them that whoever could interpret the words would be given new clothes and jewelry and would be made third ruler in the kingdom. Yet none of the men could tell the king what the writing on the wall meant.

Then Belshazzar became even more fearful. While he sat in the hall, full of terror, the queen came to find him. She told the king of a man named Daniel, a captive Jew who lived in the kingdom and had interpreted many things for Nebuchadnezzar.

Belshazzar called Daniel to come to him. He told Daniel that if he could interpret the writing on the wall, then he would be given gifts and made a ruler. Daniel told the king he would read the writing but accept no gifts.

Daniel reminded the king of all that had happened to his father, Nebuchadnezzar. He went on to explain that, because Belshazzar was not humble, he too would be punished. Daniel warned, "The God who holds your breath in His hand and owns all your ways, you have not glorified" (Daniel 5:23).

Then Daniel explained the writing on the wall to the king. The words themselves were "MENE, MENE, TEKEL, UPHARSIN" (Daniel 5:25). Then Daniel interpreted each word: "MENE: God has numbered your kingdom, and finished it; TEKEL: You have been weighed in the balances, and found wanting; PERES: Your kingdom has been divided, and given to the Medes and Persians" (Daniel 5:26–28).

Because Belshazzar had not followed God, God would give his kingdom over to another nation. Although the news was not good, the king insisted on dressing Daniel in a new robe and proclaimed him to be the third ruler in the kingdom.

Questions

1. Belshazzar used the gold and silver _____ from Israel's temple in his celebration.

2. Belshazzar saw _____ of a hand writing on the wall.

3. The words written on the wall were _____, MENE, _____, UPHARSIN.

Thought Question

How was Daniel able to bravely stand in front of a king who did not know him and tell him that he was doing evil before the Lord?

Catechism

Question 9: What is God?
Answer 9: God is a Spirit and does not have a body like men.

Memory Verse

Psalm 1:4
The ungodly are not so, but are like the chaff which the wind drives away.

LESSON 142

Persians Capture Babylon

Daniel 5:30

At this time, a king named Cyrus ruled over the kingdom of Persia. This new, powerful king was conquering many countries. First he had conquered the neighboring country of Media. Then he went on to conquer Babylon. Much of Babylon's land was taken, yet the city of Babylon itself would not fall before Cyrus.

So Cyrus went on to conquer other countries that surrounded the city of Babylon. Soon the Persian king's empire was three times as big as Nebuchadnezzar's had been. Soon only the city of Babylon was left unconquered.

In this city, Belshazzar and his lords were having a feast, the very same feast where the writing appeared on the wall. Behind the high, strong city walls, the people of Babylon felt safe. They were certain that Cyrus could not break through their city walls.

Cyrus and his men were camped outside the city. They could not surround the city and try to starve the people out, for the people had enough food for many years to come. The mighty Euphrates River flowed under the walls, right into the city, so the Babylonians would not go thirsty. The Persians could not break down the walls or climb over them.

Instead, Cyrus and his men thought of a clever way to get into the city. While Belshazzar and his lords feasted, Cyrus and his men dug a new channel for the Euphrates River. Then they turned the water of the river into its new riverbed, away from the city.

The old riverbed was now empty. Quietly, Cyrus and his men walked through the old channel, right under the city walls and into mighty Babylon. They quickly surrounded the palace, where Daniel had already explained that Belshazzar would not be king much longer.

The same night that Daniel spoke to Belshazzar, the king of Babylon was killed, and Cyrus took over all of Babylon. The warning that was written on the wall by the mysterious hand came true. God was done using the Babylonian kingdom. Now it was time for the Persians to rule.

This night also fulfilled other prophecies. For one, Nebuchadnezzar's dream of the image was beginning to come true, for the second kingdom, of silver, represented Cyrus and his Persian empire. Also, many years before, Jeremiah had foretold the fall of Babylon. Now the Persian Empire would be supreme, ruled by Cyrus, the greatest conqueror the world had known.

Questions

1. Cyrus conquered the city of Babylon while _____ was having a party.

2. The Persians entered Babylon by digging a new channel for the _____ and _____ walking under the _____.

Thought Question

What does it mean that "God was done using the Babylonian Empire"?

Catechism

Question 10: Where is God?
Answer 10: God is everywhere.

Memory Verse

Psalm 1:4
The ungodly are not so, but are like the chaff which the wind drives away.

LESSON 143

Darius of Persia

Daniel 6:1–9

The mighty Persian Empire was too great and large to be ruled over by a single man. Cyrus took a general named Darius the Mede and put him on the throne in Babylon to rule that area of Cyrus' land. Even though he did not live very long after he became a king, he did have an important part to play in Daniel's life.

Darius divided the kingdom into many smaller parts. He placed princes over each part of his kingdom. Over the princes, Darius placed three presidents. Daniel was one of those presidents. He was already very important, but he did such good work that Darius took notice of him and thought about making him ruler of everything in Babylon, higher even than the three presidents.

By this time, Daniel's wisdom and knowledge were well known, so it was natural for him to be placed in a position of power and influence. However, Daniel's high position did not make everyone happy.

Some of the other rulers in the land were jealous of Daniel.

They began to try to think of ways to get him into trouble. They watched him to see if they could find anything wrong in what he did. Yet Daniel was a faithful worker, and the other rulers could find no problems. Finally, they said to each other, "We shall not find any charge against this Daniel unless we find it against him concerning the law of his God" (Daniel 6:5).

So the rulers conspired together to trap Daniel. Together, the men went to Darius. They told the king that all the rulers of the land had spoken together and decided that a royal decree should be spoken. This decree should say that no man in all the land would be allowed to pray to any man or god for thirty days. Instead, everyone in the kingdom was supposed to pray only to Darius, the king. Anyone who disobeyed would be thrown into a den of lions.

Darius was pleased. He liked to be worshiped by the people as if he were a god. He did not know that his princes were trying to get Daniel in trouble. So Darius signed the royal decree.

Questions

1. Darius wanted to make _____ the ruler in Babylon.

2. King _____ was supposed to be worshiped for _____ days.

3. Those who disobeyed the royal decree would be thrown into a _____ of _____.

Thought Question

Why do wicked people so often try to get Christians like Daniel in trouble for being faithful to God?

Catechism

Question 12: Does God know all things?
Answer 12: Yes. Nothing can be hidden from God.

Memory Verse

Psalm 1:4
The ungodly are not so, but are like the chaff which the wind drives away.

LESSON 144

Cumulative Review 12

Job–Daniel

Word Bank: Abed-Nego Daniel David Eli Elijah God Job Jonah Josiah Naboth Saul

1. Which two kings were anointed by Samuel? _____, _____

2. Who lost all his possessions but refused to curse God? _____

3. Who fought 400 prophets of Baal? _____

4. Who was swallowed by a huge fish? _____

5. Who raised Samuel in the tabernacle? _____

6. Who was killed so Ahab could have his vineyard? _____

7. Who read the writing on the wall? _____

8. When Shadrach, Meshach, and _____ refused to bow to the king's idol, they were thrown into the fiery furnace.

9. Who found the Law of God and read it to the people? _____

10. Who was Israel's rightful king? _____

Catechism

Question 11: Can you see God?
Answer 11: No. I cannot see God, but he always sees me.

Memory Verse

Psalm 1:4
The ungodly are not so, but are like the chaff which the wind drives away.

LESSON 145

Week 29 Review

Memory Verse

Psalm 1:1–4

Catechism

Question 9: What is God?

Question 10: Where is God?

Question 11: Can you see God?

Question 12: Does God know all things?

Question 83: Is God displeased with those who do not love and obey him?

Question 84: What is the first commandment?

Activity

Maze

Help Cyrus and his soldiers sneak into the city of Babylon.

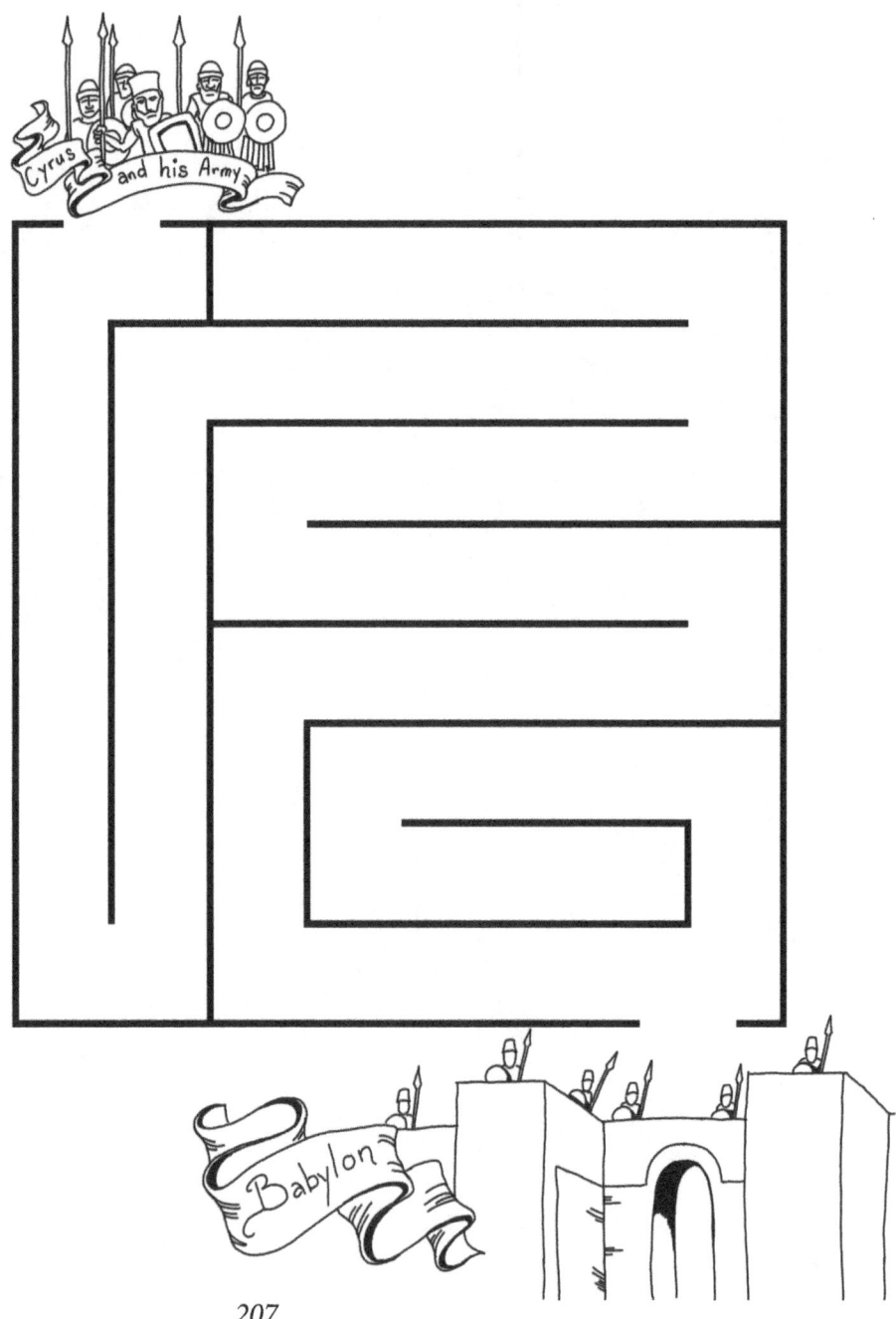

Unit 30 Daniel's Final Days and Ezra

LESSON 146

The Jealous Princes' Plot

Daniel 6:10–17

All through his captivity, Daniel had remembered God's promise that if His people repented of their sins and prayed to Him, then He would hear their prayer and rescue them. Three times every single day, Daniel opened the windows of his room towards Jerusalem, knelt down, and prayed to the Lord.

Of course, the jealous princes knew of Daniel's habit. They knew Daniel would refuse to stop praying to God.

Soon Daniel heard of the king's new decree. He was not supposed to worship anyone other than the king for thirty days. Daniel knew that the king's decree could not be changed. He also knew that disobeying the king meant almost certain death by being thrown to the lions. Yet Daniel went into his bedroom, opened his windows, knelt down, and began praying to the one true God.

The jealous princes were watching. When they saw Daniel begin to pray, they became very excited and ran straight to the king. They reminded King Darius of his decree and of the punishment for disobeying the king. Then they told the king, "That Daniel, who is one of the captives from Judah, does not show due regard for you, O king, or for the decree that you have signed" (Daniel 6:13).

When he heard what his princes said, Darius was very sad that he had ever signed the decree. All day he tried to come up with a way to save Daniel's life. At the end of the day, the princes returned and reminded him that the law of the people forbade anyone from changing a decree given by the king.

The king knew he had been tricked. He could do nothing. So Darius commanded Daniel to come before him. Daniel was thrown into the lions' den. Before he left, Darius told Daniel, "Your God, whom you serve continually, He will deliver you" (Daniel 6:16). Then Darius' soldiers placed a stone over the mouth of the lions' den, and Darius placed his own seal on it so that no one would open it.

Questions

1. Daniel's daily habit was to pray _____ times a day.

2. Who was Daniel supposed to worship for thirty days? _____

3. Since Darius had been _____, he became very sad about throwing Daniel to the lions.

Thought Question

Why was the king upset when he thought Daniel was going to die? Should not the king have been angry with Daniel since Daniel disobeyed him?

Catechism

Question 13: Can God do all things?
Answer 13: Yes. God can do all his holy will.

Memory Verse

Psalm 1:5
Therefore the ungodly shall not stand in the judgment, nor sinners in the congregation of the righteous.

LESSON 147

Daniel in the Lions' Den

Daniel 6:18–28

With a deeply sorrowful heart, Darius returned to the palace. He ate nothing that night, and he could not sleep either. He worried for Daniel.

Very early in the morning, Darius got up and went quickly to the lions' den. He commanded his soldiers to remove the stone from the den and cried out anxiously for Daniel, hoping to hear Daniel call back to him.

Sure enough, Darius heard Daniel's voice calling to him. Daniel said, "O king, live forever! My God sent His angel and shut the lions' mouths, so that they have not hurt me, because I was found innocent before Him; and also, O king, I have done no wrong before you" (Daniel 6:21–22).

God had kept Daniel perfectly safe from the lions! Darius was very glad, and he commanded his soldiers to bring Daniel out of the den. Not a single injury was found on Daniel because he believed in God.

Then Darius called for the jealous princes who had gotten Daniel in trouble. This time, they were the ones thrown into the lions' den. King Darius also threw the jealous princes' families into the lions' den.

This time, the lions' mouths were not closed. The lions crushed the men before they could even reach the bottom of the den. So all the jealous princes, who tried to kill Daniel in the lions' den, were themselves killed by the lions.

Finally, Darius made a new decree. He commanded all the people of the land to worship and fear the one true God of Daniel. He told the people that Daniel's God was the living God, and that He delivers and rescues His people. Darius also knew that God's kingdom was the only kingdom that would never be destroyed.

After all of this, Daniel became an important man during the rule of Darius. The Lord made him prosper, even after Darius died and King Cyrus took over control of the area. Daniel had many visions from the Lord, and the Lord continually blessed His servant and made him prosperous in all that he did.

Questions

1. Daniel was saved when God _____ the lions' mouths.

2. The jealous, wicked _____ were thrown to the lions instead of Daniel.

3. King Darius commanded all the people to worship and fear the _____ of _____ .

Thought Question

Why could God save Daniel when the king of the land could not?

Catechism

Question 14: Where do you learn how to love and obey God?
Answer 14: In the Bible alone

Memory Verse

Psalm 1:5
Therefore the ungodly shall not stand in the judgment, nor sinners in the congregation of the righteous.

LESSON 148

Cyrus, King of Persia

Ezra 1:1–11

Daniel had been a young boy when he first came as a captive to Babylon. He had lived through seventy years of captivity and was now an old man. He had survived the reigns of several kings from two different nations. He had been an important man to both nations' kings. The Lord truly had cared for and lifted up His faithful servant.

Now Daniel lived to see the beginning of the reign of King Cyrus. At the beginning of the captivity, the prophet Jeremiah had written that the Jews' captivity would last for seventy years. That time had ended, and the people were beginning to look forward to returning to their promised land.

In the very first year of King Cyrus' reign, he made a proclamation to the Jews, for the Lord had stirred up the spirit of Cyrus. His proclamation read: "All the kingdoms of the earth the Lord God of heaven has given me. And He has commanded me to build Him a house at Jerusalem which is in Judah. Who is among you of all His people? May his God be with him, and let him go up to Jerusalem which is in Judah, and build the house of the Lord God of Israel (He is God), which is in Jerusalem. And whoever is left in any place where he dwells, let the men of his place help him with silver and gold, with goods and livestock, besides the freewill offerings for the house of God which is in Jerusalem" (Ezra 1:2–4).

Now Cyrus' proclamation was amazing, but it was not entirely unexpected. Isaiah the prophet had mentioned Cyrus by name 150 years before, prophesying that Cyrus would be the king to let the Jews return to their land (Isaiah 44:28).

The captive people of Judah were very happy. Soon the heads of all the houses were meeting to plan who should return and when. Most of the men returned, along with the Levites that were in captivity, to rebuild the temple of the Lord.

Not everyone could return, for it was a long journey back home, and the land they were traveling to had been destroyed. Clearing away the rubbish and building new homes would take a long time. Only the strongest people returned to begin the hard work of rebuilding the nation.

Daniel was one of the old men who did not return to Judah. Yet the people like him who stayed behind still rejoiced and helped those who were returning as much as they could. They gave presents of money, animals, and other helpful things.

Even King Cyrus helped out. He brought the gold and silver dishes that Nebuchadnezzar had stolen from the temple and gave them back to the Levites. So it was that the first group of Jews began to return out of their exile, back to the Promised Land, just as the Lord had promised.

Questions

1. Which prophet foretold the coming of Cyrus? _____

2. How many years were the Jews in captivity? _____

3. Since it was a long, hard trip, only the _____ people returned to Israel right away.

Thought Question

What does the phrase "the Lord stirred up the spirit of Cyrus" mean?

Catechism

Question 15: Who wrote the Bible?
Answer 15: Chosen men who were inspired by the Holy Spirit

Memory Verse

Psalm 1:5
Therefore the ungodly shall not stand in the judgment, nor sinners in the congregation of the righteous.

LESSON 149

The Second Temple

Ezra 2:64–3:13

Fifty thousand people made the journey out of captivity and back to Jerusalem. They carried many things that would help them rebuild their lives in Israel.

After many long days, the captives arrived home. Sadly, they were greeted only by ruins and rubbish. Jerusalem had been destroyed. The people came to where the temple had once stood, but all that was there now were piles of broken pillars and heaps of stones.

Some of the men took gold and other treasures from what they brought with them and donated them to the temple. This money would be used to rebuild the temple. Then all the people returned to their own cities. God had given each family a plot of land when Israel first entered the land. Even though they had been in captivity, the people still knew where their own land was. Now they moved their families back to the land that had belonged to their fathers.

After a little while, the priests and Levites who had returned built an altar to God in Jerusalem. All the people gathered in Jerusalem to worship God and offer sacrifices on the new altar. They also kept the Feast of Tabernacles, as God had commanded them to do. Not only had they physically returned to the land, but they were also spiritually returning to the worship of God.

About a year after they returned, the people of Israel gathered in Jerusalem to begin rebuilding the temple. The Levites were in charge of the rebuilding process.

When the builders laid the foundation for the new temple, the priests stood in their robes and blew their trumpets while the people sang and rejoiced. They praised God, singing, "For He is good, for His mercy endures forever toward Israel" (Ezra 3:11). The people rejoiced greatly, for the foundation of the Lord's house had been laid.

Yet many of the older men, priests, and heads of the houses began to weep when the foundation was laid. These men were old enough to have lived through the whole captivity in Babylon and Persia. They remembered the wonderful splendor of the first temple that Solomon built. These men knew that the new temple could never match the wonderful glory of the old temple. They wept for what they had lost.

The shouting, singing, and weeping all mixed together. The noises could not be separated from each other. Instead, the noise of the people mixed together made such a loud sound that it could be heard from a long way away.

Questions

1. When the people returned, they lived in their own _____.

2. The Levites were in charge of rebuilding the _____.

3. When the temple foundation was laid, the old men wept because it could never match the _____ of the old temple.

Thought Question

Why was it important for the people to return to worshiping God as well as to return to the land that they called home?

Catechism

Question 16: Who were our first parents?
Answer 16: Adam and Eve

Memory Verse

Psalm 1:5
Therefore the ungodly shall not stand in the judgment, nor sinners in the congregation of the righteous.

LESSON 150

Week 30 Review

Memory Verse

Psalm 1:1–5

Catechism

Question 13: Can God do all things?

Question 14: Where do you learn how to love and obey God?

Question 15: Who wrote the Bible?

Question 16: Who were our first parents?

Question 85: What does the first commandment teach you?

Question 86: What is the second commandment?

Activity

Number the Order of Events

Number the parts of Daniel's story in order from one to five.

_____ Daniel is thrown into the lions' den.

_____ The jealous princes catch Daniel praying to God.

_____ Darius commands all the people to worship only Daniel's God.

_____ Darius makes a decree that no one can worship anyone other than the king.

_____ God shuts the lions' mouths and saves Daniel.

Unit 31   *Rebuilding the Temple*

LESSON 151

Rebuilding the Temple

Ezra 4:1–5:2; Haggai 1:1–2:9

As you remember, the ten tribes of Israel had been taken into captivity by Assyria. The king of Assyria had then filled the empty land of Samaria with people from foreign nations.

These strangers had been living in Samaria the entire seventy years that Judah was in captivity. When they saw that the Jews were back and were rebuilding the temple, they came to talk to the high priest, Zerubbabel, who was in charge of the building process.

The foreigners asked Zerubbabel to let them help build the temple. Zerubbabel answered, "You may do nothing with us to build a house for our God; but we alone will build to the Lord God of Israel" (Ezra 4:3). After they heard this, the people from Samaria did their best to stop the rebuilding of the temple.

Judah's enemies discouraged the people who were trying to build. They hired people to cause trouble wherever they could.

During this time, Cyrus king of Persia died. Knowing that Cyrus was the king who had given the Jews permission to return to their land and rebuild, the enemies of Judah sent a letter to the new king, Artaxerxes. In that letter, the wicked men told the new king that the Jews had rebuilt much of their city already. If they were allowed to finish building the city, then they would refuse to pay taxes and become a rebellious city.

This, of course, was a lie. Nevertheless, the king of Persia searched his records anyway. He concluded that the city of Jerusalem had been a rebellious city in the past, and he did not want it to be rebuilt. Artaxerxes sent a letter back to Judah's enemies and commanded them to tell the Jews to stop building.

As soon as they got the letter, Judah's enemies hurried to Jerusalem. They forced the Levites to stop working on the temple. Work on the temple stopped completely until a new king, Darius I (the First), came to rule in Persia. Note that King Darius I is different from Darius the Mede, who conquered Babylon for King Cyrus seventeen years earlier.

At this time, God spoke to two prophets, Haggai and Zechariah, so that they prophesied to the people in Jerusalem. They told the people to begin rebuilding the temple once more. Zerubbabel obeyed.

Through Haggai, God encouraged Zerubbabel to be strong in his building, for "I am with you … My Spirit remains among you; do not fear!" (Haggai 2:4–5). God also promised that the glory of the new temple would be greater than that of the old, for God would give peace in the new temple.

Questions

1. Which man was in charge of rebuilding the temple? _____

2. The enemies of Judah convinced the king of _____ to stop the Jews from working on the temple.

3. Whom did God send to prophesy and encourage the people to restart building the temple? _____ _____ _____ and _____

Thought Question

Why was it important for Zerubbabel to know that God was with him and would bless the rebuilding of the temple?

Catechism

Question 18: Of what were our first parents made?
Answer 18: God made Adam's body out of the ground and Eve's body out of a rib from Adam.

Memory Verse

Psalm 1:6
For the Lord knows the way of the righteous, but the way of the ungodly shall perish.

LESSON 152

A Decree from Persia

Ezra 5:3–6:22

As soon as the Jews began building the temple again, the governor demanded to know who had said the building could start again. The Jews replied that God was the One who had commanded them to build. So the governor sent a letter to King Darius I.

The letter told everything that had happened. It included the names of the men who were building the temple. It also added what the men of Judah had said: "We are servants of the God of heaven and earth, and we are rebuilding the temple that was built many years ago, which a great king of Israel built and completed" (Ezra 5:11). The Jews also explained why they had been sent into captivity and why their temple had been destroyed. They also told how King Cyrus had allowed them to return in order to rebuild the temple.

The governor told King Darius everything the Jews said. He also recommended that the king look up old records to see if what the Jews were saying was true. Darius read the letter and commanded the old records to be brought out. Without any trouble, Darius found King Cyrus' decree to send the Jewish captives back to their own land to rebuild the temple of God.

Then Darius sent a letter back to the governor. He told him, "Let the work of this house of God alone; let the governor of the Jews and the elders of the Jews build this house of God on its site" (Ezra 6:7). Darius also told the governor and his officials to help the Jews in whatever way they could find. They were to give gifts of money from the king's treasuries and animals for sacrifices to God.

Darius wanted animals given to the Jews every day so that they could sacrifice continually. He also wanted the Jews to pray for him, the king, and his sons. Finally, Darius said that anyone who tried to undo his decree would be hanged.

The governor and his officials obeyed and began to help the Jews build. So the Jews continued building the temple and finished it. The work had taken about twenty years. After the building was finished, the people dedicated the temple and offered hundreds of sacrifices. They also set up the priests and Levites as Moses had once commanded.

Last of all, they celebrated the Passover with great joy. For the Lord made the people joyful by turning Darius' heart to help them rebuild the temple.

Questions

1. Which Persian king originally commanded the Jews to build the temple? _____

2. Darius told the governor to let the Jews work on the _____ of _____ and to help them build.

3. What feast did the Jews celebrate when the temple was done? _____

Thought Question

Why might King Darius I have wanted the Jews to pray for him and his sons?

Catechism

Question 19: What else did God give Adam and Eve besides bodies?
Answer 19: He gave them souls that will last forever.

Memory Verse

Psalm 1:6
For the Lord knows the way of the righteous, but the way of the ungodly shall perish.

LESSON 153

King Ahasuerus

Esther 1:1–9

Although 50,000 Jews had returned to Israel, many stayed behind for one reason or another. These people were scattered all throughout the kingdom of Persia. Wherever they went, they carried the knowledge of God with them.

At this time, King Darius I was dead and his son Ahasuerus, or Xerxes, was ruling. Ahasuerus was not a wise or God-fearing man. Instead, he was rather foolish.

The capital of the empire had been moved to a new city. Babylon's splendor was destroyed, and the whole city was in ruins.

The new capital was called Shushan and was even more magnificent than Babylon had been. Ahasuerus lived in Shushan in great splendor. From that city, he ruled his huge empire.

In the third year of his reign, Ahasuerus invited all the princes and nobles from his empire to come to a feast in Shushan. This was a large, wonderful gathering with many important people.

For half a year, Ahasuerus entertained all the princes and nobles from his entire empire. He showed them all the splendor and majesty of his kingdom.

At the end of this time, he held a feast for all the people of Shushan. The greatest and smallest of people were all invited. No one was left out, for everyone was invited.

The feast was held in the king's garden. The whole place was extravagantly decorated with white and blue linen curtains tied to silver rods with cords of fine purple linen. The ground was paved with red, blue, white, and black marble. The king generously served an abundance of wine in golden cups.

Now only men from the city could attend the feast in the garden. At this time in history, men and women did not gather together in public. Instead, the king's wife, Queen Vashti, gave a feast for the women of the city while the king gave his feast for the men of the city.

The feasting lasted for a whole week. Everyone was happy and in a mood of celebration. Yet trouble was not far away.

Questions

1. The feast for all the people lasted for a whole _____.

2. What was the queen's name? _____

3. The king and queen held separate _____ because it was seen as improper for men and women to feast together in public.

Thought Question

Why might the king and queen have wanted to give such extravagant feasts for all the people?

Catechism

Question 20: Do you have a soul as well as a body?
Answer 20: Yes. And my soul is going to last forever.

Memory Verse

Psalm 1:6
For the LORD knows the way of the righteous, but the way of the ungodly shall perish.

Cumulative Review 13

Josiah–Ezra

Word Bank: Babylon   Daniel   Jeremiah   Son   Zedekiah

1. What nation captured Judah? _____

2. Who was the last king of Judah? _____

3. _____ said that Judah would remain in captivity for seventy years.

4. Who interpreted Nebuchadnezzar's dreams? _____

5. In the fiery furnace, Nebuchadnezzar saw a fourth person, like the _____ of God, along with Shadrach, Meshach, and Abed-Nego.

Oral Questions

1. How did Josiah die?

2. Why did Judah's princes throw Jeremiah into a pit?

3. Why would Daniel and his friends not eat Nebuchadnezzar's food?

4. How did Cyrus take over Babylon?

Catechism

Question 17: How did God create man?
Answer 17: God created man, male and female, after his own image.

Memory Verse

Psalm 1:6
For the Lord knows the way of the righteous, but the way of the ungodly shall perish.

LESSON 155

Week 31 Review

Memory Verse

> *Psalm 1:1-6*

Catechism

Question 17: How did God create man?

Question 18: Of what were our first parents made?

Question 19: What else did God give Adam and Eve besides bodies?

Question 20: Do you have a soul as well as a body?

Question 87: What does the second commandment teach you?

Question 88: What is the third commandment?

Activity

True or False

1. The ten tribes of Israel were taken into captivity by Assyria. *True/False*

2. Zebulun was in charge of rebuilding the temple. *True/False*

3. The prophet Haggai encouraged Zerubbabel. *True/False*

4. The Jews tried to convince Artaxerxes to stop the Jews' building. *True/False*

5. King Darius I ordered the governor to help build the temple. *True/False*

6. Ahasuerus was a wise, godly king. *True/False*

7. Ahasuerus invited all the men of Shushan to a party. *True/False*

8. Ahasuerus had a wife named Ruth. *True/False*

Unit 32   Esther, Mordecai, and Haman

LESSON 156

Searching for a Queen

Esther 1:10–2:23

On the seventh day of the feast, King Ahasuerus, who had drunk too much wine, sent seven of his servants into the hall where Queen Vashti was holding her feast. He told his servants to have the queen wear her crown and come out to the garden. Ahasuerus wanted all the men to see his queen's beauty.

Queen Vashti refused King Ahasuerus' request. When the servants came back to the king and told him that his queen had refused, Ahasuerus became furious. He consulted with his wise men and asked them what should be done to Vashti because of her actions.

One wise man answered that the queen had wronged not just the king, but all the people of the city. He said, "the queen's behavior will become known to all women, so that they will despise their husbands in their eyes…. Thus there will be excessive contempt and wrath" (Esther 1:17–18). The wise man suggested that because of her actions, Vashti should no longer be the queen. If the king made an example of Vashti and chose himself a new wife, then all women in the land would be more obedient to their husbands.

King Ahasuerus liked this advice. He sent letters throughout all the kingdom proclaiming that each man should be master in his own house.

Soon after this, the king's servants suggested that the king find a new wife by gathering together all the beautiful young women of the land. All the girls would be brought before the king. Whichever girl pleased the king most would be his wife.

Again, Ahasuerus liked this advice. He commanded his servants to begin hunting everywhere for beautiful young girls.

A Jew named Mordecai was living in Shushan at this time. He had a beautiful young cousin named Esther. Esther's mother and father had died, so Mordecai was raising his cousin as his own daughter.

Esther was beautiful, and she was chosen as one of the girls who would go before the king. She was brought to the palace along with many other girls, but she told no one that she was a Jew, for Mordecai had warned her not to.

Many women were brought to the palace, and one man was in charge of all of them. Esther pleased this man, and he gave her special treatment. She was given seven of the best maidservants, and they lived together in the best room in the house of the women.

Each young woman prepared for twelve whole months before she was allowed to see the king. One by one, each woman was sent to see the king. When Esther's turn finally came, she pleased Ahasuerus and won his favor. He loved her more than all the other women. The king gave Esther a crown, and she became his queen in place of Vashti.

Meanwhile, Esther's cousin Mordecai walked before the court of the women's house and sat in the palace gate every day to find out how Esther was. While he lingered there, he discovered a plot, which two servants had made, to kill the king.

Mordecai told Esther of the plot so that she could warn Ahasuerus. The plot was proved, and the two servants were hanged. What Mordecai had done was written down in the king's records, but Ahasuerus forgot to reward the man who had saved his life.

Questions

_____

1. Vashti's crime was that she _____ the king's command.
   _____

2. Esther's cousin _____ raised her.
   _____

3. The king chose _____ to be his new queen.
   _____

4. Mordecai discovered a _____ to kill the king.

Thought Question

Why might Mordecai have told Esther not to tell anyone she was a Jew?

Catechism

Question 21: How do you know your soul will last forever?
Answer 21: Because the Bible tells me so

Memory Verse

Philippians 2:13
For it is God who works in you both to will and to do for His good pleasure.

LESSON 157

Haman, a Hateful Prince

Esther 3:1–15

King Ahasuerus had many princes to help him rule his empire. The king liked a prince named Haman and promoted him so that he ruled over the other princes. The king's other princes and servants had to bow down whenever they saw Haman.

Haman loved the attention and the power. He liked being bowed down to, and he liked to think he was a very important person.

The only man who refused to bow before Haman was Mordecai, Esther's cousin. The king's servants were shocked that Mordecai would not bow. They asked him why he would not bow and told him that he should bow. Yet Mordecai continued to stand whenever Haman passed by. So the king's servants told Haman that Mordecai was not bowing to him.

Because he was such a proud man, Haman could hardly believe someone would ignore his command to bow. He became furious. With the power he had, he could probably have just killed Mordecai himself. However, Haman was so insulted that killing Mordecai was not good enough for him. Someone had told Haman that Mordecai was a Jew. Now nothing would satisfy Haman except for destroying all the Jews in the empire.

Still, Haman could not destroy an entire race of people without the king's permission. Thousands of Jews lived in the empire and paid taxes to the king. The king would lose money if they were all killed. Also, if the king did not want the Jews killed, he could just as easily kill Haman for asking such a thing.

So Haman, who was a superstitious man, decided to cast lots to find a lucky day for him to attack the Jews. Then Haman went to speak to the king.

Haman told the king, "There is a certain people scattered and dispersed among the people in all the provinces of your kingdom; their laws are different from all other people's, and they do not keep the king's laws. Therefore it is not fitting for the king to let them remain. If it pleases the king, let a decree be written that they be destroyed, and I will pay ten thousand talents of silver into the hands of those who do the work, to bring it into the king's treasuries" (Esther 3:8–9).

Haman was a rich man, but the king was even more rich. He told Haman to keep his money and to do whatever he wanted with the people he disliked. Ahasuerus gave Haman his seal ring. Haman could write whatever he wanted and put the king's seal on it so that his decree could never be changed.

Of course, Haman immediately wrote a decree stating that on the thirteenth day of the twelfth month, all the Jews in the empire were to be destroyed. Old, young, men, and women were all to be killed.

The law went everywhere throughout the kingdom, and wherever it went, it brought sadness and fear to the Jews. The entire Jewish race was about to end.

Questions

1. Who was the king's favorite prince? _____

2. Haman hated _____ because he did not bow down to him.

3. Haman wanted to kill all the _____.

Thought Question

Why did Haman feel he had to kill all the Jews in order to get even with Mordecai for not bowing to him?

Catechism

Question 22: In what condition did God make Adam and Eve?
Answer 22: He made them holy and happy.

Memory Verse

Philippians 2:13
For it is God who works in you both to will and to do for His good pleasure.

LESSON 158

Esther's Bravery

Esther 4:1–5:9

When Mordecai heard that all the Jews were to be killed, he tore his clothes, put on sackcloth and ashes, and went into the middle of the city with a loud, bitter cry. He came to the front of the king's palace and wept at the gate. He could not enter, however, for no one wearing sackcloth could enter the palace.

Some of Queen Esther's servants told her that Mordecai was outside the gate wearing sackcloth and ashes. Not knowing about Haman's wicked scheme, Esther sent Mordecai some clothes to wear. Mordecai, however, refused to accept them.

So Esther sent a servant out to ask Mordecai what was wrong. Mordecai told the servant the entire story. He also gave the servant a copy of Haman's decree, sealed with the king's ring. Mordecai asked Esther to go before the king and beg him for her peoples' lives.

Esther was afraid when she heard what Mordecai had to say. She sent a message back to her cousin and reminded him that anyone who approached the king in his inner court without being called by the king would be killed. The only exception was if the king held out his golden scepter to the one who entered. Esther had not been called before the king for thirty days. If she went into the king's court without being called, the king could kill her just as easily as he had replaced Vashti, his former queen.

Mordecai knew the danger. Yet he also knew that the Jews were in terrible danger. Even Esther, the queen, was in danger because of this decree. Mordecai told Esther that she must speak out. If she did not, deliverance would be brought from a different place, but Esther and her family would die.

Then Mordecai said, "Yet who knows whether you have come to the kingdom for such a time as this?" (Esther 4:14).

Esther was still afraid, but she knew that Mordecai was right. She sent one last message to Mordecai asking him to gather all the Jews in the city of Shushan to fast for her for three days. She and her servants would fast, as well. At the end of that time, Esther would go before the king. If she died, then she died. If not, perhaps she could do something to help the Jews. Mordecai did what Esther asked.

At the end of three days, Esther put on her royal robes and went into the king's inner court. When the king saw his beautiful young queen, he held out his golden scepter to her and let her approach.

Esther came closer to the king, and he asked her what she wanted. He offered to give her up to half of his kingdom. Yet Esther asked only if the king and Haman would come to a banquet she had prepared for them that day.

The king was delighted, and so was Haman. He thought he was now the queen's favorite, as well. Both men went to Esther's banquet. While there, the king once again asked what Esther wanted. Esther asked if the king and Haman would come to another banquet the next night.

Both men agreed. The king was curious to know what the queen would tell him the next night. Haman, meanwhile, was joyful to be getting special attention from the queen.

Haman's joy disappeared when he walked out of the king's gate, though. There at the gate was Mordecai the Jew, and he was once again not bowing.

Questions

1. It was dangerous for Esther to go before the king because, if he did not call her, he could _____ her.

2. Esther asked the king to attend a banquet with _____.

3. Haman got upset when he left the palace because he saw _____.

Thought Question

Why might Esther have asked the king to a banquet instead of immediately asking him to save the Jews?

Catechism

Question 23: What covenant did God make with Adam?
Answer 23: The covenant of life

Memory Verse

Philippians 2:13
For it is God who works in you both to will and to do for His good pleasure.

LESSON 159

Cumulative Review 14

The Captives

Word Bank: Assyria   Babylon   Cyrus   forever   Hoshea   Nebuchadnezzar   seventy years   temple
Zedekiah   Zerubbabel

1. What nation captured the ten tribes of Israel? _____

2. Who was the last king of the ten tribes? _____

3. How long were the ten tribes in captivity? _____

4. What nation captured the two tribes of Judah? _____

5. Which king captured the two tribes? _____

6. Who was the last king of the two tribes? _____

7. How long were the two tribes in captivity? _____

8. Which king allowed Judah to return to Israel? _____

9. Who was in charge of rebuilding the temple? _____

10. The older generation wept when they saw the new temple because it was not like Solomon's _____.

Catechism

Question 24: What is a covenant?
Answer 24: A relationship that God establishes with us and guarantees by his word

Memory Verse

Philippians 2:13
For it is God who works in you both to will and to do for His good pleasure.

LESSON 160

Week 32 Review

Memory Verse

Philippians 2:13

Catechism

Question 21: How do you know your soul will last forever?

Question 22: In what condition did God make Adam and Eve?

Question 23: What covenant did God make with Adam?

Question 24: What is a covenant?

Question 89: What does the third commandment teach you?

Question 90: What is the fourth commandment?

Activity
Matching

Match the people on the right to what they did on the left. Names can be used more than once.

_____1. Raised his young cousin

_____2. Became angry with and banished his wife

_____3. Pleased the king and won his favor

_____4. Invited the king and Haman to dinner

_____5. Uncovered a plot to kill the king

_____6. Hated the Jews and wanted to kill them

_____7. Refused to bow down to Haman

_____8. Bravely went before the king without being invited

A. Ahasuerus

B. Esther

C. Haman

D. Mordecai

228

Unit 33 — Esther Saves Her People

LESSON 161

Haman's Arrogance

Esther 5:10–6:13

Haman went home and gathered his family and friends around him. He reminded them of how rich he was, how many children he had, and how the king had promoted him above most everyone in the kingdom. Then he told them that Esther had invited him to another banquet the next night, but he also said that he could find no joy when Mordecai was still alive and not bowing to him.

Seeing her husband was distressed, Haman's wife suggested that Haman build a huge gallows. He would ask the king's permission to hang Mordecai on the gallows, and then he could go to the queen's banquet in peace.

Haman was delighted with this idea. He commanded his servants to start building the gallows immediately.

That night, the king could not sleep. He commanded one of his servants to bring him the book of records. As the servants read through the book, they came to the part that told how Mordecai had saved King Ahasuerus from a plot to murder him. The king stopped his servants and asked what had been done for Mordecai as a reward for his loyalty. The servants answered that nothing had been done. Then and there, the king decided to reward Mordecai. He asked his servants who was in the court. The servants answered that Haman was in the court.

Although it was early, Haman had indeed entered the court. He wanted to ask the king to hang Mordecai on the gallows he had built. So the king called Haman before him.

Ahasuerus asked Haman what should be done for a man whom the king wanted to honor. Haman was so arrogant that he thought to himself, "Whom would the king delight to honor more than me?" (Esther 6:6).

Haman thought of what he wanted most. He said that servants should bring clothes that the king himself had worn. They should bring out the king's own horse, as well. One of the king's most noble princes should take the clothes and put them on the man whom the king wanted to honor. Then the prince would put that man on the king's horse and lead him all throughout the city shouting before him that this was how the king honored those who pleased him.

The king was pleased with Haman's idea. He told Haman, "Hurry, take the robe and the horse, as you have suggested, and do so for Mordecai the Jew who sits within the king's gate! Leave nothing undone of all that you have spoken" (Esther 6:10).

Haman did as the king commanded, but he did not do it joyfully. He was bitterly angry that he was not being honored. Worse still, the man he most wanted to kill was enjoying the reward Haman thought belonged to himself.

The people in the streets honored Mordecai, and Haman continued to grow more angry. When the procession ended, Haman went home in mourning. He told his wife and friends what had happened, and his wife warned him that he would fall before Mordecai.

Questions

1. When the king looked through the book of records, he discover that Mordecai stopped a _____ on his life.

2. When asked for advice, _____ thought the king wanted to honor him.

3. Everything Haman suggested was done to honor _____.

Thought Question

Why do you think the king could not sleep and ended up wanting to honor Mordecai at the very time that Haman was trying to kill Mordecai?

Catechism

Question 25: In the covenant of life, what did God require Adam to do?

Answer 25: To obey God perfectly

Memory Verse

Philippians 2:14

Do all things without complaining and disputing,

LESSON 162

Haman's Reward

Esther 6:14–8:2

Soon men came to bring Haman to Esther's banquet. Haman went to enjoy the banquet. That night the king asked Esther again what it was that she wanted.

Esther answered, "If I have found favor in your sight, O king, and if it pleases the king, let my life be given me at my petition, and my people at my request. For we have been sold, my people and I, to be destroyed, to be killed, and to be annihilated" (Esther 7:3-4). The word *annihilated* means "to destroy to the point as if [they] never existed."

She went on to say that if her people had only been sold as slaves, then she would have requested nothing. Yet she could not sit by and watch her entire nation be destroyed. Esther asked the king to help her and her people.

When the king heard his wife's request, he became very angry. He wanted to know who would do such a thing as threaten to kill the queen and all her people. Esther answered that the enemy was Haman, a truly wicked man.

The king rose from the table in anger and went out to walk in the palace garden. Haman knew he was in danger. He got up from his place at the table and fell across the queen's couch to beg Esther for his life. At that moment, the king returned and became even angrier with Haman. He did not like Haman to be so close to his wife.

Some servants recognized how angry King Ahasuerus was. They covered Haman's face with a cloth so that the king did not have to see his face anymore. They knew Haman was about to die. Then one servant told the king about the gallows Haman had made for Mordecai. The king immediately commanded that Haman was to be hanged on the gallows he had built.

So Haman died on the gallows he had built for Mordecai. The Lord punished his wickedness and protected His people, the Jews.

Then Esther told the king about Haman's plot to destroy the Jews. The king knew about the decree, but he had not known why the decree had been made.

Finally, Esther told Ahasuerus that Mordecai was her cousin. The king was pleased and made Mordecai his new prince. Haman was dead, so the king needed a new man to overlook his affairs. Thus, Mordecai was given the highest office in all of Persia next only to the king.

Questions

1. The king was _____ when he heard Esther's request.

2. Haman died by hanging on the _____ he had built for Mordecai.

3. Whom did the king promote to take over Haman's old job? _____

Thought Question

Why did Esther choose this time to tell Ahasuerus that she was a Jew?

Catechism

Question 26: What did God promise in the covenant of life?

Answer 26: To reward Adam with life if he obeyed God perfectly

Memory Verse

Philippians 2:14

Do all things without complaining and disputing,

LESSON 163

Purim

Esther 8:3–9:32

Haman was dead, but the evil he had done could not be completely undone. His decree had gone throughout all the land with the king's seal. Even the king could not change the decree.

Once more Esther spoke to the king. She fell at his feet and, weeping, begged him to spare the lives of her people. Esther still found favor in the king's sight, and he held out his golden scepter to her.

This time, Esther suggested that the king undo the decree Haman had written. The king told Esther that he could not undo what had been done. However, he did tell Esther that Mordecai, now a powerful and important man, could write a second decree with the king's seal.

Mordecai quickly wrote the second decree and sent it throughout the entire kingdom. This decree was also signed in the king's name and sealed with the king's seal. The new decree said that on the day that all the Jews were to be killed, the Jews were allowed to fight back. Jews could defend themselves and kill anyone who tried to kill them.

The Jews throughout the kingdom rejoiced. They had been saved! The entire land knew of both proclamations, and they were amazed. Some even became Jews themselves because the fear of the Jews came upon them.

When the day of the proclamations finally arrived, the Jews were ready. The people who hated the Jews thought they would defeat the Jews. Instead, the opposite happened. Many powerful people helped the Jews because they feared Mordecai now that he was such an important man. The Jews overcame all of their enemies and captured the ten sons of Haman.

Esther asked the king to allow the Jews in Shushan to defend themselves the next day. Also, she wanted Haman's sons to be hanged. So the next day, Haman's sons were all hanged on the gallows their father had built while the Jews continued to defend themselves from anyone who tried to harm them.

The rest of the kingdom had also been fighting. Thousands of wicked people had been killed. The second day, while the Jews of Shushan were hanging Haman's sons, the rest of the Jews throughout the nation rested and celebrated.

Then Mordecai sent letters to the Jews throughout the entire nation. He commanded the Jews to celebrate the fourteenth and fifteenth days of the month each year in remembrance of the terrible times the Jews had survived.

These two days were called the Feast of Purim. To this day, Jews keep that Feast of Purim and remember the time when their race was saved from destruction.

Questions

1. The king helped Esther's people by letting them defend themselves against those who tried to _____ them.

2. All of Haman's sons were _____ .

3. The Feast of _____ is celebrated each year to remember when the Jews were saved from destruction.

Thought Question

Why was it important to remember the time the Jews were saved from destruction?

Catechism

Question 27: What did God threaten in the covenant of life?
Answer 27: To punish Adam with death if he disobeyed God

Memory Verse

Philippians 2:14
Do all things without complaining and disputing,

LESSON 164

Cumulative Review 15

The Women

Word Bank: Abigail Athaliah Bathsheba Esther Hannah Jezebel Michal servant girl Vashti wife

1. Job's _____ told him to curse God and die.

2. Who was Samuel's mother? _____

3. Who was David's first wife, the daughter of King Saul? _____

4. Who saved her husband from David by bringing David's army food? _____

5. David killed Uriah so he could have Uriah's wife, _____ .

6. Who was King Ahab's wicked wife? _____

7. Which wicked queen killed her own grandchildren? _____

8. An Israelite _____ _____ told Naaman to go to Elisha for help for his leprosy.

9. Who was Ahasuerus' first queen? _____

10. Whom did God use to save His people from Haman? _____

Catechism

Question 28: Did Adam keep the covenant of life?
Answer 28: No. He sinned against God.

Memory Verse

Philippians 2:14
Do all things without complaining and disputing,

<hr>

LESSON 165

Week 33 Review

Memory Verse

Philippians 2:13–14

Catechism

Question 25: In the covenant of life, what did God require Adam to do?

Question 26: What did God promise in the covenant of life?

Question 27: What did God threaten in the covenant of life?

Question 28: Did Adam keep the covenant of life?

Question 91: What does the fourth commandment teach you?

Question 95: What is the fifth commandment?

Question 96: What does the fifth commandment teach you?

Activity

Fill in the Blank

Word Bank: banquet   defend   gallows   hanged   honor   Jews   Mordecai   Purim

1. Haman was excited because Esther invited him to a _____.

2. Haman built a _____ on which to hang Mordecai.

3. Ahasuerus wanted to know how to _____ a man who pleased the king.

4. Haman had to walk through the city and honor _____.

5. Esther was upset because Haman wanted to kill all the _____.

6. The king _____ Haman on the gallows meant for Mordecai.

7. The king proclaimed that the Jews could _____ themselves.

8. The day the Jews were saved came to be called _____.

234

Unit 34   *Ezra and Nehemiah*

LESSON 166

Ezra, Teacher of the Law

Ezra 7:1–28

Back in Judah, where some captives had returned and rebuilt the temple, the people still lived under the rule of the Persian king. Judah had no king of its own.

A Jewish man named Ezra was living in Persia at this time. He had spent his whole life studying the Law of God. Ezra also spent much time teaching other people about God's Law. He was known for teaching God's Law throughout all of Persia. Even the king knew of Ezra.

God gave Ezra the desire to go to Judah and to teach the holy Law of God to the people who had returned there. So Ezra asked the King Artaxerxes to let him return to Judah.

The king was kind. Not only did he let Ezra go to Judah, but he also said that any other Jews who wanted to, could go with Ezra. The king also gave the Jews more gold and silver as an offering to God.

Judah was carried into captivity as punishment for their sins. Yet not all the Jews were wicked, and many righteous men had become a good influence throughout Persia. God had blessed the kings of Babylon and Persia through the Jews.

Through the Jews, Nebuchadnezzar had learned of God's power and might. All the people were astounded by God's power when He saved Shadrach, Meshach, and Abed-Nego from the fiery furnace. Nebuchadnezzar had even praised God with his own mouth after his return from living seven years as a beast in the field.

King Darius had seen God's power when Daniel was delivered from the lion's den. King Cyrus had allowed the Jews to return home. Then he and King Darius had both sent money and provisions with the Jews who were returning to Judah for the first time.

Many people within the kingdom of Persia had never heard of God before. Now they were seeing His power, truth, and goodness through the lives of His people. Many heathen people turned from their sin and trusted in the God of the Jews.

So the captivity of the Jews had brought blessing and knowledge of the one true God to the heathen people of the kingdoms of Babylon and Persia. The knowledge of God would never completely leave this land, for we know that the wise men who came to visit the baby Jesus came from these lands.

Still, it was time for more Jews to return to the land God had promised them. Now, as Ezra prepared to bring a second group of captives home, King Artaxerxes gave all kinds of provisions for the temple. Other nobles from Persia gave gifts to the Jews, as well. Finally, the king gave Ezra the authority to set up judges over the people, to teach the Law of God to the Jews, and to keep them all living according to that Law.

Questions

1. Ezra spent his life studying and _____ the Law of God.

2. Ezra wanted to teach the _____ of _____ when he went to Judah.

3. The Jews brought _____ and knowledge of God to the people who had taken them captive.

Thought Question

Why might God have used the punishment of the Jews to bring blessing to other people?

Catechism

Question 29: What is sin?
Answer 29: Sin is any lack of conformity to, or transgression of, the law of God.

Memory Verse

Philippians 2:15
That you may become blameless and harmless, children of God without fault in the midst of a crooked and perverse generation, among whom you shine as lights in the world.

LESSON 167

Ezra Travels to Jerusalem

Ezra 8:15–36

About 7,000 people returned to Judah with Ezra. For three days, the company camped by the side of a river. There, before they had actually started, Ezra proclaimed a fast. They spent the time in prayer, asking God to guide them and to take care of them on their long journey.

Ezra and the people had 700 miles of land to travel across, and they would meet many dangers on the road. Ezra knew they would need God's help. He said, "I was ashamed to request of the king an escort of soldiers and horsemen to help us against the enemy on the road, because we had spoken to the king, saying, 'The hand of our God is upon all those for good who seek Him, but His power and His wrath are against all those who forsake Him'" (Ezra 8:22). So the people fasted and prayed, and God listened to their prayers.

While they were at the river, Ezra discovered that no Levites could be found among his company. So he sent for some Levites to come with them so they could have some ministers of the house of God. More than 250 Levites answered Ezra's call and joined the company of Israelites at the river. Ezra chose twenty-two of the priests and charged them to take care of the gold and silver objects that the king had given to the Israelites.

Then the people began their journey. It was a very long, hard journey. Yet God was watching over His little group of people. God led them safely the entire way.

Four months after they left, Ezra and the rest of the people with him finally arrived at Jerusalem. Eighty years had passed since the first group of Israelites had returned home, and many of the people who had made that first journey were now dead.

When they reached Jerusalem, Ezra and the priests put the gold and silver objects in the temple and offered sacrifices as a burnt offering to the Lord. They were thankful for His provision for them and joyful to be in Jerusalem.

Questions

1. Ezra was _____ to ask the king for protection because he did not want the king to think God could not do it.

2. Who was missing from the group that was going back to Jerusalem? _____

3. Who protected the Israelites on their journey? _____

Thought Question

Why was it better to trust God than the king for protection?

Catechism

Question 30: What is meant by lack of conformity?
Answer 30: Not being or doing what God requires

Memory Verse

Philippians 2:15
That you may become blameless and harmless, children of God without fault in the midst of a crooked and perverse generation, among whom you shine as lights in the world.

LESSON 168

What Ezra Found

Ezra 9:1–10:44

After Ezra arrived, some of the princes of Israel who had been living there for some time came to Ezra and told him that, sadly, many of the Jews who lived in Judah had forgotten God's command that they should never marry any of the heathen people living around them. Some of the rulers had been the worst and led the way in this sin. Many of the people had fallen into sin and were now married to women from the surrounding heathen nations.

Ezra was horrified when he heard this. He tore his clothes and began to mourn. Others who sorrowed over this sin came and mourned with him. It was right for them to mourn, for Israel had just suffered captivity because of their idolatry. If the Jews married heathen wives, they would soon slip right back into idolatry and forget God completely.

Ezra mourned all day. In the evening, he fell to his knees and prayed to God. He was ashamed to lift his face before God, but still he confessed his peoples' sins and asked that the Jews should not be forgotten forever.

While Ezra was praying, a great company of men, women, and children came together, weeping because of their sins. One man said to Ezra, "Let us make a covenant with our God to put away all these wives and those who have been born to them" (Ezra 10:3).

So they called a meeting. It was decided that all the men who had taken heathen wives must come before Ezra, the priest, and one or two other chief men. After due judgment was given, the guilty men confessed their sin and put away their heathen wives and the children of their heathen wives.

Questions

1. The Jews who had returned had fallen into the sin of marrying heathen _____.

2. Ezra tore his clothes and _____ when he heard the news of this sin.

3. The guilty men _____ their sin and put away their foreign wives.

Thought Question

Why was it important for the Jews to put away their heathen wives and never see them again?

Catechism

Question 31: What is meant by transgression?
Answer 31: Doing what God forbids

Memory Verse

Philippians 2:15
That you may become blameless and harmless, children of God without fault in the midst of a crooked and perverse generation, among whom you shine as lights in the world.

LESSON 169

Nehemiah, the King's Cupbearer

Nehemiah 1:1–2:10

Back in Persia, a Jewish man named Nehemiah held the important office of king's cupbearer. This position was only given to very trustworthy people. The king's cupbearer had to taste every cup of wine that he handed to the king so that no one would have a chance to poison the king.

One day, a man who had been living in Judah came back to the royal city of Persia. This man brought bad news. The people in Jerusalem were in great trouble and distress. He said, "The wall of Jerusalem is also broken down, and its gates are burned with fire" (Nehemiah 1:3).

When Nehemiah heard this news, he was filled with sorrow. Nehemiah fasted and prayed, but he still had to work. As he went about his work, he prayed to God to help Jerusalem. His sadness for his people showed on his face.

The king, Artaxerxes, noticed that his cupbearer was sad. Nehemiah had never been sad in the king's presence before. So the king asked him what was wrong. Nehemiah was afraid, but he answered the king anyway. He asked the king why he should not be sad when the city of his fathers was laid waste and its gates were burned with fire.

The king answered very graciously and asked what he could do to help Nehemiah. This was the same king who had allowed Ezra to return to Jerusalem about fifteen years earlier. This fact, and the king's gracious answer, helped Nehemiah answer the king boldly.

Nehemiah prayed to God and then answered, "If it pleases the king, and if your servant has found favor in your sight, I ask that you send me to Judah, to the city of my fathers' tombs, that I may rebuild it" (Nehemiah 2:5).

Then the king asked how long Nehemiah would be gone and when he would return. Nehemiah asked to be gone for twelve years. Then he asked the king for letters to the governors of the countries beyond the Euphrates River so that they would all let him travel safely through their countries. Finally, Nehemiah asked the king for a letter to the keeper of the king's forest, telling him to give the Jews wood to build the wall of the city and a palace for their governor.

The king granted everything that Nehemiah had asked because God's hand was upon him. Artaxerxes also sent soldiers and horsemen with Nehemiah to keep him safe. So Nehemiah reached Jerusalem safely.

Questions

1. Nehemiah was the _____ for the king.

2. Nehemiah was sad because Jerusalem's walls were _____ and its gates burned.

3. How many years did Nehemiah get to stay in Jerusalem? _____

Thought Question

What does it mean that the Persian king granted all Nehemiah's requests because the hand of the Lord was upon him?

Catechism

Question 32: What does every sin deserve?
Answer 32: The wrath and curse of God

Memory Verse

Philippians 2:15

That you may become blameless and harmless, children of God without fault in the midst of a crooked and perverse generation, among whom you shine as lights in the world.

LESSON 170

Week 34 Review

Memory Verse

Philippians 2:13–15

Catechism

Question 29: What is sin?

Question 30: What is meant by lack of conformity?

Question 31: What is meant by transgression?

Question 32: What does every sin deserve?

Question 97: What is the sixth commandment?

Question 98: What does the sixth commandment teach you?

Question 99: What is the seventh commandment?

Question 100: What does the seventh command-ment teach you?

Activity

Dot-to-Dot

Connect the dots to see what Nehemiah's job was when he worked for the king.

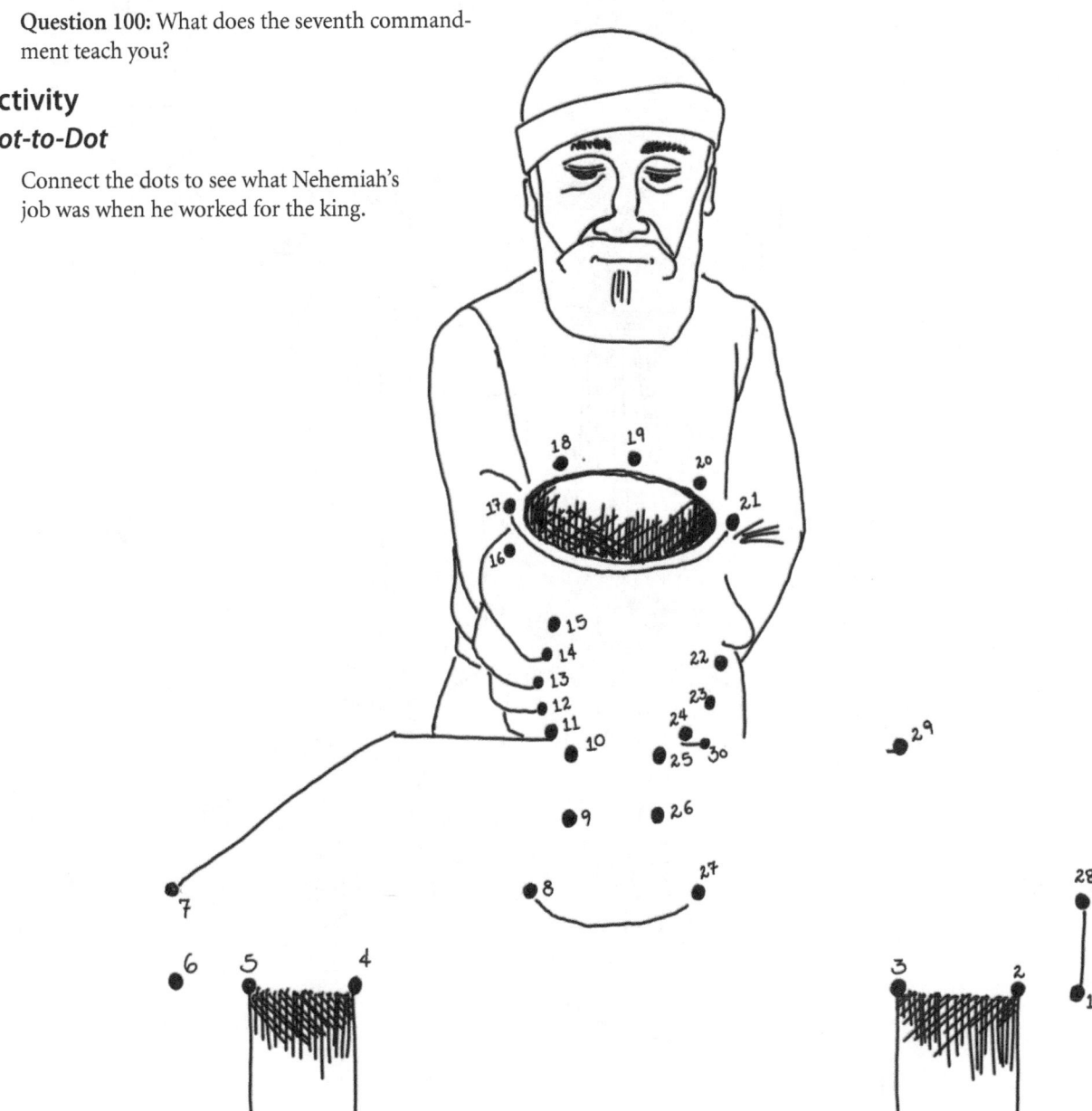

Unit 35 — Rebuilding the Walls of Jerusalem

LESSON 171

The Walls of Jerusalem

Nehemiah 2:11–4:20

After a short rest, Nehemiah and a few other men mounted horses. At night and in secret, these men rode all the way around the city of Jerusalem to see what condition it was in.

They discovered that Jerusalem was in very bad shape. The walls were broken down, and the gates were burned. Heaps of rubbish lay throughout the city. The city's desolate condition disturbed Nehemiah very much. The next day, he went to the rulers of Jerusalem and told them they were going to rebuild the walls of Jerusalem.

The rulers were eager to rebuild the walls. Because the Persian king had made him governor, Nehemiah gave orders. He portioned out the wall, all the way around the city. Each family was to rebuild the part of the wall that was closest to their house.

Some of the Samaritans who lived in or near Jerusalem began to make trouble for Nehemiah. They laughed scornfully as the people began to rebuild. They came and asked Nehemiah what he was doing and if he planned on rebelling against the king of Persia. Nehemiah answered, "The God of heaven Himself will prosper us; therefore we His servants will arise and build, but you have no heritage or right or memorial in Jerusalem" (Nehemiah 2:20).

So the Jews continued to rebuild the wall. Then the Samaritans came again. This time, they mocked the Jews mercilessly. They would not leave the builders alone. This time,

Nehemiah cried out, "Hear, O our God, for we are despised" (Nehemiah 4:4).

The Jews continued building the wall. They worked well and quickly. Soon the wall was almost done. When the Samaritans realized that the Jews were ignoring their mockery, they planned to come and fight against the Jews, to stop the work.

Once again, Nehemiah and the Jews prayed to God and continued building. This time, they set up a guard of men with swords, spears, and bows to protect the people who were building the wall. Nehemiah told the people not to be afraid, for God was on their side, and He is mighty and strong. He told them to fight for their wives, mothers, brothers, and children.

The Samaritans heard that the Jews were ready to fight, and they knew they had been defeated already. From that time on, half of Nehemiah's men built the wall while the other half stood guard with weapons. Also, the people who were building, built with one hand and carried a sword in the other. Everyone had a sword by his side.

Nehemiah also had a man with a trumpet stand near him. Because the wall was so large, it was hard to hear what was happening at other places along the wall. Nehemiah told the workers to come quickly to wherever they heard the call of the trumpet, for that would be their signal that they were being attacked. Nehemiah knew that God would fight for them and the wall would be built.

Questions

1. Whom did Nehemiah turn to for help when the Samaritans caused trouble? _____

2. Nehemiah and his servants set up a _____ to protect themselves when they heard that the Samaritans were planning an attack.

3. The trumpet call was a _____ that they were being attacked and to come and help fight.

Thought Question

Why was it important for the builders to build with one hand and hold a sword with the other?

Catechism

Question 33: What was the sin of our first parents?
Answer 33: Eating the forbidden fruit

Memory Verse

Philippians 2:16
Holding fast the word of life, so that I may rejoice in the day of Christ that I have not run in vain or labored in vain.

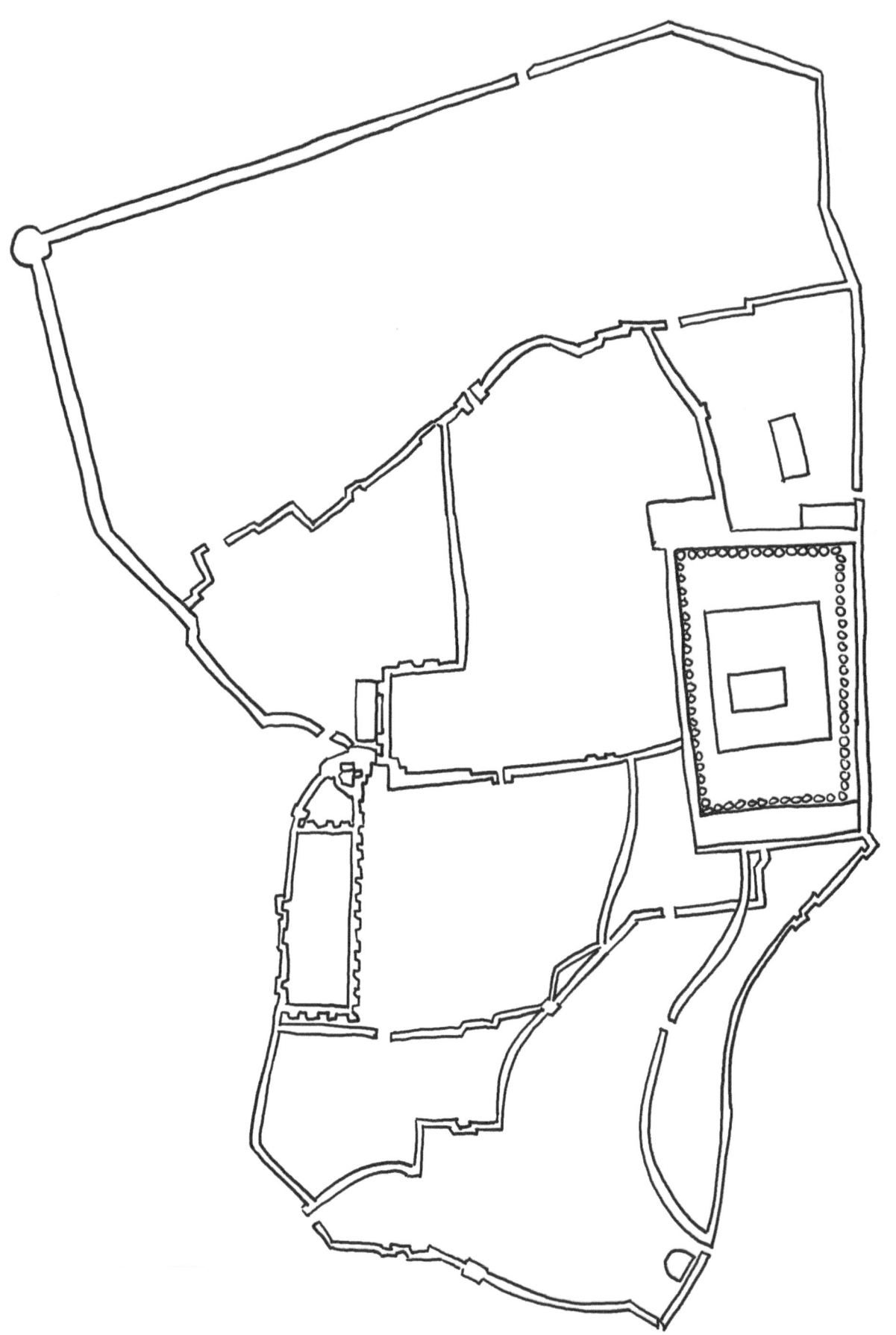

LESSON 172

The Wall of Jerusalem Is Finally Rebuilt

Nehemiah 4:21–7:73

Nehemiah and his men worked hard to rebuild the walls and keep them safe. They worked all day and then stayed in the city at night as guards. They were so busy and stayed so alert that none of the men took their clothes off at all except to wash them. They were always prepared to fight.

During this time, many of the Jews were very poor. Governors before Nehemiah had made life hard for the people and taken many taxes from them. Nehemiah, however, made life as easy as he could for the people. He did not even accept payment for his role as governor, and he fed as many people as he could from his own provisions because he knew how poor and hungry the people were.

At last, the wall was almost complete. All the men had to do was hang the gates in the walls. Once more, the Samaritans came to cause trouble.

The leaders of the Samaritans sent a message to Nehemiah asking him to come down and meet with them. Yet Nehemiah knew that they only wanted to hurt him and try to stop the building of the wall. So he told the men he was doing a great work and was too busy to meet with them.

The Samaritans kept sending messages to Nehemiah. Four times they sent for him, and four times he refused. The fifth time, they sent a new message and accused Nehemiah of building the walls so that he could become king of Jerusalem himself. They threatened to tell the king of Persia what Nehemiah was doing.

So Nehemiah answered and told them that he was doing no such thing. He also continued to pray to God for protection from the wicked men and their lies.

Finally, the wall was finished. It took fifty-two days to build the wall of Jerusalem. When their enemies heard that the wall was complete, they were afraid, for they knew that the work was God's doing.

Nehemiah had done a remarkable thing in completing the wall in less than two months. He and all the men had worked very hard, with all their might, and God had blessed their efforts.

After the wall was complete, Nehemiah gathered all the families that had come back from Babylon. He found an old book that contained a list of all the true Jewish families. He looked up the record in this book to see if anyone before him that day was not a true Jew.

This was a long task, for there were forty-two thousand people gathered before him. When the task was complete, several families of the priests had not been mentioned in the book. These families were no longer allowed to serve as priests in God's temple.

Then all the people went to live in their own homes in their own towns.

Questions

1. While the men of Jerusalem rebuilt the wall, they did not take their clothes off except to wash them because _____

    they needed to stay _____ for an enemy attack.

2. The Samaritans threatened to tell the king of Persia that _____ wanted to make himself king.

3. How many days did it take to build the wall? _____

Thought Question

When the enemies of the Jews realized that the walls of Jerusalem were rebuilt, why were they afraid?

Catechism

Question 34: Who tempted Adam and Eve to this sin?
Answer 34: Satan tempted Eve first, and then he used her to tempt Adam.

Memory Verse

Philippians 2:16
Holding fast the word of life, so that I may rejoice in the day of Christ that I have not run in vain or labored in vain.

LESSON 173

Celebrating the Law of God

Nehemiah 8:1–10:39; Malachi 3:1–4:6

After all of these things, Nehemiah and Ezra, who was still alive and teaching God's Law to the Jews, called the people together to a great meeting. Ezra stood up on a high wooden platform and blessed the Lord, the great God. The people answered "Amen, Amen!" (Nehemiah 8:6). They lifted up their hands to God, bowed their heads, and worshiped the Lord with their faces to the ground.

Ezra and his helpers read from the Book of the Law of God. They explained the meaning of what was read so that the people would understand God's Law. From morning to noon they read. The people listened closely. As they listened, they wept, for many of them had never heard the Law of God read before.

Then Nehemiah, the governor, and Ezra, the scribe, said to the people, "This day is holy to the LORD your God; do not mourn nor weep…. Go your way, eat the fat, drink the sweet, and send portions for whom nothing is prepared; for this day is holy to our Lord. Do not sorrow, for the joy of the LORD is your strength" (Nehemiah 8:9–10). So all the people returned to their homes to eat, drink, and celebrate what the Lord had done for them. They were glad to return to the worship of their God.

On the next day, the people came together again. Again, Ezra read the Book of the Law of God. It was found in this book that the people were supposed to dwell in booths to celebrate the feast of the seventh month. Booths were temporary shelters made with tree branches and willows. These booths were to remind the people of the time when the Israelites left Egypt and lived in temporary shelters while they were in the wilderness for forty years. So the Jews obeyed and went to the Mount of Olives and cut olive, pine, and palm branches.

They made booths on the roofs of their houses and in their gardens.

Many people were happy to be returning to God and becoming true Israelites in His sight. They no longer wanted to be like the heathen nations around them. Yet some people still lived in wickedness.

Ezra read each day from the Law of God. The people confessed their sin to God and praised His name for being their God. They made a solemn promise to God to walk in His Law and to keep all His commandments.

While Nehemiah was governor in Jerusalem, a prophet named Malachi lived and prophesied. He wrote what is now the last book of the Old Testament in our Bibles.

Malachi told the people that the promised Savior of God's people would come very soon. He said, "But to you who fear My name the Sun of Righteousness shall arise" (Malachi 4:2). He also foretold the coming of John the Baptist, saying, "Behold, I will send you Elijah the prophet" (Malachi 4:5). Malachi used the name of Elijah, but we know from the New Testament that he meant John the Baptist (Matthew 3:2, 11:14, 17:10–13; cf. Isaiah 40:3).

To comfort the people who tried to serve God, Malachi reminded them that Jehovah listened to those who feared the Lord. Their names would be written in the Lord's book of remembrance, and those people would be the Lord's.

That is a comforting thought. Those who love God, and who often meet together to talk about Him, are the ones whom God will call His own. God loves those who serve Him, and He promises to always be with them, His own people.

Questions

1. Ezra read the Book of _____ _____ before the people.

2. Ezra and Nehemiah told the people that that day was a _____ day.

3. Malachi prophesied about the coming of _____ the Baptist and _____ .

Thought Question

Throughout all of Nehemiah, there is one thing Nehemiah does first whenever trouble arises. What is it? How is this an important lesson for how those who serve God ought to live?

Catechism

Question 35: How did Adam and Eve change when they sinned?
Answer 35: Instead of being holy and happy, they became sinful and miserable.

Memory Verse

Philippians 2:16
Holding fast the word of life, so that I may rejoice in the day of Christ that I have not run in vain or labored in vain.

LESSON 174

Cumulative Review 16

The Captives Return

Word Bank: cupbearer Cyrus Jesus Christ John Law marrying rebuilt swords teach walls Zerubbabel

1. Who decreed that the captives should return to Judah? _____

2. Who was in charge of rebuilding the temple? _____

3. When Ezra returned to Jerusalem, he wanted to _____ the Law of God to the people.

4. When Ezra returned, he found the people had sinned by _____ heathen wives.

5. Nehemiah's job for the king was _____.

6. Nehemiah was sad because the _____ of Jerusalem were broken down.

7. Nehemiah and his men _____ the walls of Jerusalem.

8. The people needed to keep _____ with them at all times while they built the walls.

9. When the wall was complete, Ezra read the _____ of God to the people.

10. Malachi prophesied the coming of _____ the Baptist and _____ _____, the Savior of God's people.

Catechism

Question 36: Did Adam act for himself alone in the covenant of life?
Answer 36: No. He represented the whole human race.

Memory Verse

Philippians 2:16
Holding fast the word of life, so that I may rejoice in the day of Christ that I have not run in vain or labored in vain.

LESSON 175

Week 35 Review

Memory Verse

Philippians 2:13–16

Catechism

Question 33: What was the sin of our first parents?

Question 34: Who tempted Adam and Eve to this sin?

Question 35: How did Adam and Eve change when they sinned?

Question 36: Did Adam act for himself alone in the covenant of life?

Question 101: What is the eighth commandment?

Question 102: What does the eighth commandment teach you?

Question 103: What is the ninth commandment?

Question 104: What does the ninth commandment teach you?

Activity

Matching

Match the items on the right to their descriptions on the left.

1. ____ Nehemiah had to repair this.

2. ____ He prospered the Jews in their work.

3. ____ Nehemiah set these up to protect the working people.

4. ____ Each builder held this in one hand while he built.

5. ____ The number of days it took to build the wall.

6. ____ Ezra read this to the people when the wall was done.

A. Sword

B. God

C. Fifty-two

D. Guards

E. Book of the Law of God

F. wall of Jerusalem

Unit 36   Review

LESSON 176

Final Review 1

True or False

1. Job was a righteous man who never cursed God. **True/False**

2. Samuel's mother was named Sarah. **True/False**

3. Saul's oldest son was named Jonathan. **True/False**

4. David had one of his own men, Uriah, killed. **True/False**

5. David's son Solomon tried to kill his father. **True/False**

6. When Rehoboam did not listen to wise advisors, Israel split in two. **True/False**

7. Jezebel rewarded Naboth for having a beautiful vineyard. **True/False**

8. Lions came and mauled the boys who mocked Elisha. **True/False**

9. Joash acted righteously until Jehoiada the priest died. **True/False**

10. Isaiah prophesied the coming of Jesus Christ. **True/False**

11. Josiah became king when he was thirty. **True/False**

12. God gave Hezekiah twenty extra years to live. **True/False**

13. Baruch was Jeremiah's scribe. **True/False**

14. Daniel and his friends refused to eat vegetables. **True/False**

15. Nebuchadnezzar became like an animal for seven years. **True/False**

16. Belshazzar saw a hand writing on the wall. **True/False**

17. Mordecai raised his cousin Ruth, a young Jewish girl. **True/False**

18. Zerubbabel was in charge of rebuilding the temple. **True/False**

LESSON 177

Final Review 2

Maze

Help David and his mighty men escape from Saul.

LESSON 178

Final Review 3

Matching

Draw lines to match the people on the right to their descriptions on the left.

1. ten of his children were killed in one day   Hannah

2. died when he heard the ark was captured   Job

3. prayed diligently for a son   Eli

4. killed a lion and bear with a sling and stone   Bathsheba

5. Solomon's mother   David

---

6. The Lord called him Jedidiah.   Judah

7. one of the two tribes left to Rehoboam   Elisha

8. the most wicked king of Israel   Solomon

9. had 400 prophets of Baal killed   Ahab

10. helped Naaman get rid of his leprosy   Elijah

---

11. saved from wicked Queen Athaliah by his aunt   Daniel

12. the Law of God was found during his reign   Haman

13. was thrown in a pit of mud   Jeremiah

14. was thrown into a lions' den   Joash

15. wanted to kill Mordecai, Esther's cousin   Josiah

LESSON 179

Final Review 4

Dot-to-Dot

Connect the dots to see who appeared before the king's throne.

LESSON 180

Week 36 Review

Memory Verse

1 Timothy 3:16–17; Psalm 23; Galatians 5:22–23; Exodus 20:1–18; Psalm 1; Philippians 2:13–16

Catechism

Question 105: What is the tenth commandment?

Question 106: What does the tenth commandment teach you?

Question 107: Can you keep the Ten Commandments perfectly?

Question 108: Of what use are the Ten Commandments to you?

Activity

Fill in the Blank

Word Bank: bow Esther fiery furnace Goliath Jezebel Jonathan letter Mordecai Naboth prayed send

1. David killed _____ and was friends with _____.

2. Ahab's wife, _____, killed _____ for his vineyard.

3. God called Isaiah, and he answered, "Here am I—_____ me."

4. Hezekiah was afraid, so he took his enemy's _____, spread it before the Lord, and _____ with all his might.

5. Daniel's three friends refused to _____ to the idol and were thrown into a _____.

6. _____ uncovered a plot to kill the king and also told _____ to go before the king to save her people.

Answer Key

Lesson 1
1. ten
2. Satan
3. permission

Lesson 2
1. fire
2. wind
3. blessed (or worshiped)

Lesson 3
1. sick
2. curse
3. friends

Lesson 4
1. sins
2. sinned
3. glorify

Lesson 5
Week 1 Review
4 Job's three friends come to visit.

3 Job gets boils.

1 Satan first appears before God.

2 Job's children are killed.

Lesson 6
1. no
2. alive, God
3. sinning

Lesson 7
1. young
2. greater
3. God

Lesson 8
1. whirlwind
2. answers
3. God

Lesson 9
1. behemoth
2. God
3. twice

Lesson 10
Week 2 Review
1. True
2. False
3. False
4. True
5. False
6. True
7. True
8. True

Lesson 11
1. Hannah
2. Eli
3. Samuel

Lesson 12
1. tabernacle
2. wicked

Lesson 13
1. Eli
2. God
3. punishment

Lesson 14
1. ark, covenant
2. captured

Lesson 15
Week 3 Review
1. Hannah
2. Philistines
3. Samuel
4. Eli

Lesson 16
1. Dagon
2. cows
3. afraid

Lesson 17
1. Samuel
2. God

Lesson 18
1. king
2. sad
3. Saul

Lesson 19
1. Samuel
2. hiding
3. Saul

Lesson 20
Week 4 Review
1. Philistines
2. face
3. judge
4. king
5. God
6. Saul
7. Benjamin
8. hid

Lesson 21

1. eyes
2. Saul
3. no

Lesson 22

1. Jonathan
2. offering (or sacrifice)

Lesson 23

1. armorbearer
2. God
3. eat

Lesson 24
Cumulative Review 1

1. Samuel
2. king
3. Saul
4. Jonathan

Oral Questions

1. Satan could take away all Job's possessions, children, and health; but he could not kill Job.
2. They thought Job had sinned and would not confess and repent.
3. God is above man, His ways are not our ways, and we have no right to question God.
4. (*The student is required to give only three answers.*) seas, waves, clouds, thunder, lightning, …

Lesson 26

1. Amalekites
2. regret
3. kingdom

Lesson 27

1. Jesse's

2. David
3. harp

Lesson 28

1. Goliath
2. David

Lesson 29

1. God
2. five
3. sword

Lesson 30
Week 6 Review

__C__ Saul
__E__ God
__B__ Samuel
__D__ Goliath
__A__ David

Lesson 31

1. Jonathan
2. Michal
3. jealous

Lesson 32

1. David
2. kill

Lesson 33

1. crazy
2. killed
3. Jonathan

Lesson 34

1. Saul
2. spared
3. king

Lesson 35
Week 7 Review

__1__ Saul throws a spear at David, trying to kill him.

__3__ Saul kills the priest who helped David.
__2__ Jonathan tells David to run away.
__4__ David spares Saul's life in the cave.

Lesson 36

1. rudeness
2. Abigail
3. died

Lesson 37

1. spear, pitcher
2. Ziklag

Lesson 38

1. afraid
2. Samuel
3. sons

Lesson 39

1. Philistines
2. Ziklag

Lesson 40
Week 8 Review

1. False
2. True
3. True
4. True
5. False
6. False
7. True
8. True

Lesson 41

1. sword
2. buried
3. Song of the Bow

Lesson 42

1. Abner

2. Judah
3. Jerusalem

Lesson 43

1. ark of God
2. disobeying (or breaking)
3. David's son

Lesson 44

1. five
2. Jonathan's

Lesson 45
Week 9 Review

1. David
2. Asahel
3. Uzzah
4. Joab
5. Abner
6. Saul
7. Jonathan
8. Mephibosheth

Lesson 46

1. Uriah
2. He died.
3. Jedidiah

Lesson 47

1. Absalom
2. hearts
3. fled

Lesson 48

1. Absalom
2. spy
3. stones, cursed

Lesson 49
Cumulative Review 2

1. mourned, cursed
2. God

3. ark, covenant
4. Saul
5. sword
6. Jonathan
7. king
8. fell
9. Solomon

Lesson 50
Week 10 Review

1. Bathsheba
2. Uriah
3. Nathan
4. Solomon
5. Jedidiah
6. Absalom
7. David
8. Hushai

Lesson 51

1. Hushai
2. well

Lesson 52

1. gently
2. hair
3. Joab

Lesson 53

1. wept (or mourned)
2. disgraced
3. yes

Lesson 54

1. mercy (or kindness)
2. Jerusalem
3. praised, sang

Lesson 56

1. Bathsheba
2. Adonijah

Lesson 57

1. temple
2. wisdom

Lesson 58

1. temple
2. obeyed

Lesson 59
Cumulative Review 3

1. Job
2. Hannah
3. God
4. Samuel
5. Jonathan
6. Goliath
7. Abigail
8. Uriah's
9. Absalom
10. Joab

Lesson 60
Week 12 Review

1. **B**
2. **D**
3. **A**
4. **E**
5. **C**
6. **A**
7. **D**
8. **B**

Lesson 61

1. palace (or home), cities
2. queen

Lesson 62

1. idols (or false gods)
2. Jeroboam
3. Judah, Benjamin

Lesson 63

1. calves
2. Asa

Lesson 64

1. heathen
2. Ahijah
3. Baasha

Lesson 65
Week 13 Review

2 Rehoboam, Solomon's son, became king of Israel.

1 The queen of Sheba visits Israel.

4 The king of Israel splits into two kingdoms—Israel and Judah.

3 Rehoboam increases the taxes against the advice of his wise, older advisors.

5 Jeroboam builds golden calves for Israel to worship.

Lesson 66

1. million
2. God
3. disobeyed

Lesson 67

1. Ahab, Jezebel
2. Jericho
3. Elijah

Lesson 68

1. ravens
2. food
3. lived (or breathed)

Lesson 69

1. cave
2. troubler
3. Ahab

Lesson 70
Week 14 Review

1. True
2. False
3. True
4. True
5. False
6. True
7. True
8. False

Lesson 71

1. fire
2. wicked, Baal

Lesson 72

1. Jezebel
2. loved, obeyed
3. 7,000

Lesson 73

1. Elisha
2. Ben-Hadad

Lesson 74
Cumulative Review 4

1. Samuel
2. Saul
3. battle
4. Solomon

Oral Questions

1. God's ways are mightier and better than man's ways, and sometimes His ways are beyond our understanding.

2. He knew that the people liked David and that David would be Israel's next king.

3. Daily God sent ravens to bring food to Elijah.

Lesson 75
Week 15 Review

1. Baal
2. God
3. water
4. kill
5. Jezebel
6. Elijah
7. voice
8. Elisha

Lesson 76

1. hills
2. city wall
3. brother

Lesson 77

1. vineyard
2. God's Law
3. Naboth

Lesson 78

1. friends, Ahab
2. Jehoshaphat
3. bad things (or only evil)

Lesson 79

1. Ahab
2. prison
3. arrow

Lesson 80
Week 16 Review

1. hills
2. brother
3. vineyard
4. blasphemy
5. stone
6. eat
7. Law
8. lie

Lesson 81

1. window
2. burned, fire
3. spared (or saved)

Lesson 82

1. choir
2. fight, kill

Lesson 83

1. double portion
2. chariot
3. heaven

Lesson Lesson 84
Cumulative Review 5

1. Absalom
2. wisdom
3. Judah, Benjamin
4. Ahab, Jezebel
5. obeyed
6. Elisha
7. Naboth's
8. battle

Lesson 86

1. salt
2. bears
3. slaves

Lesson 87

1. room
2. Gehazi
3. sneezed

Lesson 88

1. servant
2. Jordan River
3. clean (or healthy)

Lesson 89

1. God
2. Gehazi
3. leprosy

Lesson 90
Week 18 Review

1. **B**
2. **C**
3. **A**
4. **F**
5. **G**
6. **D**
7. **H**
8. **E**

Lesson 91

1. Elisha
2. army
3. blindness

Lesson 92

1. siege
2. noise

Lesson 93

1. Hazael
2. king, Syria
3. cruel, wicked (or evil)

Lesson 94
Cumulative Review 6

1. Hannah
2. God
3. Saul
4. Goliath
5. Rehoboam
6. vineyard
7. chariot
8. servant

Lesson 95
Week 19 Review

2 The four lepers go into the Syrian camp.

4 Hazael kills Ben-Hadad.

1 The Lord made the Syrians hear a loud noise.

3 The hungry people trampled Jehoram's guard at the gate.

Lesson 96

1. killed
2. king, Israel
3. trumpets

Lesson 97

1. Jehoram
2. Jezebel

Lesson 98

1. sacrifice
2. God's Law
3. four

Lesson 99

1. killed
2. aunt
3. Jehoiada

Lesson 100
Week 20 Review

1. False
2. False
3. True
4. False
5. True
6. False
7. True
8. True
9. True
10. False

Lesson 101

1. Jehoiada
2. Zechariah
3. servants

Lesson 102

1. Jehoash
2. lived

Lesson 103

1. Amaziah
2. Israel
3. Lachish

Lesson 104
Cumulative Review 7

1. Jonathan
2. wept
3. Sheba
4. Jezebel
5. Elijah

Oral Questions

1. The prophets of Baal prayed all day, but Baal did not answer. Elijah prayed once to God, and He sent fire down to burn up Elijah's sacrifice.
2. God's army of horses and chariots surrounding them
3. His aunt hid him and his nurse from Athaliah.

Lesson 105
Week 21 Review

1. Zechariah
2. Hazael
3. Jehoiada
4. Joash
5. two servants
6. Elisha
7. Jehoash
8. Amaziah

Lesson 106

1. Nineveh
2. storm
3. prayed

Lesson 107

1. believed
2. withered
3. mercy

Lesson 108

1. Amos, Hosea
2. captivity

Lesson 109

1. incense
2. leper
3. high places

Lesson 110
Week 22 Review

1. Nineveh
2. ship
3. storm
4. overboard
5. fish
6. three
7. repented
8. angry
9. worm
10. mercy
11.

Lesson 111

1. send me
2. Christ (or Jesus)

Lesson 112

1. slaves
2. heathen altar
3. Damascus

Lesson 113

1. Assyria
2. disobeyed
3. lions

Lesson 114
Cumulative Review 8

1. Elihu
2. Eli
3. David
4. Jonathan
5. Solomon
6. Elijah
7. Elisha
8. Joash
9. Jonah
10. Christ

Lesson 116

1. mother
2. temple
3. Passover

Lesson 117

1. God
2. Sennacherib (or the Assyrians)
3. afraid (or fear)

Lesson 118

1. letter
2. stabbed
3. wept, prayed

Lesson 119
Cumulative Review 9

1. temple
2. Rehoboam
3. Israel
4. Judah
5. Ahab

6. Zechariah

7. Assyria

Oral Questions

1. He hid David while he spoke to King Saul, then helped David run away.

2. His hair caught him in a tree; when Joab found him, he killed him.

3. He spread the letter before the Lord and prayed over it.

Lesson 120
Week 24 Review

1. **D**
2. **G**
3. **E**
4. **A**
5. **B**
6. **F**
7. **H**
8. **C**

Lesson 121

1. fifty-five
2. captured
3. servants

Lesson 122

1. eight
2. God's Law
3. curses

Lesson 123

1. prophet
2. Bethel
3. shot (or killed, or wounded)

Lesson 124

1. Jeremiah
2. young
3. stocks

Lesson 125
Week 25 Review

2 Josiah commands his men to destroy the idols.

5 Josiah is shot by the archers of Egypt.

3 Hilkiah finds the Law of Moses.

4 Josiah has the Law read out loud to all the people.

1 Josiah becomes king at age eight.

Lesson 126

1. prison
2. Baruch
3. scroll, prophecies

Lesson 127

1. Nebuchadnezzar
2. pit, dungeon

Lesson 128

1. killed, eyes
2. seventy
3. punish

Lesson 129
Cumulative Review 10

1. Elisha
2. Micaiah
3. Isaiah
4. Jeremiah
5. Baruch

Oral Questions

1. Many wicked people were trying to kill him, he had been driven into the desert, and he did not know of any other righteous people who loved God.

2. The prophets of Baal prayed all day, but Baal did not answer. Elijah spoke one prayer to God, and He sent down fire to burn up Elijah's sacrifice.

Lesson 130
Week 26 Review

1. False
2. True
3. False
4. False
5. True
6. True
7. False
8. True

Lesson 131

1. wine, meat (or food)
2. God's Law
3. health, wisdom

Lesson 132

1. magicians
2. kill
3. prayed

Lesson 133

1. Kingdom
2. amazed

Lesson 134

1. idol, music
2. Shadrach, Meshach, Abed-Nego

Lesson 135
Week 27 Review

1. Nebuchadnezzar
2. Daniel
3. God
4. wise men
5. image (statue)
6. his and future kingdoms

7. golden idol

8. fiery furnace

Lesson 136

1. never

2. killed

3. fourth man

Lesson 137

1. tree, stump

2. silent

Lesson 138

1. Nebuchadnezzar

2. greatness (or power)

3. animal

Lesson 139
Cumulative Review 11

1. Saul

2. David

3. Solomon

4. Rehoboam

5. Jeroboam

6. Ahab

7. Hezekiah

8. Joash

9. Manasseh

10. Josiah

11. Hoshea

Lesson 140
Week 28 Review

1. music

2. seven

3. killed

4. four

5. God

6. fire

7. dream

8. animal

Lesson 141

1. dishes

2. fingers

3. MENE, TEKEL

Lesson 142

1. Belshazzar

2. river, walls

Lesson 143

1. Daniel

2. Darius, thirty

3. den, lions

Lesson 144
Cumulative Review 12

1. Saul, David

2. Job

3. Elijah

4. Jonah

5. Eli

6. Naboth

7. Daniel

8. Abed-Nego

9. Josiah

10. God

Lesson 146

1. three

2. Darius

3. tricked

Lesson 147

1. shut

2. princes

3. God, Daniel

Lesson 148

1. Isaiah

2. seventy

3. strongest

Lesson 149

1. cities

2. temple

3. glory

Lesson 150
Week 30 Review

3 Daniel is thrown into the lions' den.

2 The jealous princes catch Daniel praying to God.

5 Darius commands all the people to worship only Daniel's God.

1 Darius makes a decree that no one can worship anyone other than the king.

4 God shuts the lions' mouths and saves Daniel.

Lesson 151

1. Zerubbabel

2. Persia

3. Haggai, Zechariah

Lesson 152

1. Cyrus (or King Cyrus)

2. house, God

3. Passover

Lesson 153

1. week

2. Vashti

3. feasts

Lesson 154
Cumulative Review 13

1. Babylon

2. Zedekiah

3. Jeremiah

4. Daniel

5. Son

Oral Questions

1. He was shot with an arrow in battle.
2. They were angry with him for prophesying evil against them for their wickedness.
3. It was against God's Law for them to eat such food.
4. *Answers may vary.* He dug a new channel for the river that ran under the city walls, and he and his army walked on the riverbed under the walls.

Lesson 155
Week 31 Review

1. True
2. False
3. True
4. False
5. True
6. False
7. True
8. False

Lesson 156

1. refused (or disobeyed)
2. Mordecai
3. Esther
4. plot

Lesson 157

1. Haman
2. Mordecai
3. Jews

Lesson 158

1. kill
2. Haman
3. Mordecai

Lesson 159
Cumulative Review 14

1. Assyria
2. Hoshea
3. forever
4. Babylon
5. Nebuchadnezzar
6. Zedekiah
7. seventy years
8. Cyrus
9. Zerubbabel
10. temple

Lesson 160
Week 32 Review

1. D. Mordecai
2. A. Ahasuerus
3. B. Esther
4. B. Esther
5. D. Mordecai
6. C. Haman
7. D. Mordecai
8. B. Esther

Lesson 161

1. plot
2. Haman
3. Mordecai

Lesson 162

1. angry
2. gallows
3. Mordecai

Lesson 163

1. kill
2. hanged
3. Purim

Lesson 164
Cumulative Review 15

1. wife
2. Hannah
3. Michal
4. Abigail
5. Bathsheba
6. Jezebel
7. Athaliah
8. servant girl
9. Vashti
10. Esther

Lesson 165
Week 33 Review

1. banquet
2. gallows
3. honor
4. Mordecai
5. Jews
6. hanged
7. defend
8. Purim

Lesson 166

1. teaching
2. Law, God
3. blessing

Lesson 167

1. ashamed
2. Levites
3. God

Lesson 168

1. wives
2. mourned
3. confessed

Lesson 169

1. cupbearer
2. broken
3. twelve

Lesson 171

1. God
2. guard
3. signal

Lesson 172

1. alert
2. Nehemiah
3. fifty-two

Lesson 173

1. God's Law
2. holy
3. John, Jesus Christ

Lesson 174
Cumulative Review 16

1. Cyrus
2. Zerubbabel
3. teach
4. marrying
5. cupbearer
6. walls
7. rebuilt

8. swords
9. Law
10. John, Jesus Christ

Lesson 175
Week 35 Review

1. **F**
2. **B**
3. **D**
4. **A**
5. **C**
6. **E**

Lesson 176

1. True
2. False
3. True
4. True
5. False
6. True
7. False
8. False
9. True
10. True
11. False
12. False
13. True
14. False

15. True
16. True
17. False
18. True

Lesson 178

1. Job
2. Eli
3. Hannah
4. David
5. Bathsheba
6. Solomon
7. Judah
8. Ahab
9. Elijah
10. Elisha
11. Joash
12. Josiah
13. Jeremiah
14. Daniel
15. Haman

Lesson 180

1. Goliath, Jonathan
2. Jezebel, Naboth
3. send
4. letter, prayed
5. bow, fiery furnace
6. Mordecai, Esther

Appendix: Catechism Questions 1–57

Question 1: Who made you?

Answer 1: God

Question 2: What else did God make?

Answer 2: God made all things.

Question 3: Why did God make you and all things?

Answer 3: For his own glory

Question 4: How can you glorify God?

Answer 4: By loving him and doing what he commands

Question 5: Why are you to glorify God?

Answer 5: Because he made me and takes care of me

Question 6: Is there more than one true God?

Answer 6: No. There is only one true God.

Question 7: In how many Persons does this one God exist?

Answer 7: In three Persons

Question 8: Name these three Persons.

Answer 8: The Father, the Son, and the Holy Spirit

Question 9: What is God?

Answer 9: God is a Spirit and does not have a body like men.

Question 10: Where is God?

Answer 10: God is everywhere.

Question 11: Can you see God?

Answer 11: No. I cannot see God, but he always sees me.

Question 12: Does God know all things?

Answer 12: Yes. Nothing can be hidden from God.

Question 13: Can God do all things?

Answer 13: Yes. God can do all his holy will.

Question 14: Where do you learn how to love and obey God?

Answer 14: In the Bible alone

Question 15: Who wrote the Bible?

Answer 15: Chosen men who were inspired by the Holy Spirit

Question 16: Who were our first parents?

Answer 16: Adam and Eve

Question 17: How did God create man?

Answer 17: God created man, male and female, after his own image.

Question 18: Of what were our first parents made?

Answer 18: God made Adam's body out of the ground and Eve's body out of a rib from Adam.

Question 19: What else did God give Adam and Eve besides bodies?

Answer 19: He gave them souls that will last forever.

Question 20: Do you have a soul as well as a body?

Answer 20: Yes. And my soul is going to last forever.

Question 21: How do you know your soul will last forever?

Answer 21: Because the Bible tells me so

Question 22: In what condition did God make Adam and Eve?

Answer 22: He made them holy and happy.

Question 23: What covenant did God make with Adam?

Answer 23: The covenant of life

Question 24: What is a covenant?

Answer 24: A relationship that God establishes with us and guarantees by his word

Question 25: In the covenant of life, what did God require Adam to do?

Answer 25: To obey God perfectly

Question 26: What did God promise in the covenant of life?

Answer 26: To reward Adam with life if he obeyed God perfectly

Question 27: What did God threaten in the covenant of life?

Answer 27: To punish Adam with death if he disobeyed God

Question 28: Did Adam keep the covenant of life?

Answer 28: No. He sinned against God.

Question 29: What is sin?

Answer 29: Sin is any lack of conformity to, or transgression of, the law of God.

Question 30: What is meant by lack of conformity?

Answer 30: Not being or doing what God requires

Question 31: What is meant by transgression?

Answer 31: Doing what God forbids

Question 32: What does every sin deserve?

Answer 32: The wrath and curse of God

Question 33: What was the sin of our first parents?

Answer 33: Eating the forbidden fruit

Question 34: Who tempted Adam and Eve to this sin?

Answer 34: Satan tempted Eve first, and then he used her to tempt Adam.

Question 35: How did Adam and Eve change when they sinned?

Answer 35: Instead of being holy and happy, they became sinful and miserable.

Question 36: Did Adam act for himself alone in the covenant of life?

Answer 36: No. He represented the whole human race.

Question 37: What effect did the sin of Adam have on you and all people?

Answer 37: We are all born guilty and sinful.

Question 38: How sinful are you by nature?

Answer 38: I am corrupt in every part of my being.

Question 39: What is the sinful nature that we inherit from Adam called?

Answer 39: Original sin

Question 40: Can anyone go to heaven with this sinful nature?

Answer 40: No. Our hearts must be changed before we can believe in Jesus and go to heaven.

Question 41: What is this change of heart called?

Answer 41: The new birth, or regeneration

Question 42: Who can change a sinner's heart?

Answer 42: The Holy Spirit alone

Question 43: Can anyone be saved through the covenant of life?

Answer 43: No. No one can be saved through the covenant of life.

Question 44: Why can't anyone be saved through the covenant of life?

Answer 44: Because all have broken it and are condemned by it

Question 45: How did you break the covenant of life?

Answer 45: Adam represented all people, and so I fell with Adam in his first sin.

Question 46: How, then, can you be saved?

Answer 46: By the Lord Jesus Christ through the covenant of grace

Question 47: Whom did Christ represent in the covenant of grace?

Answer 47: His elect people

Question 48: How did Christ fulfill the covenant of grace?

Answer 48: Christ obeyed the whole law for his people and then suffered the punishment due for their sins.

Question 49: Did Jesus ever sin?

Answer 49: No. He lived a sinless life.

Question 50: How could Christ suffer?

Answer 50: Christ, the Son of God, became a man so that he could obey and suffer in our place.

Question 51: For whom did Christ obey and suffer?

Answer 51: For all whom God the Father gave to Christ

Question 52: What kind of life did Christ live on earth?

Answer 52: A life of obedience, service, and suffering

Question 53: What kind of death did Jesus die?

Answer 53: The painful and shameful death of the cross

Question 54: What is meant by the atonement?

Answer 54: Christ satisfied God's justice by his suffering and death as a substitute for sinners.

Question 55: What does God the Father guarantee in the covenant of grace?

Answer 55: To justify and sanctify all those for whom Christ died

Question 56: How does God justify you?

Answer 56: God forgives all my sins and accepts me as righteous through Christ.

Question 57: How does God sanctify you?

Answer 57: God makes me more and more holy in heart and conduct.